Application Performance Management (APM) in the Digital Enterprise

Application Performance Management (APM) in the Digital Enterprise

Managing Applications for Cloud, Mobile, IoT and eBusiness

Rick Sturm

Carol Pollard

Julie Craig

MORGAN KAUFMANN PUBLISHERS

AN IMPRINT OF ELSEVIER

elsevier.com

Morgan Kaufmann is an imprint of Elsevier
50 Hampshire Street, 5th Floor, Cambridge, MA 02139, United States

Library of Congress Cataloging-in-Publication Data
A catalog record for this book is available from the Library of Congress

British Library Cataloguing-in-Publication Data
A catalogue record for this book is available from the British Library

ISBN: 978-0-12-804018-8

For information on all Morgan Kaufmann publications visit
our website at https://www.elsevier.com/books-and-journals

Working together
to grow libraries in
developing countries

www.elsevier.com • www.bookaid.org

Publisher: Todd Green
Acquisition Editor: Brian Romer
Editorial Project Manager: Kattie Washington
Production Project Manager: Punithavathy Govindaradjane
Cover Designer: Mark Rogers

Typeset by TNQ Books and Journals

Contents

About the Authors

Rick Sturm, MBA, has more than 30 years of experience in the computer industry. He is CEO of Enterprise Management Associates (EMA), a leading industry analyst firm that provides strategic and tactical advice to major corporations and government agencies on the issues of managing computing and communications environments and the delivery of those services. He was co-chair of the IETF Applications MIB Working Group that developed the standards for managing application software with SNMP. Rick has authored hundreds of articles about various aspects of enterprise management that have appeared in leading trade publications in the United States, Europe, and Asia. He has also co-authored five books: *CMDB Systems: Making Change Work in the Age of Cloud and Agile, The Foundations of Application Management, Foundations of Service Level Management, SLM Solutions: A Buyer's Guide,* and *Working With Unicenter TNG.*

Carol Pollard has more than 25 years of experience in IS education and industry consulting in the United States, Canada, and Australia. She is a full professor of computer information systems and supply chain management at Appalachian State University and holds an MBA and PhD in management information systems and business administration from the University of Pittsburgh. She also has ITILv3 certification.

Carol's consulting, teaching, and research focus is on application lifecycle management, IT service management, IT project management, and IT for sustainability. Carol is internationally recognized for her leading-edge IS research that she has presented at international academic and practitioner conferences, including the International Conference on Information Systems, Hawaii International Conference on Systems Sciences, Australasian Conference on IS, Pacific Asia Conference on IS, PINK, IBM Pulse, and IBM Innovate. She has also authored more than 100 publications in top-tier academic journals, including *MIS Quarterly, Journal of MIS, International Small Business Journal, Group Decision and Negotiation,* and *International Journal of Sustainability in High Education,* and in practitioner-oriented journals, including *Communications of the ACM* and *IT Professional.* Currently, Carol has served as chair of the Australasian Conference on Information Systems, associate editor for the *Journal of Global IT Management* and *International Journal of Decision Sciences,* and research analyst/faculty advisor to leading software companies.

Julie Craig has more than 25 years of deep and broad experience in software engineering, IT infrastructure and integration engineering, and application management. She holds a BA degree in psychology from Lycoming College, an associate's degree in computer science from the Pennsylvania College of Technology, and an MS degree in computer information technology from Regis University.

As a former software engineer and IT infrastructure engineer for global software companies, she managed development teams, developed software including enterprise management products, and deployed multiple commercial system, application, and performance management solutions. Her experience in commercial software companies also included development of communications software supporting television broadcasting and commercial integration applications.

She is internationally recognized for her thought leadership in the application management space, with numerous webinars, videos, and speaking engagements to her credit. She has been broadly quoted and continues to contribute to a wide variety of industry publications.

Acknowledgments

A book is rarely produced through the efforts of just the authors, and this book is no exception. Many people contributed to its creation, both directly and indirectly. There are so many people that it's not possible to list them all!

This book's genesis was in 1999, when Rick Sturm and Winston Bumpus collaborated to produce *Foundations of Application Management* (John Wiley and Sons, 1999). Sixteen years and millions of air miles later, Winston approached Rick with the suggestion that, since so much had changed regarding application management in the intervening period, they produce a new book on the topic. In 1999, application management was truly in its infancy. While application management will not be fully mature for decades, if ever, huge advances were made in the past 16 years. Although Winston ultimately decided that he was unable to proceed with the project, without the initial impetus he provided, this book would never have been written. For that reason, he deserves special thanks.

Major contributions were made by the research team at Enterprise Management Associates, Inc. (EMA). In particular, Steve Brasen contributed to the chapter about Mobile Applications and David Monahan contributed substantially to the Application Security and the Internet of Things chapters. The appendix about CMDB was largely derived from *CMDB Systems: Making Change Work in the Age of Cloud and Agile* (Morgan Kaufman, 2015). Dennis Drogseth was one of the authors of that book and assisted with the appendix.

Amy Anderson of EMA deserves special credit for her editorial assistance. She reviewed and edited approximately 75% of this book, some of the chapters more than once. Cecilia Kiely, also of EMA, needs to be recognized for her editorial efforts in editing Chapters 9–12. Together, their work resulted in a book that is much easier to read and understand.

A special thanks goes to IBM's Arun Biligiri and his team for providing a review of and input to Chapter 12, "Application Performance Management and User Experience Management (UEM)." Their comments were invaluable in ensuring the accuracy and readability of the chapter. Additionally, their contribution of a topology graphic provides a "real world" glimpse into the complexities of modern application delivery.

Many thanks to Gene Kim for providing a quote as part of the introduction to Chapter 10 and to AppDynamics for their contribution of a topology graphic for Chapter 9 ("Distributed, Tiered, and Component-Based Applications") to help explain component-based applications. It isn't always easy to find the right words or images for technical writing so we greatly appreciate those contributions!

Finally, we would like to thank the team at Elsevier, including Brian Romer, Kattie Washington, Amy Invernizzi, and Punithavathy Govindaradjane. They provided the necessary guidance and support to translate the vision of this book into a reality.

To everyone involved, we want to say "Thanks! We couldn't have done it without you."

Introduction

Nothing is more visible to users and business unit managers than an application that does not work! In the age of the digital enterprise, superior performance is critical to maintaining a competitive advantage. In order to meet those requirements, applications must be managed as efficiently and effectively as possible. Over the years, as applications have become increasingly complex, they require increasingly sophisticated management tools as well as techniques tailored to meet the unique requirements of each new application technology. This makes it imperative to stay abreast of new trends in application management processes, techniques, and tools.

At the same time, applications are now running in an expanding array of operating environments (mainframes, servers, personal computers, mobile devices, Internet of Things devices, etc.). Each of those environments is unique and in turn necessitates that application management tools and techniques be adapted accordingly. In *Managing Applications in the Digital Enterprise,* we aim to provide the reader with a solid understanding of application management in each of the diverse environments where it is required and to explain how to effectively manage applications in each of those environments.

WHO WILL BENEFIT FROM THIS BOOK?

This book is aimed at four primary audiences: information technology (IT) practitioners, IT managers, designers and developers of applications, and line of business managers. The first three share the responsibility for applications being available and functioning as intended. The designers and developers have the unique responsibility of creating and maintaining applications that meet the requirements of users and are reliable. The fourth group (line of business managers) relies on the applications to enable them to do their work. This book is designed to give the advice and direction to enable each of these groups to meet their unique objectives.

FEATURES

Managing Applications in the Digital Enterprise provides a comprehensive discussion of application management processes, techniques, tools, and standards, along with the history, current art, and future promise of application management in the multifaceted environment of mobile and cloud computing. Topics covered in-depth include:

- How application management has evolved over the years
- How to manage
  - Traditional applications
  - Applications in the cloud environment
  - Virtualized systems
  - Mobile applications
  - Web-based applications

- Application security
- Distributed, tiered, and componentized application architectures
- DevOps and continuous delivery
- Application programming interfaces and connected systems
- Application performance and the user experience
- Containerized applications
- Software-defined data center
- Internet of Things
- The Case for Application Management Standards
- What to expect in application management in the future

From the Authors

In this book, we have created a unique and useful reference on the evolution of applications, the current state of affairs in application management, existing tools, major application management standards, and expectations in the application management arena as it moves forward. It is our hope that in doing so, we can equip applications managers and developers with the information and skills required to implement best practice application management strategies for both today and into the future.

In writing this book, we have drawn on our joint expertise in IT operations and application development. If you're ready to improve your application management and people management skills, this book is a must-read.

OVERVIEW

Application management provides tremendous benefits by improving the productivity of application users and lines of business.
Wayne Morris, VP, Corporate Marketing, BMC Software, Inc.

Application management has become one of the critical challenges for all large IT organizations today since it is where IT groups often have the most visibility with their business clients.
Theo Forbath, Global VP, Digital Transformation at Cognizant Technology Solutions

INTRODUCTION

In many organizations, applications that were developed 20 or 30 years ago are still in use, and the most recently developed applications can be expected to have a similar longevity. To ensure high performance and productivity, these applications and their related data structures must be systematically monitored, enhanced, renewed, and retired. The question is, "How do we best manage applications in the complex world of mobile and cloud computing?"

In the following pages, we provide the answer to this question through an enlightening discussion focused on the various aspects of application management and its evolving role in mobile and cloud systems. To achieve this, we take a brief look at application management in traditional standalone systems as a necessary starting point, followed by a systematic discussion of the ways in which application management processes, techniques, tools, and standards have changed to successfully manage today's complex application environment. In those chapters where it is appropriate, a list of vendors who offer products in the topic space is provided at the end of each chapter.

CHAPTER 2—EVOLUTION OF APPLICATION MANAGEMENT

Application management is closely coupled to the technologies of application software and the associated networks, systems, and databases. As such, application management is always constrained and at the same time driven by those technologies. It is important to understand the development and **evolution of application management** in order to help the reader better understand and give context to modern application management.

Chapter 2 explains the process through which the management of modern applications, though built on innovations of the past, was revolutionized since the beginning of the 21st century. It also discusses how and why the complexity of the management challenge increased tremendously as applications became componentized and virtualized with the introduction of mobile and cloud computing.

CHAPTER 3—MANAGING TRADITIONAL APPLICATIONS

The primary functions of application management are Fault, Configuration, Accounting, Performance, and Security. Key roles for application management are frontline staff (e.g., system administrator, help desk technician, service desk analyst, etc.), applications specialists (e.g., Tier II or Tier III support, etc.), and application developers. The key objectives of application management are to ensure that applications are available to users and deliver an acceptable level of performance, in accordance with a service-level agreement.

Chapter 3 focuses on how traditional applications created 10–20 years ago were managed. We use this as our starting point to embark on the application management journey since it is a simpler environment than is found with more modern applications, and consequently the role of application management was much less complex than it is in today's distributed environment.

CHAPTER 4—MANAGING APPLICATIONS IN THE CLOUD

Cloud computing is a key enabler of the distributed information technology (IT) environment. The use of public and private cloud environments by organizations around the globe continues to grow at a rapid pace and shows no signs of abating in the near future, and the financial benefits of cloud computing will continue to drive its adoption. However, cloud computing brings unique challenges for managing the applications that run in those environments. Chapter 4 discusses the multifaceted nature of **application management in cloud environments**. It also addresses the user and service provider dimensions that exist in each of the public cloud environments, along with the different capabilities and responsibilities in each instance. In addition, it presents a discussion of IaaS and private cloud environments, the responsibilities of the customer's IT department for active management of the applications, and their power to install the appropriate tools as needed.

CHAPTER 5—MANAGING VIRTUALIZED SYSTEMS

A key concept in the distributed environment is **virtualization,** which can be viewed as a logical abstraction of a physical system that allows multiple physical systems to appear as a single logical system, or as a single physical system that is partitioned to appear as multiple independent logical systems. Chapter 5 addresses the various forms of virtualization, including virtualized desktops, virtualized applications, virtual appliances, network virtualization, storage virtualization, and service virtualization. It will also discuss how virtualization is evolving as an innovative concept designed to enable organizations to gain better control over their IT resources, reduce network equipment costs, and reduce power and space requirements. Also addressed are the benefits and challenges of managing virtual machines.

CHAPTER 6—MANAGING MOBILE COMPUTING

Hardware also enabled the distributed environment. Laptop computers, tablets, and smartphones dramatically changed the ways in which people work, interact with each other, and even how they think. It is not just the mobile devices themselves, but those devices together with the applications that run on them and (usually) network connectivity that provide access to additional application functionality and additional data. Chapter 6 addresses the new set of management challenges that **mobile applications** bring to application management, particularly in the realm of security. Also addressed is how the role of "bring your own device" (BYOD) simultaneously complicated and simplified the challenges of management mobile applications. BYOD made managing mobile applications more complicated because of the diversity of devices on which applications may run and, alternatively, how BYOD simplified the management challenges since most of the responsibility for managing performance and availability of mobile applications shifted to the user of the device.

CHAPTER 7—MANAGING WEB-BASED APPLICATIONS

Internally hosted, cloud-hosted, or software as a service **web-based applications** compose a significant and growing majority of today's business applications and are transforming the ways in which enterprise-class applications are built, deployed, consumed, and managed. There are differing opinions as to whether web applications are easier to develop and require less management than traditional desktop applications. Regardless of the position taken on this debate, most people would agree it is impossible for any organization to prosper without implementing, executing, monitoring, and ultimately retiring dozens of web applications across many different platforms. The challenge is to determine the best way to achieve these goals while expending minimum effort, time, and money to manage them throughout their lifecycle. Chapter 7 discusses the management of web-based applications throughout the system development lifecycle with a particular emphasis on skills, concepts, principles, and challenges related to their development, maintenance, and operations. Finally, protection of corporate and customer data in a web-based environment is discussed, and a set of web application security management principles are recommended.

CHAPTER 8—APPLICATION MANAGEMENT SECURITY

Applications are at the heart of an organization's security. If compromised, they can become an avenue to exploiting or destroying valuable organizational assets. The initial development of an application is where critical decisions must be made. Correct decisions then lead to the creation of much more secure applications and less vulnerability for organizational assets.

Chapter 8 explores the need to secure those applications and how to achieve this objective. Topics covered include the need to secure applications and how to accomplish that, and Chapter 8 describes steps that can be taken to prevent problems from arising or minimize the impact if they do arise. In addition, Chapter 8 identifies 25 of the worst application coding errors that can create vulnerabilities and describes steps that can be taken to prevent problems from arising and/or minimizing their impact. Finally, protection of corporate and customer data in a web-based environment is discussed, and a set of web application security management principles are explained.

CHAPTER 9—DISTRIBUTED, TIERED, AND COMPONENTIZED APPLICATION ARCHITECTURES

The definition of "application" is exceedingly broad, defined differently in many different contexts. Often, the only things "applications" have in common are the fact that they are created from code and designed to perform a discrete task or set of tasks.

For example, in the network management space, file transfer protocol (FTP) is considered to be an "application." In the desktop space, Microsoft Word and Virtual Private Network (VPN) software are considered to be "applications." On a mobile device, an application could be either a tiny native "app" running on the device *or* a traditional web application running on a mobile browser. A mobile "app" and a massive enterprise resource planning (ERP) system consisting of hundreds of modules and thousands of functions are both examples of "applications."

This diversity can be extremely confusing to potential application performance management (APM) buyers. It can be time-consuming to navigate the sea of potential vendors and solutions in search of the one single product that best meets the buyer's needs.

Chapter 9 discusses the management challenges inherent in complex **distributed and componentized application architectures.** Tiered/distributed applications, services built over service-oriented architectures (SOA), hybrid applications executing across on-premise and public cloud, and even complex web applications can be grouped into this category. All traverse multiple infrastructure elements, software components, network segments, platforms, and often data centers/locations during end-to-end execution.

The growth of this level of heterogeneity means that cross-functional skills, instrumentation/insight from multiple vantage points, and collaborative processes and tools are the new normal. For IT organizations already grappling with support costs and expertise shortfalls, the impact can be overwhelming. Automated toolsets are virtually the only way to ensure the quality of complex applications while also mitigating the support costs and workforce effort required to manage massively complex application systems.

CHAPTER 10—DEVOPS AND CONTINUOUS DELIVERY

DevOps and continuous delivery are separate but related IT practices that are neither institutionalized by standards nor uniformly defined and understood. They differ, for example, from IT service management (ITSM) practices, which are now well-defined across the industry and provide a common language and framework, enabling cross-functional IT practitioners to collaborate more effectively.

From the tools perspective, both of these terms are often defined by vendors as "whatever we have that may fit into these 'hot topic' categories." They are likewise defined differently by industry thought leaders and by DevOps and continuous delivery zealots, all of whom cast a somewhat different flavor to their definitions based on their personal experience and that of the companies with which they have worked or consulted.

Chapter 10 explores these two topics separately and together, lending a generic twist to the definitions and descriptions of these concepts. The history and underlying drivers for both DevOps and continuous delivery are discussed, along with how and why they captured center stage in recent years, and the implications for both IT and business stakeholders are described.

CHAPTER 11—MANAGING APPLICATION PROGRAMMING INTERFACES AND CONNECTED SYSTEMS

We live in a world of massively **interconnected applications** and supply chains. In recent years, the use of **application programming interfaces (APIs)** has largely replaced technologies such as electronic data interchange (EDI) and custom-written programs for the development of new system integrations. APIs are now the de facto industry standard for integrating data and functionality across diverse application ecosystems.

The growth of public cloud, mobile devices, containers, microservices, and Internet of Things (IoT) has accelerated the need for software integration. Industry standards such as representational state transfer (REST), simple object access protocol (SOAP), and hypertext transfer protocol/secure (HTTP/S) facilitated the process.

APIs built over these protocols simplify and, to some degree, standardize the integration process. They reduce the need for the "bespoke" integrations of the past—which were required to support exotic protocols and proprietary operational systems. In short, APIs became the standard currency of exchange connecting applications, devices, and companies.

There are two sides to the API coin: "providing" and "consuming" APIs. Growing numbers of companies are consuming APIs to access data and functionality exposed by other entities. A large number of companies are acting as API providers, exposing their systems to those of customers, partners, and suppliers. Many companies are doing both, and some are monetizing access to data or internal systems as part of revenue generation. Both business-to-business (B2B) and business-to-consumer (B2C) interactions are supported by API connections, and usage grows on a daily basis.

The speed and breadth with which standards-based APIs have proliferated are affecing APM in a big way. Applications relying on APIs to provide data or functions necessary to complete a transaction—an Internet sale, for example—can be slowed or stalled by many of the same factors as tiered, distributed transactions. At the same time, APIs are supported by new protocols, connection methodologies, and architectures that are largely unsupported by many traditional APM solutions.

Chapter 11 points out that while APIs are the new standard of B2B and B2C interchanges, they also introduce new management challenges that many companies are not equipped to address.

CHAPTER 12—APPLICATION PERFORMANCE MANAGEMENT AND USER EXPERIENCE MANAGEMENT

The term **"application performance management" (APM)** is defined differently by virtually every vendor delivering any sort of performance-related toolset. Whether the tool monitors data centers, containers, virtual ecosystems, or networks, APM is the new hot topic, and nearly every enterprise management vendor wants to hop on that bandwagon.

Closely related to APM, **user experience management (UEM)** is a complementary discipline, often with a different set of drivers and always supported by a variety of diverse data collection methodologies. UEM is often viewed as a subset of APM, and the two are particularly valuable when the metrics delivered by each are consolidated, correlated, and analyzed in context with one another.

Although the loose definitions of these terms can be confusing, the reality is that the application performance product family must be versatile enough to accommodate a wide variety of application types and architectures. Since the applications themselves often execute across heterogenous and geographically separated infrastructure elements, the monitoring infrastructure supporting them must be equally diverse and distributed.

It is also true that by its nature, application performance "management" (versus simple "monitoring") requires a level of root-cause analysis functionality. From this perspective, multiple instrumentation points and perspectives supporting insights into application execution all contribute to building an end-to-end perspective.

Chapter 12 explores the various facets of APM and UEM. We also examine the types of products that deliver the multidimensional visibility necessary to manage complex applications, as well as the performance metrics required to support sophisticated modern users. Two models—a "semantic cube" focusing on product capabilities supporting the full spectrum of IT service management and an "application management semantic model" focusing specifically on instrumentation supporting the APM discipline round out the chapter content.

CHAPTER 13—MANAGING CONTAINERIZED APPLICATIONS

Containerized applications represent a major shift in the evolution of IT. Building on the tenets of virtualization, containerization is often referred to as "lightweight virtualization" because of its ability to run applications on a variety of hosts, reduce memory requirements, increase ease of migration and use of applications, enable faster deployment, and back up and free up server capacity.

Chapter 13 explores the history and underlying concepts of containerized applications and container-based virtualization, explores their relationship to virtualization, describes the areas of computing that benefit most from using container-based virtualization, and evaluates how containerized applications can be managed by various categories of IT personnel to provide the greatest value. Finally, we discuss containerization management challenges and the creation of the Open Container Project, a move spearheaded by many of the largest technology organizations to develop a containerization industry standard.

CHAPTER 14—APPLICATION MANAGEMENT IN THE SOFTWARE-DEFINED DATA CENTER

In the past decade, data centers evolved into mission-critical assets whose availability, performance, power, efficiency, security continuity, and overall effectiveness must be guaranteed to avoid critical downtime and revenue losses. The planning, design, implementation, operation and control, maintenance, evolution, and eventual disposal at the end of the data center's useful life consist of a set of complex processes. Managing these processes was difficult, and data center managers had to use a plethora of IT tools and techniques to achieve optimal integration, interoperability, security, reliability, serviceability, manageability, controllability, scalability, security, virtualization, energy efficiency, and overall performance to effectively deploy and operate their data centers. As organizations transitioned to a cloud-based infrastructure, data centers became virtualized. In turn, virtualization led to the emergence of the **software-defined data center** (**SDDC**) that facilitates the integration of the various infrastructure silos, optimizes resource usage and balances workloads, and maximizes operational efficiency through dynamic workload distribution and network provisioning.

Chapter 14 describes the innovative concept of SDDC and discusses the managerial implications of its potential impact, risks, and benefits. The need for new IT management approaches is examined, new approaches are presented, and ways to implement the new approaches are recommended. Finally, challenges to transitioning to the SDCC are identified and solutions offered.

CHAPTER 15—APPLICATION MANAGEMENT IN THE INTERNET OF THINGS

The **Internet of Things (IoT)** is an explosion in progress that promises to change the lives of nearly every human being. IoT is only possible because of advances in technology that have allowed miniaturization of components and drastic reduction in power requirements.

In Chapter 15, the remote application that resides on or in close proximity to the IoT system that collects data from associated sensors, and the IoT component that receives data that was captured by the remote application, are explained and discussed. The importance of security in the management of IoT is of particular interest since IoT systems are frequently unattended and may not be physically secured.

CHAPTER 16—THE CASE FOR STANDARDS

As industry leaders recognize the importance of developing standardized technologies to instrument IoT-related applications and in response to customer demands for increased efficiency and effectiveness in application manageability, several organizations have stepped up to develop **standards** to guide deployment and management of software and hardware components. These organizations, made up of industry leaders, recognize the importance of developing standardized technologies to instrument applications. They include the Internet Engineering Task Force (IETF), Desktop Management Task Force (DMTF), Institute of Electronic Engineers (IEEE), Tivoli, ASL-BiSL Foundation, and the International Organization of Standards (ISO).

Chapter 16 discusses the various industry and government organization standards and explains the standards developed by these influential organizations vis-à-vis the different aspects of the application management lifecycle. Finally, the pros and cons of using standards to facilitate the management of applications are presented and discussed. The primary utility of this chapter is that it presents a timeline of the development of application management standards and an overview of the many standards that were published over the past 25-plus years in a single, concise resource.

CHAPTER 17—LOOKING AHEAD

As organizations in the future continue to leverage mobile and cloud computing to enable users to connect on a 24/7 basis to applications and data centers through a wide range of devices, the professionals who build and manage them will face an increasing application performance gap.

As a result, in the next several years, considerable changes will occur in how applications are managed. For example, digital transformation will emerge as an important business strategy. Organizations that embrace the next wave of innovative opportunities to digitally transform applications and free themselves of outdated legacy business models will be the big winners in application lifecycle management.

In Chapter 17, digital transformation and other important future developments in application management are presented and discussed, including expected changes in the nature of applications, evolution of software-defined everything, importance of advanced predictive analytics, need for integrated dynamic policy rules, heightened levels of security, autonomics and cognitive computing, and the increased development and impact of standards.

To address topics that are tangential, yet relevant to application management, we have provided three appendices to explain the configuration management database, service-level management, and the NIST definition report.

APPENDICES
APPENDIX A—SERVICE-LEVEL MANAGEMENT

While **service-level management (SLM)** is not specifically about application, applications are generally central to SLM and the associated service-level agreements (SLAs). Ultimately, SLM is about setting realistic expectations for the clients and holding the service provider (IT) accountable for meeting those expectations—expectations that were mutually agreed on.

Appendix A provides the reader with an overview of the SLM process, its components, and how they integrate with application management.

APPENDIX B—CONFIGURATION MANAGEMENT DATABASE

There are a multitude of views as to what a **configuration management database (CMDB)** really is. Some define the CMDB and the configuration management system (CMS) by the strict IT Infrastructure Library (ITIL) definitions, while others rely on one of the many descriptions put forth by vendors of CMDB-related products. A CMDB is a repository that acts as a data warehouse for IT installations. It holds data relating to a collection of IT assets [commonly referred to as configuration items (CIs)], as well as to descriptive relationships between such assets. When populated, the repository provides a means of understanding.

While a CMDB does contain CIs about servers and devices in the infrastructure, it is not limited to those. A CMDB may also contain information about applications, middleware, documentation, people, processes, service providers, and other relevant information in addition to the basic infrastructure components.

Appendix B examines ITIL processes and associated CMDB-related technologies that are the foundations of the CMDB.

APPENDIX C—NIST DEFINITION REPORT

The NIST definition of cloud computing characterizes important aspects of cloud computing and is intended to serve as a means for broad comparisons of cloud services and deployment strategies.

Appendix C present the NIST definition, which is a baseline for discussion from "what is cloud computing" to "how best to use cloud computing." The service and deployment models defined in the NIST definition forms a single taxonomy designed to better inform system planners, program managers, technologists, and others adopting cloud computing as consumers or providers of cloud services.

SUMMARY

Application management has become increasingly complex during the past 20 years. The various chapters of this book are packed with valuable information and insights into best practices in application management in the digital enterprise. The overviews provided in this chapter assist the reader in targeting the areas that interest them most.

THE EVOLUTION OF APPLICATION MANAGEMENT

2

Living systems are never in equilibrium. They are inherently unstable. They may seem stable, but they're not. Everything is moving and changing. In a sense, everything is on the edge of collapse.
Michael Crichton, Jurassic Park.

One general law, leading to the advancement of all organic beings, namely, multiply, vary, let the strongest live and the weakest die.
Charles Darwin, On the Origin of Species.

Authors' note: *Some readers may be tempted to skip this chapter, feeling that the evolution of application management is a look into the past with little relevance to the challenges faced with application management today. However, this chapter is important because just as the roots shape a tree, the technical decisions of the past shape the future directions of technology. While it is not necessary to memorize every line of this chapter, we encourage you to spend a few minutes with this section. It will pay dividends in the subsequent chapters.*

In the above quotes, Crichton and Darwin understate the scope of change. Change is not limited to living systems. The entire universe is in a constant state of flux. Stars are being born while others are dying or exploding. If you stop and reflect, you can surely think of at least a few things that seem unchangeable. However, that appearance is the result not thinking in the long term—the *really* long term. For example, the movement of tectonic plates continuously reshapes the surface of the earth, but it happens not even for generations, but rather over millions or billions of years.

The biases of Victorian England influenced Charles Darwin. He presumed that evolution, through survival of the fittest, would inevitably lead a better species—to a better state. Unfortunately, that is not true for plants and animals, and it is definitely not true for computer systems.

HISTORICAL PERSPECTIVE

To understand the evolution of **application management**, it is necessary to first look at the evolution of computers and of the **applications** that ran on them. Some people will argue that the Jacquard loom deserves recognition as the first "computer." However, that, at best, could be considered the forerunner of numerically controlled manufacturing equipment. The looms did earn distinction for their use of a series of punched cards to control complex operations by the looms. While those series of cards bore a resemblance to paper tape that was used two centuries later, the looms did not process data (Fig. 2.1).

Application Performance Management (APM) in the Digital Enterprise. http://dx.doi.org/10.1016/B978-0-12-804018-8.00002-4

FIGURE 2.1

Jacquard loom.

Of course, some argue that the first programmable computer was either the Difference Engine or the Analytical Engine designed by Charles Babbage in the mid-19th century. Both were the result of the sheer genius of Babbage. Unfortunately, only small parts of the machines designed by Babbage were built during his lifetime. Despite that, they represented brilliant, groundbreaking work. Strictly, it would be a stretch to consider the Difference Engines to be more than an elaborate calculator—an incredible achievement for the day, to be sure, but a calculator nonetheless. They were much closer in nature to a mechanical clock than to a computer.

The Analytical Engine was a much more sophisticated device. The Analytical Engine is much more than a calculator and marks the progression from the mechanized arithmetic of calculation to something that was the mechanical precursor to the modern computer. It was programmable using punched cards. The engine had a "store" where numbers and intermediate results could be held and a separate "mill" where the arithmetic processing was performed. It was also capable of functions used in modern computing systems, like conditional branching, looping (iteration), microprogramming, parallel processing, iteration, latching, and detection and handling of errors (Fig. 2.2).

It was during World War II that the first modern electronic data processing computers, known as Colossus, were developed. Little is known about the machines because they were developed and

FIGURE 2.2

Analytical Engine.

successfully used by Britain to decrypt coded German messages. These machines were considered ultra secret and were so effective that they continued to be used during the Cold War. Because of the secrecy surrounding them and the very effectiveness of the devices, when they were superseded by more powerful equipment, these early electronic computers were quietly and secretly destroyed.

The next major advance in computing came with the creation of ENIAC in 1946. It was programmed with patch cables and switches. Patch cables continued as a form of programming into the early 1970s. The next advance was the replacement of relay switches with vacuum tubes and later with transistors. Another advance was the introduction of random access storage devices. Programs moved from patch cables/boards to paper tape and then to punch cards.

In the late 1960s and early 1970s, programs began to be referred to as applications. Individual programs were run in a series of steps. Initially, these pieces were loaded (run) manually. Eventually, they came to be connected via **Job Control Language (JCL)**. These interconnected programs became application systems such as payroll, accounts receivable, general ledger, etc. Also in the 1970s, online systems and computer networks made their appearance.

DEFINITION

Before proceeding any further, it is important to establish a common understanding of the term **application management**. In the broadest sense, an application may be considered any software or any program that runs on a computer. It may be "firmware"—that is, software that is written on a chip. It may be the **operating system (OS)** or associated utilities. However, in general, the term **application** refers to those collections of programs that are designed to perform a particular function that entails the processing of data and subsequently generating some form of output.

> Application management consists of the monitoring and control of application software with objective of optimizing its performance, availability, and security in order to meet service-level commitments.

In the world of information technology (IT), to manage something means to monitor it and to control it. Therefore, application management means the monitoring and control of application software with the objective of optimizing its **performance** and availability in order to meet service-level commitments. That management may be done by humans or by other software. The objective is to optimize the performance, availability, and **security** of the application. This is discussed in greater depth in Chapter 3, "Managing Traditional Applications."

> Management is always an afterthought.

THE EARLY DAYS

This is a good time to lay out a universal, but unfortunate, principle of management: *management is always an afterthought.* It does not matter what the technology is. The innovators initially rush to build, prototype, and deploy. Only after some initial success is the need for management and instrumentation (i.e., the ability to monitor and to measure) recognized and addressed. The need may be recognized by the creator/builder/engineer or it may be the user of the technology who demands that manageability be incorporated into the product.

Consider the Wright Brothers. On December 17, 1903, near Kitty Hawk, North Carolina, Orville Wright made the first powered flight in the Wright Flyer. This was only a little more than a glider with an engine strapped to it, but it was revolutionary. Management of the aircraft was almost nonexistent. The only instrument included was a handheld anemometer that was taped to a wing strut. It did not have any of the instruments that became quickly standard. However, it did not take long for pilots and designers to realize that there were some basic components that were critical, including a tachometer, altimeter, compass, fuel indicator (later a gauge was introduced), airspeed indicator, bank or turn indicator, climb indicator, oil pressure gauge, and oil temperature gauge.

Like the Wright brothers' early aircraft, applications and the management of them were equally primitive in the beginning. In the early years of computing, computer pioneer Grace Hopper (Fig. 2.3) coined the term "bug" to refer to system (including program) malfunctions. Moths, attracted to the heat of a computer, would crawl inside of a computer. Once inside, a moth had the potential to interfere with the operation of one of the relay switches, which was how program instructions were executed. One time, on finding a moth causing of malfunction of a relay switch, Ms. Hopper declared that she had found the "bug," thus coining the now ubiquitous term. Moths could also get stuck on a paper tape containing a program or data. This would prevent the holes in the tape from being detected, thereby altering the program or the data that were encoded on the tape.

Also like the Wright brothers, the people leading the way in computing learned by trial and error. They waited for something to break, tried to figure out why it had happened, and then tried to fix it and find a way to prevent it from happening again. Therefore, in the late 1940s and very early 1950s, application management largely consisted of waiting for something to break and then fixing it. At that time, the primary cause of failures was the complex array of hardware components (particularly vacuum tubes, relay switches, and complex circuitry). If there was a problem, the immediate and natural

FIGURE 2.3

Grace Hopper and team at the console of an early UNIVAC mainframe computer.

assumption was that the cause would be found somewhere in the hardware. Only after exhausting the hardware possibilities was the software considered as the possible explanation. Tracking an application's progress was relatively a straightforward thing to do since only one program could run at a time.

THE 1960s

Fast forward to the 1960s. Led by the introduction of IBM's System 360 and with it OS/MFT, operating systems of computers had matured to the point that applications were no longer single-threaded (i.e., only one application could run at the same time on a single computer). Now it was possible to run multiple applications at the same time on one computer. These applications ran in separate partitions of the computer's memory, isolated from each other. Data sharing between applications was generally done through files rather than through a direct exchange of data between the applications. While multiple applications could run on a single computer, those applications still ran in batch mode. That is, an application would be started, process the data it was given, and then terminate (i.e., shut down). In the 1960s, online, real-time systems were still the stuff of fantasy and research laboratories focused on the most advanced technologies.

By the 1960s, the hardware had also matured; it was much more stable and reliable. True, computer systems were still large and ran in special air-conditioned rooms, with special air filters and "conditioned power" (i.e., run through special equipment to minimize fluctuations in voltage or amperage); in some cases, chilled water was required for cooling the computer(s). If there were hardware problems, the OS could often give some indication of the nature of the problem and where it occurred (Fig. 2.4).

FIGURE 2.4

System 360.

Few products in American history have had the massive impact of the IBM® System/360—on technology, on the way the world works or on the organization that created them. Jim Collins, author of Good to Great, *ranks the S/360 as one of the all-time top three business accomplishments, along with Ford's Model T and Boeing's first jetliner, the 707. It set IBM on a path to dominate the computer industry for the following 20 years.*

Most significantly, the S/360 ushered in an era of computer compatibility—for the first time, allowing machines across a product line to work with each other. In fact, it marked a turning point in the emerging field of information science and the understanding of complex systems. After the S/360, we no longer talked about automating particular tasks with 'computers.' Now, we talked about managing complex processes through 'computer systems.'

At the time, however, success was far from clear. Thomas Watson Jr.'s decision to pursue this vast, US$5 billion investment in something that would cannibalize the company's existing product lines was an epic 'bet the business' move—one that emerged as much from Watson's determination to prove he could live up to the legacy of his father, IBM's legendary founder Thomas Watson Sr., as from changes in technology. Within IBM, the S/360 project sparked an extraordinary period of technological and business creativity, internal conflict and self-reflection for thousands of IBMers. When the S/360 was announced on April 7, 1964, it not only changed computing forever, but also IBM. The company learned, in Watson Jr.'s words, that 'there was nothing IBM couldn't do.'

The S/360 replaced all five of IBM's computer product lines with one strictly compatible family, using a new architecture that pioneered the eight-bit byte still in use on every computer today. The announcement was revolutionary in concept and unprecedented in scope. Six processor models were announced, covering a fifty-fold range in performance, as well as 54 different peripheral devices.

The System/360 announcement changed the way customers thought about computer hardware. Companies for the first time could buy a small system and add to it as they grew. Companies other than IBM found they could make peripheral equipment that worked with the S/360. An entire industry was soon created, consisting of companies making and supplying plug-compatible peripheral products....

In 1989, a quarter of a century after IBM System/360 debuted, products based on S/360 architecture and its extensions accounted for more than half of IBM's total revenues. They also accounted for more than 50 percent of the US$260 billion worldwide inventory of all computers made by all companies and priced over US$100,000 each.

http://www-03.ibm.com/ibm/history/ibm100/us/en/icons/system360/

A **master console operator (MCO)** would sit at a terminal and watch the console for signs of problems with hardware or software. The MCO would manually start applications by loading punch cards containing the program into a card reader. At that point, the execution of the application would either be controlled by the JCL commands or manually by the MCO. The MCO would also watch the progress of applications and their completion. The MCO would receive a notification when an application required some action to be taken (e.g., mount a specific magnetic tape, or a particular disk pack, etc.). If an application failed, an error message would usually be given to indicate the nature of the nature of the problem that caused the failure. In some specific cases, the MCO could resolve the problem; however, the MCO had to contact the application programmer to troubleshoot and resolve the problem. Often, if a job (i.e., the running of an application with a specific set of data) failed, after the problem was resolved, it would be necessary to run the entire job again—from the very beginning. With jobs that took a long time to run or ran on computers that had little or no extra capacity, this could be a serious problem.

Some applications were very large, with instruction sets of thousands of punch cards. While today that may seem trivial, an important management feature consisted of punching a sequence number on each of the program's cards. That was a safety measure so that when, sooner or later, someone inevitably dropped some (or all) of the cards, they could be quickly resorted into the correct order.

In short, in the 1960s and into the early 1970s, application management was still largely a manual process and that was becoming more complex and difficult. Thinking back to the example of aviation, the progress of application management in the 1960s was comparable to the early instrumentation and navigation aids available to pilots by the outbreak of World War I. By that time, pilots had the bare minimum required in terms of instrumentation and navigation aids (a compass and a window). Of course, the airframes were better and stronger, the engines were infinitely more powerful and reliable, and speeds had increased dramatically. All of this is surprisingly similar to how the computing environment was evolving.

THE 1970s

It was in this decade that computing really began to mature. No longer was the use of computers limited to just the largest companies or government agencies needing to process large amounts of data. As the cost of computer components followed Moore's Law, prices continued to fall and computers became affordable to more and more companies. Also during this period, computer systems continued to become faster and more complex and, with that, the management of the applications became more difficult.

> **"Moore's Law"** states that the number of transistors in an integrated circuit doubles every 24 months. This concept was introduced by Gordon E. Moore, co-founder of Intel.

Developers of the OSs of that era sought to provide some relief for the management problem with some basic functionality incorporated into those systems. They improved the ability of the OS to recognize the cause of an application failure and report it when the job terminated. The OS also tracked resource utilization by each application. The information was useful for job **accounting**, charge-back systems, and capacity planning. The latter was the analysis done to determine when it was necessary to purchase a new computer or upgrade an existing one. Reports were developed from this information to permit system programmers, application programmers, and MCOs to study the utilization of the **central processing unit (CPU)**, I/O (input/output) channel and storage (disk and tape), and how long it took for programs to run. This data could be used to determine if programs were running efficiently. Those that appeared to be inefficient or had high resource usage ("resource hogs") would be analyzed to determine what changes could be made to the programs (e.g., processing techniques, file structures, etc.) to make them more efficient. Small changes could sometimes lead to a significant reduction run times, resource consumption, or the overall system load.

It was in the 1970s that online, real-time processing began to be become mainstream. Initially it was a novelty, with terminals that were similar to an electric typewriter. These devices were universally slow. Their speed was constrained by the speed of the connection to the mainframe and even more by the speed at which they could print the output. In 1971, IBM introduced the 3270 CRT terminal (often referred to as a "green screen" because of the color of the characters on the original models). These terminals were attached, through a control unit, to a mainframe (Fig. 2.5).

Online, real-time processing meant that users could have immediate feedback. Agents at airline ticket counters, bank tellers, or even data entry clerks could have immediate access to information or get immediate feedback about their input. Similarly, the data entered by these people could be immediately entered into corporate files (if the business chose to do that). For application programmers in

FIGURE 2.5

3270 Terminal.

particular, this was a paradigm shift. Gone were the days of submitting test jobs and then waiting, perhaps 24 hours, to get the results. Now they could have very quick turnaround for their test jobs, provided that resources were available to allow the test jobs to run.

The arrival of online, real-time processing was the tipping point for application management in **mainframe computers**. It was no longer acceptable for resolving an application failure to take several hours. Now, users were interacting with the applications on a real-time basis and businesses required that availability and interaction in order to be able to function. Downtime (i.e., system outages) was expensive: revenue could be lost and/or unnecessary expenses could be incurred because staff were unable to do work when scheduled. IT turned to automation to improve the management of applications. Larger organizations created some programs to automate certain critical functions. However, most turned to their system supplier (which was increasingly IBM) and to third-party software developers.

It was also in the 1970s that the minicomputer (e.g., IBM System 32, DEC VAX, etc.) made its debut. Although minicomputers generally used a different OS than their larger, mainframe cousins, in terms of application management, there were no significant differences.

Some of the early application management functions to be automated are shown in Table 2.1.

The IT world was not and is not perfect. It never will be. It never can be. There were still unplanned application outages and some of them were protracted. However, overall, both performance and availability of applications improved significantly over what they had been in the 1970s. Some of that could be attributed to the automation of application management and some was attributable to improved hardware reliability.

Minicomputers appeared on the IT scene in the 1970s. To borrow from Yogi Berra, it was "Déja vu all over again." There was a stampede to deploy this new technology without sufficient thought given to how it would be managed. IT had to work through the same problems that it had faced in the mainframe environment.

Table 2.1 Examples of Early Application Management Tools

Role	Description
Tape management	Mapped the location of files to specific reels of magnetic tape and allowed the application to request that a specific reel be mounted on a tape drive.
Data backup and recovery	This relieved that application programmer from having to write code to ensure that data used by the application would be regularly backed up. It also greatly simplified the process of restoring a data set.
Job scheduling	This was intended primarily for applications that were run in batch mode. It allowed someone in operations to define the sequence in which jobs would be run. It also allowed dependencies on other resources to be defined.
	Job scheduling was also useful for ensuring that online systems were started at the required time. It eliminated the problem of an operator forgetting to start the online system.
Checkpoint restart	This tool would monitor an application. If the application failed or if the process was otherwise interrupted, this tool could be used to restart the application at the point in its processing where it was when it failed.

THE 1980s

Within the data center, automation of application management functions continued throughout the 1980s. Increasingly, IT departments turned to automation tools sold by third parties, also known as **independent software vendors (ISVs)**, rather than by IBM (whose hardware technology, by the late 1980s, was the de facto standard for mainframes). Top priority was given to tools that would monitor **application performance** and availability.

With the 1980s came the adoption of the **personal computer (PC)** for business uses. Initially, they were dismissed by IT departments as not being "real computers." The early ones had only 64 KB of memory and were prone to frequent crashes. Data and applications were stored on and loaded from 5¼" floppy diskettes that held a mere 110 KB of data. In fact, those early PCs were relatively expensive when their limited functionality is taken into account, especially comparing the price and capabilities of today's PCs. They were capable of limited word processing, running basic spreadsheets, and playing games. In short, they were fine for a hobbyist but not for doing serious work.

However, the PC began to mature. As they matured, businesses began to adopt them. Initially, the use of PCs was confined to small, specialized tasks within a department. As **line of business (LOB)** managers saw what PCs could do for them and that it could be done without incurring the charge-backs for IT assessed by the accounting department, with who-knows-what included (floor space? part of the break area? etc.), they continued to proliferate. Next came the demand to connect the PCs to a mainframe or minicomputer. Once connected to the mainframe, they acted as smart terminals, capable of pushing data to the mainframe as well as receiving and storing information.

In terms of application management, PCs bore a very strong resemblance to mainframes of the 1960s. Since there were no management tools, if you knew how to get to it and interpret it (most users did not know), there was some management information available from the operating system. However, it was very limited and arcane. The user filled the roles of both MCO and the application user. Again, like the mainframe operators in the 1960s, the user would run their application (just one at a time) and pray that it would not crash. If the application did fail, they would either have to figure out why it did and fix the problem, or find someone willing and able to help them.

An application management issue of particular concern that arose as the use of PCs became widespread was that of software distribution/version control. It became important to make sure that PCs scattered across the enterprise were all running the same version of each application that interfaced with the mainframe. It was a problem that was never completely solved and still it persists with PCs and servers in the current **distributed computing** environment.

THE 1990s

The mainframe continued its evolution in the 1990s, as pundits around the world proclaimed its imminent demise. Tools for application management became more sophisticated and powerful. The use of them grew and provided benefits in the form of improved availability and performance. Similarly, PCs became ubiquitous in the enterprise. However, the application management issues faced on the PC were more intractable.

In the 1990s, two "elephants" that pushed their way into the room were the Internet and client/server computing. At first glance, it does not seem like the Internet should have had a significant impact on application management. It did not have to have a material impact and it would not have, if organizations were content run corporate "intranets" and not connect the enterprise to the global Internet. Unfortunately, the temptation to grab that shiny new toy was too great to resist. Organizations, first in the United States, and gradually around the globe, started to connect their private networks to the public Internet. Usually, this was done with little regard to whether there would be material benefits from doing so. There was no risk-versus-reward assessment. It was a shiny new toy and every self-respecting technologist has to have all of the latest toys. It was *really cool* and what could possibly go wrong? (A lot!) Furthermore, it held the promise of saving money by eliminating some of an enterprise's private network expense (the same technology that enabled the Internet also enabled the deployment of corporate **local area networks (LANs)** and **wide area networks (WANs)**).

Each organization that connected their infrastructure to the Internet opened Pandora's box. The problems were not immediately apparent. It took time, but gradually the consequences started to be exposed. As the hackers started to knock on the "door," it became obvious that applications had to be better protected. Certainly network security was required, but that is not truly application management. The applications needed to have a higher level of security than the application developers were incorporating into their applications. Ever since then, there has been an ongoing struggle between the hackers and those trying to defend the corporate assets. Short of businesses disconnecting from the Internet, this struggle is going to continue indefinitely.

With almost any new technology, there is a lag between the time innovation occurs and the widespread adoption of it. With client/server, widespread adoption really took off in the 1990s. When compared by most metrics to a mainframe, those servers were cheap, *really* cheap. Like the adoption of PCs in the 1980s, the servers were cheap but did not come with management tools. It was another case of "back to the future."

Similarly, the adoption of new networking technologies for similar reasons brought comparable management problems. Of course, by this time there was a burgeoning community of third-party software developers that were ready to charge in to the gap to fill the management void in both the server and the network domains. That included addressing the full set of application management functions. By the end of the decade, developers in Silicon Valley and around the world had responded to the needs created by these new technologies, and application management in the client/server was able to be as robust as what was being done in a mainframe environment. In some cases, it was even more advanced than on the mainframes.

Together, innovations in networking, **client/server architecture**, and distributed computing led to demand from clients for the vendors of products used in these areas to support open, standards-based management. That is, the users wanted to be able to decide which management tools they would use to manage any part of the IT infrastructure. For example, they did not want to be forced to use a specific tool from the manufacturer of a router to manage those routers. The significance of this for application management was that it led to a drive to enable integrated management of the entire IT infrastructure. Just as an application did not exist or run in the absence of a computer, it could not be managed while ignoring the infrastructure that enabled it. This became even more important in the 21st century.

It may seem like the emergence of client/server, Internet, and distributed computing were just one more step along the path in the evolutionary journey of information technology. In a sense, that is true. However, taken together, they represented something much greater—a watershed period for the changes that were to follow. They opened the door for the explosive changes that have taken place since then.

Cloud computing, **virtualization**, **componentization**, etc., can all trace their routes to those changes that took place in the 1990s.

THE 21ST CENTURY: THE FIRST DECADE

The period of 2000–09 saw dramatic changes in how applications were built, how they were deployed, where and how they were run, and how they were managed. The discussion of the advances in this decade and the next will be brief. That is because they will be discussed in much greater depth in later chapters of this book. With that caveat, we can begin a quick review of the developments of the 21st century.

This was a period of changes that were simultaneously revolutionary and evolutionary. It was during this period that **service-oriented architecture (SOA)** began to be widely adopted. It meant that an application was now seen as being comprised of components, each providing a **service** when invoked by another component or by a user. It standardized the exchange of data between components and exponentially increased the complexity of applications and the management of them. Software companies in the business of building management tools were somewhat slow to respond to this demands of this new paradigm. Initial attempts were expensive, complex, labor-intensive to implement, and difficult to use. The ability of IT departments to manage applications actually regressed during this period.

Cloud computing comes in three forms: private, public, and hybrid. **Private clouds** do not have a material impact on application management. The applications are still running on infrastructure that is owned and operated within the enterprise. Therefore, it is possible to use the same management tools and disciplines as are used on other systems. **Public clouds** can create new challenges for the management of applications. Whether or not a public cloud presents those challenges really depends on the nature of the cloud and the relationship between the cloud provider and the client. If the "cloud" is really just a **platform as a service (PaaS)** (i.e., the client is contracting for exclusive use of a computer and other resources), then this is essentially the same as a private cloud. The **hybrid cloud** reflects a situation in which organizations can be thought of as having a foot in both worlds. That is, hybrid reflects the use of a combination of both public and private cloud.

It is when the "cloud" entails multiple enterprises running applications on the same computer that management challenges arise. In that type of environment, actions that a client can take are limited and tightly controlled. The client can see whatever management information is provided by the application itself. Anything beyond that is a matter of the policies of the cloud service and the agreement with the client. Similarly, the corrective actions that the client can take are generally very limited.

Virtualization is an essential technology that is the underpinning of cloud computing. It introduces a significant increase in the complexity of the environment in which applications run. However, it does not directly impact the management of applications.

Software as a service (SaaS) really had its roots in the dot-com bubble of the late 1990s. Survivors of the crash that followed the bubble learned important lessons. They proceeded to build companies to offer the use of an application software solution. One of the more famous and successful SaaS companies is SalesForce.com. From the perspective of application management, the SaaS environment is a problem. The client is not able to instrument the application or the system on which it runs. In short, the client is not able to manage SaaS applications. The decision to use SaaS applications has to be a risk-versus-reward tradeoff.

Mobile applications also appeared in this decade. However, initially, the apps on them largely targeted consumers. For that reason, we will wait to discuss them in the next section.

THE TEENS (2010—PRESENT)

As we begin our look at the last period, it is worth noting that the demarcation between this period and the preceding one is not as sharp as we perceive in those between other decades. Part of that is because we are still living through it. Also, much of what is happening reflects the continuation of changes begun in the previous decade.

Today, SOA is the norm. Everything is componentized and parts can be reused (management of componentized applications will be addressed in Chapter 9). Applications morphed from being encapsulated entities in a single, unified environment that once was the option. Now, applications are spilling across the enterprise and out of the enterprise via **application programming interfaces (APIs)** into a fabric that is forming and reforming again, bonding with various components as needed to satisfy a particular service call. Applications have become dynamic and capable of constant change, like a virulent virus.

Because of that dynamism, we are faced with the challenge of simultaneously managing each component as a discrete piece, plus managing all of the components involved in processing a transaction as a single entity. It requires a holistic view that is not limited to just the application software as the "managed object." It is necessary to take into account the resources that an application uses (e.g., systems, networks, databases, etc.). Each of those resources has the potential to impact the performance of an application, while masquerading as a problem with the application.

You may be able to look at a single component and, if you are lucky, discover that it is the cause of the problem that you are addressing. However, the odds are against you. The number of pieces has soared exponentially, and the cause of a problem may not even lie with a single piece but rather the interaction between the pieces.

Manual management of such a complex and fluid environment is not a reasonable strategy. Fortunately, tools for application management have become very intelligent and much easier to use. So far in this decade, there has been an exponential leap in the capabilities of tools for application management. For example, one application management tool (AppDynamics) is able to provide up to the minute real-time **topology** mapping (of properly instrumented applications). Autonomic application management is becoming a reality.

Despite the growing body of powerful tools for application management, research by Enterprise Management Associates (EMA) repeatedly found that less than half of enterprises are actually using tools intended specifically for application management. How can this be reconciled with the statement above that manual management of modern, dynamic applications is not a reasonable strategy? The answer is twofold. First, many organizations have not made the transition to these modern apps or have only done so on a very limited basis. Traditional applications are the mainstay for those organizations. Management of those applications will be discussed in Chapter 3, "Management of Traditional Applications." The other half of the answer is that some organizations have deployed modern applications, but are still relying on the old "break/fix" approach to management of them—a very shortsighted approach that is certain to lead to missed service-level commitments and disgruntled users.

There two other major changes in this decade: mobile applications and the **Internet of Things (IoT)**. Particular challenges in each are connectivity, security, and massive scale. Mobile will be discussed in Chapter 6, "Management of Mobile Applications," and IoT is discussed in Chapter 15, "Application Management in the Internet of Things."

SUMMARY

The history and development of application management have been inexorably tied to the evolution the entire spectrum of the associated technology (networks, computer systems, operating system software, etc.). While tightly coupled with the other parts of the IT infrastructure, management technologies (including application management) have always lagged behind the other areas of innovation and evolution. Table 2.2 summarizes the developments discussed in this chapter.

Table 2.2 The Evolution of Application Management

Period	Key IT Technology Advances	Application Management
1950–59	Commercial adoption of computers	Application management happened in a reactionary mode without the aid of tools.
1960–69	Mainframe computers	Error logs were the primary tool for application management.
1970–79	Online, real-time processing	Rudimentary information for application management began to be provided, primarily by the operating systems.
1980–89	Evolution of mainframes Appearance of minicomputers Personal computers	Growing body of ISV management tools for mainframe applications, less for minicomputers. Virtually no application management resources were available for PCs.
1990–99	Internet/LANs/WANs Client/server architecture Distributed computing	Open, standards-based management tools, hardware and software. An integrated, holistic approach to application management.
2000–09	Cloud computing Virtualization SaaS	Applications no longer run in a single, unified environment. Management capabilities regressed relative to the new environments. SaaS offers lower cost application functionality, but takes away from the enterprise the ability to manage those applications.
2010–present	SOA Componentized applications Mobile applications IoT	Sophisticated, automated management tools have emerged to help manage this dynamic environment. Mobile applications present challenges to application management in terms of communication, security and scale.

MANAGEMENT OF TRADITIONAL APPLICATIONS

3

But that was yesterday and yesterday's gone…
Chad Stuart, "Yesterday's Gone"

A Day in the Life at Acme Manufacturing.

Meet Dave. He is a help desk technician working at the service desk at Acme Manufacturing. He has been doing this job for almost two years. From his perspective, it's just a job—definitely not something that he wants to do for the rest of his life, but for now, it pays the bills. His responsibilities are pretty limited; he spends most of his shift on the phone with users. He just finished a call that was fairly representative of what he deals with on a daily basis.

Dave: Service Desk, this is Dave. How can I help you?

Nancy: This is Nancy in billing. I'm not able to get into the accounts receivable application. In fact, nobody in the department is able to. What's happened to the application?

Dave: Are you able to get to the login screen?

Nancy: No, I can't get to anything! What's wrong?

Dave: Is anything showing on your monitor?

Nancy: Not much. I've got a black screen with a blinking cursor.

Dave thinks to himself, "Well, at least the monitor is turned on. It's surprising how often I get a call about a supposed network problem and it turns to be a monitor or PC that's not turned on."

Dave: Let me take a look.

The accounts receivable application is a relatively old (15 years), traditional application. It runs on a single server located in the data center, which happens to be in the same building as the billing department. Dave turns to the monitoring screen to see that the accounts receivable application appears to be running. Next, he looks at the network manager, which is not showing any signs of trouble. *Following standard procedure, he "bounces" the line to the billing department. That is, he resets the circuit and the router in the department.*

Dave: Try it now. Can you get in?

Nancy: No. It's the same as it was before.

Dave: I'm going to have research this and open a trouble ticket. You'll be able to check on the status of the ticket at any time and I'll let you know when it's fixed.

Nancy: Okay, but can you make it a priority? This is the end of the month, you know.

Dave: Yes, of course. Goodbye.

At this point, Dave is honestly stumped. The tools that he has in front of him indicate that everything is working. Nothing seems out of the ordinary. Therefore, he escalates it to an application specialist. We'll return to Acme Manufacturing and the accounts receivable application problem at the end of this chapter.

Traditional **applications** are ones that were created 10 to 20 years ago, possibly even longer ago than that. Instead of calling them "traditional applications," most people in information technology (IT) refer to these applications simply as "really old," "ancient," or as a "dinosaur." These basic applications run on a mainframe environment or in a client/server environment. Architecturally, little has changed about them since they were created. They are old workhorses that have not been retired yet. They have not been "webified," componentized, containerized, or turned into a mobile app. Supporting them is not a highly sought-after programming assignment. Most developers are willing to do almost anything to avoid being assigned to maintaining one of these applications. However, they are a good place for us to start the discussion of **application management**, because in traditional applications things are (relatively) simple and easy to understand.

> Managing an application consists of monitoring and controlling that application.

The most concise definition of **management** as it applies to the management of applications is that it consists of the monitoring and control of a managed object. The managed object can be anything. It may be a router, a server, or anything else that can be monitored and controlled. In this case, an application is the object that is being managed.

Saying that management consists of a monitor function and a control function is useful as a quick pneumonic, but this hides the complexity required in order to effectively manage applications (or any other object). The monitoring and control of an application is not achieved in a vacuum. They require the use of people, processes, tools, and technologies to achieve those functions. However, that is not enough. Before an application can be managed, it is necessary to know that it exists, where it resides, when it is running, and where the code can be found when it is not running.

LOOKING BACK

In the early days of IT, knowing which application was running was the purview of the **master console operator (MCO)**. Most of the knowledge about applications was contained in run books, shift turn-over notes, handwritten notes passed from one MCO to the next, and general tribal knowledge. The environment was relatively simple and stable (although at that time it did not seem to be either simple or stable). Jobs were run in batch mode, and "everyone" knew which hard drive held a particular application. Applications could be configured and executed through a set of instructions written in

job control language (JCL). The MCO monitored the status of each application, and there were really only two results of running an application: the application could complete successfully or it could end abnormally (ABEND). The universe of applications that might be run in a medium-to-large data center typically numbered in the low hundreds and the dependencies between applications were almost always linear. For example, the order entry application ran before the accounts receivable application and that always ran before the general ledger application. Components of an application ran on one system. That is, various components of a single application were not dispersed and did not run on multiple computer systems. In fact, there may have been only one system in the entire data center.

Today, the IT environment is an infinitely more complex atmosphere. A large company will have thousands of unique applications—tens of thousands, in some cases. Applications are no longer confined to running on a single mainframe computer in a data center. Servers are scattered far and wide across the enterprise, and some of them are not even properly accounted for (i.e., are not recorded as an asset on the company's books). Some may have been purchased surreptitiously, perhaps even recorded as "HVAC repairs" or "warehouse shelving units." While such slight of hand may be helpful in concealing a server from the powers that be for a while, it is inappropriate and, in some jurisdictions (including the United States), illegal. This same practice applies to applications. That is, the purchase of **commercial-off-the-shelf software (COTS)** is concealed as a different type of expense. Staff responsible for developing applications internally may be hidden by classifying them as regular **line of business (LOB)** staff. Regardless of the ethics or legality of such practices, they occur all too frequently. The result is that it is unlikely that IT is aware of all of the systems that are running in an enterprise and even less aware of all of the applications.

Once systems moved out of the tightly controlled environment of the data center, the genie escaped from the bottle, never to return. Since that moment, it has been impossible for operations staff—whether in the IT department or in a business unit—to know with certainty what applications exist within the organization, where applications have been installed, where they will run (since not all of the pieces of an application will run on the same system and one piece may not even run on the same system every time), when they were installed, or when they were modified. Operations personnel may or may not know when a particular application is supposed to run, what dependencies it may have for other applications or resources, or even the owner of the application. It is something of a Wild West environment.

Add applications that are being run on desktop/laptop systems to this chaotic world. Many people tend to trivialize the significance or difficulty of managing the applications running on those systems, and some even question the need to manage them at all.

First, let's make a distinction between those desktop/laptop systems that are running a minimum set of productivity tools (e.g., Microsoft Office and a web browser) and those that are running a more complex set of applications. In truth, those plain vanilla desktop/laptop systems are rare in the business world. Even your elderly Aunt Martha will probably have a few extra applications that she uses on a regular basis (e.g., an eReader, an application to archive her photos, perhaps an application for playing solitaire, etc.). When considering the relative ease of using laptop/desktop systems and of installing or even upgrading applications on them, it is important to remember the sheer volume of objects to be managed and that they are often not connected for extended periods of time. Adding to the difficulty is that, universally, users seem to be incapable of resisting the temptation to make changes to their system, alter the configuration of the applications, and or installing their favorite applications. In short, what may start out as a **personal computer** with a standard set of applications configured according to a corporate standard very quickly is modified and customized according to the whims of the user.

THE MANAGEMENT IMPERATIVE

Any system, and particularly the applications that run on it, for which technical support is provided must be manageable. In conjunction with work on standards for **Open Systems Interconnect (OSI)** and **Common Management Information Protocol (CMIP)**, the **International Standards Organization (ISO)** defined management as consisting of the following functions: **fault**, **configuration**, **accounting**, **performance**, and **security (FCAPS)** (Fig. 3.1).

> Any system, and particularly the applications that run on it, for which technical support is provided must be manageable.

The first step in managing an application on a desktop/laptop system is to configure the system. The initial configuration may define the user, define the security policy (e.g., is a password required to access the total system or an individual application?), and set up the email system. In a corporate setting, it will be necessary to capture some information about this asset. This will be used for inventory and depreciation purposes (accounting) and as a reference for technical support personnel (fault and performance). We will examine application management of a desktop/laptop system in greater depth

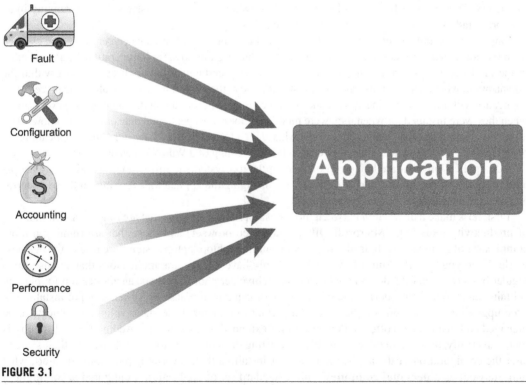

FIGURE 3.1

ISO management functions.

FIGURE 3.2

Mobile devices: the "elephant in the room."

later in this book. The key point to take away at this stage is that application management is required in these environments and it has special challenges. The era of **bring your own device (BYOD)** has further compounded the challenges of application management. We will look at those issues in Chapter 6, "Management of **Mobile Applications**."

We talked about the management of applications on **mainframe computers**, servers, and desktop/laptop systems. Next, we need to talk about the elephant in the room (Fig. 3.2): **mobile devices** (e.g., smartphones and tablets). The proliferation of mobile devices represents a new environment with management challenges that are materially greater than those seen in the other environments. All of the issues associated with applications on laptop computers exist with mobile devices in a plethora of unique **operating systems**. We will look at the management of applications on mobile devices in more depth in Chapter 6.

Taken together, application management across the various platforms is a dynamic and exciting environment. Business units are getting more benefits more quickly from the computing resources that they rely on. They have found that they can connect more tightly with their customers—increasing customer satisfaction and "stickiness" (i.e., customer loyalty).

With multiple platforms, however, comes the clear problem of how to manage them all. What we need to do is to learn to apply the principles of application management across all of these environments to maximize the performance and availability of those applications while, at the same, maintaining an acceptable level of security.

RESPONSIBILITIES

We can all agree that technology has reached a point where application management is very difficult, so how can we turn it into a manageable task? The answer is simple: break it down into smaller pieces and apply automation (Fig. 3.3).

Another way of looking at application management is that it requires two things: to know (monitor) and to do (control). Who needs to know about an application? First, there are the frontline staff who are

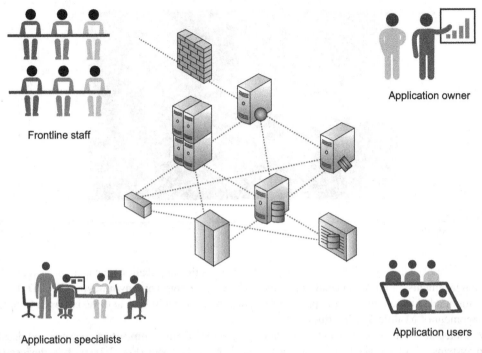

FIGURE 3.3

The players.

responsible for keeping things up and running smoothly. They have a variety of titles: system administrator, help desk technician, service desk analyst, etc. The exact titles will vary, but these are the people who actively monitor environments for problems; who receive alerts from management software and who are charged with resolving those problems when they occur. They are the firefighters.

There is another group of people who address application management problems reactively (more difficult problems are referred to them for resolution) and proactively (taking steps to prevent problems from occurring). There is not a lot of consistency in titles for people in the second group. For this discussion, we will simply refer to them as application specialists. They also install and configure applications and have the seemingly endless challenge of making sure all copies of an application are the current version. Maintenance agreements for third-party software must be kept current and updates applied when appropriate. Just maintaining an inventory of software installed and software licensed throughout the enterprise is a daunting task. Another challenge is making sure that the business has current licenses for every copy of third-party software that is in use. Finally, there are the application developers—the people who develop and maintain the applications (please note: this list is not intended to be an exhaustive list of job titles and responsibilities. Titles can vary significantly from one organization to another).

There are a couple more players that deserve to be mentioned. They are the application users and the application owner. The users are the people who actually use an application to perform some business function. They may be employees, customers, contractors, etc. The application owner is the business executive whose staff or customers are the primary users of the application. In some organizations, the application owner funds the development and maintenance (or purchase) of the application and may have some degree of limited visibility into the operational status of the application. However, neither the owner nor the user has any responsibility or authority over the management of the application.

KNOWING

Let's take a look at what each of these groups needs to know.

FRONTLINE STAFF

This group needs to know what is happening at any given point in time. They need to know the health of an application, essentially, its availability and performance. The data can come from a variety of tools, plus reports from users of the applications. The following are examples of what they need to know:

Installed applications
Application dependencies (other applications, resources, etc.)
Applications that are currently running
Applications that are supposed to be running but are not (e.g., failed, waiting on other jobs or resources, etc.)
Indicators of the **application performance** level
Application availability (running does not mean an application is available to users)
Configuration settings
License information (including status of maintenance agreements)
Ecosystem information (network, systems, databases, etc.)

As discussed in Chapter 12, a user does not see each of the unique pieces that must work together in order for that user to be able to access the application's functionality. If I am a user, I look at availability as a binary matter. I can either use the application to do my job, or I cannot. If I go to an ATM to conduct a transaction, perhaps to withdraw cash, it either works or it does not. I am totally unaware of the multiple applications that are involved in serving my request. As a user, if I cannot access the application, I do not know nor do I care what the cause is; I just want it fixed immediately. It is that simple. It is similar when thinking about performance. The application responds quickly, slowly, or somewhere in between, but I am solely focused on my use of the application. If the application is not available or its performance is degraded, I do not care if the cause is a network problem, a server issue, or a change to the configuration of the application itself. I just want to be able to get some cash so I can go to dinner with some friends on a Friday night (Fig. 3.4).

There are a myriad of things that can impact the performance or availability of the application. The management of those things that are outside of the application (e.g., network, systems, data, etc.) is beyond the scope of this book.

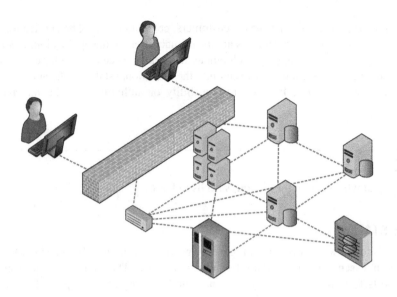

FIGURE 3.4

User perspective.

APPLICATION SPECIALISTS

Their information requirements are similar to those of the frontline staff, but they are much more concerned with information about performance, configuration, and application dependencies. While the needs of frontline staff are primarily for real-time information, application specialists tend to work from a historical perspective (except when they are installing and configuring applications). The following are key items required by application specialists:

Installed applications

Application dependencies (other applications, resources, etc.)

Indicators of the application performance level

Application availability (running does not mean an application is available to users)

Configuration settings

License information (including status of maintenance agreements)

Ecosystem information (network, systems, databases, etc.)

APPLICATION DEVELOPERS

Their need for application management capabilities parallels those of their colleagues in operations, the frontline staff and application specialists. This is because their responsibilities are not just limited to writing code. They must also test the applications that they write (or modify) before moving them into the production, meaning that they need to be able to install and configure the applications in a test environment. They also need to be able to monitor the application while it is running to see how it performs, which lets them see what happens to it under a workload similar to what will be encountered in production. In some situations, depending on company policies, application developers may be asked to help resolve a problem with an application that is in production. In that situation, they may need to access some of the same management tools in the production environment used by frontline staff and application specialists. It is also the responsibility of application developers to create applications that are manageable. We will look at that set of challenges in Chapter 9, "**DevOps** and **Continuous Delivery**."

It is in the realm of *knowing* that automation is most important. The computing resources in even a small enterprise are capable of generating a flood of data far beyond the ability of any human to absorb and analyze. Management tools are the only way to address this problem, but they are both a blessing and a curse. The strength of management tools lies in their ability to collect huge amounts of data, and then analyze, summarize, and prioritize it before presenting it as information to be acted on by the humans charged with managing the applications. This is the positive side of management tools. The negative side is that the tools are capable of collecting so much data (even when summarized) that they can flood their human counterparts. It requires both art and science to select the right management tools and to configure them optimally to ensure that the people managing the application(s) receive all of the information that they need without being buried with a flood of data.

CONTROLLING

Each of the players in the application management process needs to be able to exert nearly absolute control over the application(s) that he or she is monitoring. They have the authority to start (or restart) applications, cancel an application, modify configurations, install new versions, apply patches to the application, etc. However, only application developers have the authority to modify the application's source code. Changes to source code will normally be made separate development environment and then tested in a separate "test" environment before being moved into the production environment. When there is a crisis, though, some of the best practices may be bypassed in the rush to resolve a problem as quickly as possible. While the urgency is understandable, bypassing standard processes carries the risk of introducing new problems or creating gaps in the application's security.

In most cases in an operational environment, frontline staff and application specialists will rely upon management tools as the medium through which they exercise control of applications. While there are occasional exceptions, the use of management tools is the most efficient way to exercise control over an application and, in general, is the only practical way to do so. As an example, think of software distribution. In a single enterprise there can be thousands of systems running pieces of an application that are often scattered across many countries. Historically, installing a new application or new version of an application required someone physically going to that device and installing the software. However, in a distributed organization with thousands of systems in dozens to hundreds of locations, the cost of sending a person to each of the enterprise's locations is prohibitive. The logistics are also impractical, particularly in those cases when it is necessary to have all of the instances of the application cut over to a new version at the same time. In response to those problems, some organizations tried the "honor system" of software distribution. That is, the new software would be shipped to someone at each location. That person was given instructions about when and how to install the software.

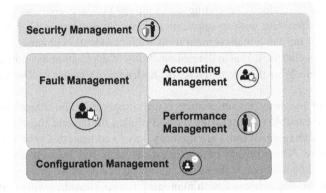

FIGURE 3.5

FCAPS model.

In theory, the "honor system" for software distribution sounded like a great idea. However, the theory ignored some simple problems, such as some people were traveling and did not receive the software before the deadline for the installation. Others felt that they had more important things to do than installing the software. In short, for a multitude of reasons (or excuses), the "honor system" for software distribution was a failure. The solution to the problem was to automate the process. Today, software is pushed to distributed systems by a software distribution system. The tool for software distribution may be a COTS product or a tool that was developed in-house.

FUNCTIONAL PERSPECTIVE

Earlier in this chapter we discussed the ISO model for management. Let's take a quick look at how those functions are realized in a traditional application management environment (Fig. 3.5).

FAULT

A management tool monitors each application for any indication of a problem with the application and frequently polls the application for information about the application's status. When a problem is detected, frontline staff will be notified. Ideally, the management tool detects the problem and notifies them early enough that failure of the application can be averted. However, too often that does not happen. Perhaps there were no early warning signs of the impending failure of an application, perhaps staff was not paying attention, or for a myriad of other reasons an application can fail and sometimes have a cascade effect on other applications, causing them also to fail.

CONFIGURATION

This is commonly done with administrator authority for the application via an interface created by the application developers for this purpose. Unfortunately, creating that interface is often done at the last minute and done poorly. Sometimes, but not always, this results in an interface that is arcane and difficult to use. Fortunately, more experienced developers recognize the importance of that human interaction and deliver an interface for application configuration that is more user-friendly.

It is in the configuration process that the application's operating parameters are set. Those parameters include such things as:

Users and their respective authority levels, a.k.a., what can each person do?
Data sources/repositories and the location(s) of them
Dependencies to other applications
Port mapping
URL specification
Network configurations

Some applications need to have multiple network cards installed on the server for additional bandwidth or parallel processing. It is also important to specify such items as **quality of service (QoS)** priorities so network settings can reflect how the application actually works. Anything involving video or even audio would need higher priority, while bulk data exchange or transfers can often proceed at a slower rate. Also, if a **virtual private network (VPN)** connection is required, that needs to be defined.

Getting the configurations right is critically important. Mistakes in configurations are a common source of application-related problems; for example, where mismatches occur between "as designed" and "as provisioned."

Note: It is important to recognize that the term "configuration" in the context of this book refers specifically to the operating parameters of an application. In the world of application development, "software configuration management" refers to the processes put in place to manage the introduction of changes to an application.

ACCOUNTING

This aspect can be divided into two primary functions: **asset management** and resource utilization. Asset management requires awareness that the application is present in the environment. That should be easier with COTS applications, or at least that is the theory. In practice, the location of each application can be very loose. Operations personnel will move applications from one system to another for any myriad of reasons, such as to balance the workload between systems, as a workaround to a problem, etc. They will sometimes install a copy of a COTS application on another system as a backup in case something happens to take down the "live" copy. In that event, they can quickly start the backup copy, which is a sound practice. However, it often occurs that the software license agreement for that application does not allow for the backup copy to be created, and by making a backup copy the staff has created a legal problem for the enterprise. Before installing a backup copy of a COTS application, it is important to make sure that license for that software allows for a backup copy.

There are two options for keeping track of applications. The first is to rely on the "tribal knowledge" of operations personnel. That is, rely on the IT organization to keep track of what it has and where each application is located. While prone to errors and omissions, this approach is widely used because it is cheap and because it has inertia on its side, i.e., the mindset of "we've always done it this way." The other option is to regularly use a management tool to discover the applications. This approach has its own challenges—especially if operations staff have attempted to hide an application. It is not sufficient to know where an application exists or even what dependencies it has. The application's attributes need to also be captured and documented. This can happen as part of the configuration management process or it can happen separately, but it must happen. More mature IT organizations store that information in a **configuration management database (CMDB)**. An overview of CMDB is provided in Appendix B.

Information about resource utilization is obviously important to operations personnel (including frontline staff and application specialists) in their daily activities of monitoring the application for problems, in performance, and tuning. Resource utilization data are also important for capacity planning and for anticipating when additional hardware will need to be added.

PERFORMANCE

Fault management and **performance management** are the two domains that account for most of the daily activities of frontline staff and application specialists. While fault management looks at an application to determine whether it is "broken" (i.e., it has failed or has another serious problem), performance management is concerned with keeping an application running "well." That is, performance management seeks to ensure that an application is operating within the parameters specified in the relevant **service-level agreement (SLA)** and **operational-level agreement (OLA)**. This is largely a question of the speed at which the application does its work. An absolute requirement for **application performance management (APM)** is a set of tools to collect and analyze data about the application. Some of the collected data will be archived to allow a historical perspective to be taken when analyzing problems. SLAs are discussed in Appendix A, **"Service-Level Management."**

SECURITY

The priority for application security is ensuring that only authorized people or other applications are allowed to make use of the application's functionality. That is, only those with permission can use the application to retrieve information or instruct it to perform an activity, such as generate a refund to a client, order more supplies, etc. Preventing intrusions into a system, while absolutely essential as part of an overall security strategy, is not part of security for the application. The role of application security is to ensure that if a hacker gains access to a system, the intruder is not able to use the application. Another piece of the application security puzzle is ensuring that only authorized changes are made to the application or to its configuration (change control). Without that protection, an intruder or a disgruntled (or inept) employee can simply change configuration settings in ways that compromise the integrity of the application. Securing applications is discussed in Chapter 8, "Application Security."

A Day in The Life (continued)…

When we left the accounts receivable application problem, it had just escalated. When the escalated ticket is referred, it gets routed (randomly) to an application specialist. In this case, it landed on the desk of Liz Winters. She has been working at Acme 12 years, eight of them in the IT department. She likes working at Acme, since she has a lot of friends there. She also enjoys the variety of challenges that her job presents.

She has a lot more experience, training, and resources than Dave, so she begins by making sure that the network is really up. She tries to ping the router in the department, which is successful.

"OK," she thinks. "It's not the network."

She can see that the accounts receivable application is up. However, when she looks at a system monitor, she can see that the application shows zero activity. She wonders, "What's going on here?" As she drills down further, she is able to see that there is no I/O activity for the application.

"Hmmm, that's odd."

Hoping for a quick fix and acting on a hunch, she decides to cancel and restart the application. A few minutes later, she checks back and is surprised to see that there is still no I/O activity for the application. Not wanting to waste time chasing phantoms, she calls Nancy in the billing department and asks her to try to log in. Unfortunately, Nancy still cannot.

Now Liz is puzzled.

"The network is up. The system is up. The application is up, but it isn't doing anything. Okay, at least at a theoretical level. I'll buy the idea that without anyone using the system there wouldn't be any noticeable activity, but why can't the users get into the app?"

She talks with a couple of coworkers. One of them suggests checking the configuration for the application and if that appears normal, then it will be necessary to call a developer for help, which she hates, as she feels that some of them are really condescending toward the application specialists. Before she does this, she pulls up the documentation from the CMDB system so she can see what the configuration settings should be. The configuration for the Accounts Receivable application is split into several files.

This is going to be a slow, methodical process. She is going to have to check every value for every setting in each of the files. There cannot be any shortcuts here. The only thing that can shorten the process is being lucky and finding the problem sooner rather than later. Before she can start, her manager calls and asks for an update. Accounting has escalated the problem at their end and now the operations director wants to know what is going on and how long it is going to take to fix it, etc. She grumbles to herself, "I'd be closer to solving this thing if they'd just let me do my job instead of sitting here explaining everything."

Explanation finished, she starts through the first config file. Based upon what she knows, she decides to start where there is a higher probability of finding the cause of the problem: the sysconfig file. As she starts checking the settings, she notices that the setting for the address of the AR database is blank.

"What the...?" she thinks. "What moron did that?"

She quickly plugs in the correct value; kills the accounts receivable application, and restarts it. While waiting for it to come back up, she reflects on how the IT department at Acme Manufacturing could be so progressive in some areas and foolishly stingy in others. Because there is not a tool in place to track and manage changes to the configuration settings, there is no way that they would ever know who deleted the setting for the location of the AR database, unless the person who did it was foolish enough to confess.

The accounts receivable application is back up. Liz checks her monitor. The accounts receivable application is now showing a low level of I/O activity. Although the application had appeared to be active before, it had never completed its startup routine, and that is why no one could log in to the application. She picks up the phone and calls Nancy in the billing department to give her the good news. Total downtime charged against the SLA: 1 h 12 min.

As she proceeds to close the trouble ticket, Liz makes a promise to herself that at her manager's next staff meeting, she should bring up the problems caused by the lack of a tool to track and control changes. It is then that a troubling thought crosses her mind: what if the problem had not been caused by a mistake; what if had been done intentionally? There is no way to know – and that will be her main message at the next staff meeting.

This is a simple example of how application management can be critical to IT being able to meet the needs of the business. We will meet the folks at Acme Manufacturing again, later in the book.

SUMMARY

Managing traditional applications is not rocket science. In fact, it is relatively simple when compared to more modern application architectures. However, it still requires a structured approach to the process, well-trained staff, and the appropriate tools. Without those tools, application management would be reduced to waiting for an application to fail or for its performance to degrade and then trying to guess at the cause as well as a solution. That is simply not tenable.

KEY TAKEAWAYS

- Application management consists of monitoring and controlling applications
- ISO model for management
  - Fault
  - Configuration
  - Accounting
  - Performance
  - Security

- Even the management of traditional applications requires tools
  - **Real-time monitoring** of the applications (fault, performance, and security)
  - Data collection, analysis, and storage
  - Application Discovery and Dependency Mapping
  - Change control
  - Service desk management tools

APPLICATION MANAGEMENT IN THE CLOUD

I've looked at clouds from both sides now
From up and down, and still somehow
It's cloud illusions I recall
I really don't know clouds at all
Joni Mitchell, "Both Sides Now"

"The Cloud"—nearly everyone has heard of it, many have used it in some form, and at least among IT professionals, nearly everyone thinks that they know what it is. In truth, most only have limited insight into a single variant of **cloud computing**. Before we can dive into the discussion of **application management** in the cloud, we must first establish some common terminology.

Let's begin with a very basic point. There is no such thing as "The Cloud." Cloud computing is not represented by a single entity as some might argue the Internet is. Rather, cloud computing is a technology that exists in hundreds of thousands (possibly millions) of unique instances.

In 2011, the **National Institute of Standards and Technology (NIST)** published a report titled, "The NIST Definition of Cloud Computing." That report became a watershed definition for cloud computing. It is particularly important because it was developed without the biases of those with commercial interests in the technology. Since that report was published, cloud computing continues to evolve. The range of types of cloud computing services must be viewed as a continuum, rather than a set of discrete types. This is partly due to each solution provider approaching the problem in a slightly different way—sometimes for technical reasons and sometimes in an attempt to set their offering apart from competitors. However, the key aspects of a cloud environment are **virtualization**, scalability, flexible resource management, data center automation (to support on-demand services), usage metering, and **security**.

Cloud computing can be broken down into three broad categories: **private cloud**, **public cloud**, and **hybrid cloud**. That seems pretty simple and straightforward and was, until cloud became the new fad topic in IT. That meant marketing organizations around the world began to weave their own messages around the theme, molding and shaping the meaning to suit their purposes. This allowed them to claim that their products were relevant, perhaps even essential, to cloud computing. The intent was not to fault those focus organizations. What they did is simply attempt to supply a definition (that is most favorable to them) to fill a void when there is no consensus about the meaning of a term. While we can't put that particular genie back in the bottle, we can at least establish a set of definitions that we will use throughout this book.

Application Performance Management (APM) in the Digital Enterprise. http://dx.doi.org/10.1016/B978-0-12-804018-8.00004-8

ESSENTIAL CHARACTERISTICS

On-demand self-service. A consumer can unilaterally provision computing capabilities, such as server time and network storage, as needed automatically without requiring human interaction with each service provider.

Broad network access. Capabilities are available over the network and accessed through standard mechanisms that promote use by heterogeneous thin or thick client platforms (e.g., mobile phones, tablets, laptops, and workstations).

Resource pooling. The provider's computing resources are pooled to serve multiple consumers using a multitenant model, with different physical and virtual resources dynamically assigned and reassigned according to consumer demand. There is a sense of location independence in that the customer generally has no control or knowledge over the exact location of the provided resources but may be able to specify location at a higher level of abstraction (e.g., country, state, or data center). Examples of resources include storage, processing, memory, and network bandwidth.

Rapid elasticity. Capabilities can be elastically provisioned and released, in some cases automatically, to scale rapidly outward and inward commensurate with demand. To the consumer, the capabilities available for provisioning often appear to be unlimited and can be appropriated in any quantity at any time.

Measured service. Cloud systems automatically control and optimize resource use by leveraging a metering capability at some level of abstraction appropriate to the type of service (e.g., storage, processing, bandwidth, and active user accounts). Resource usage can be monitored, controlled, and reported, providing transparency for both the provider and consumer of the utilized service.[1]

[1]"Characteristics of Cloud Computing." NIST. NIST SP 800-145, The NIST Definition of Cloud Computing csrc.nist.gov/publications/nistpubs/800-145/SP800-145.pdf.

Types of Cloud Computing
    Private cloud
    Public cloud
        Software as a Service (SaaS)
        Platform as a Service (PaaS)
        Infrastructure as a Service (IaaS)
    Hybrid cloud

PUBLIC CLOUD

Public cloud services are offered by companies to provide their customers with access to computing resources over a public network (Fig. 4.1). The cloud service provider is responsible for provisioning and managing the hardware and software associated with the service being offered. The public cloud actually consists of three types of services: **software as a service (SaaS)**, **infrastructure as a service (IaaS)**, and **platform as a service (PaaS)**. The main advantage offered by public cloud environments comes from the lower costs that can be realized. On the other hand, there are concerns about security of data and regulatory issues.

In the SaaS model, the customer uses an application that is owned and hosted by the service provider. In the simplest form of the pure public cloud model, there is not any interface between the hosted application and any **applications** running in the customer's organization (or any other SaaS applications hosted by a different service provider). In the public cloud environment, SaaS is the most popular public cloud service offering. Research by Enterprise Management Associates (EMA) found that 67% of enterprises surveyed were delivering at least one production service (i.e., use of an application for

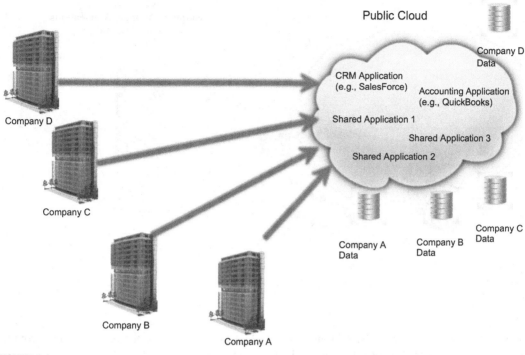

FIGURE 4.1

Public cloud.

a routine business activity) via a SaaS-based cloud application. Two examples of widely used SaaS applications are SalesForce.com and Google Docs.

PaaS provides the customers with a complete computing environment that includes **operating systems**, databases, software tools, and support services, often in a multitenant environment. PaaS is quite popular as an application development environment. Developers are freed of the need to address issues of **configuration**, management, and so on, and are able to focus specifically on the development of new software. Not only can the software be developed and tested in a PaaS environment, it can also be put into production in the same PaaS environment.

The popularity of IaaS is similar to that of PaaS. According to that same EMA research report, 55% of organizations surveyed are using IaaS, whereas 56% were using PaaS, although the data indicated that IaaS is being adopted at a faster rate than PaaS. In this service model, the customer is essentially renting computing resources such as computers (servers or mainframe), storage, operating system software, database software, and (in some cases) network capacity. The customer is responsible for configuring and managing those resources. That is simultaneously an advantage of PaaS and a disadvantage. It is particularly suited to rapid prototyping and for applications with workloads that fluctuate widely. It is an alternative to buying or leasing the equipment and associated software. Examples of IaaS are IBM BlueMix, Microsoft Azure CloudBees, and **Amazon Web Services**.

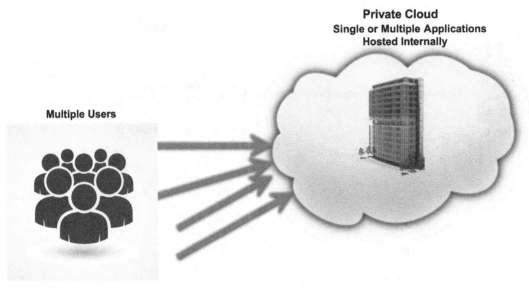

FIGURE 4.2

Private cloud.

However, PaaS does require the customer to have IT staff to configure the resources and provide ongoing management. This offsets some of the financial benefits of the PaaS model.

PRIVATE CLOUD

A private cloud has many of the same characteristics as a public cloud (Fig. 4.2). The difference is that the resources used for this service belong to the enterprise (usually the IT department). Since a private cloud is physically located within the enterprise, concerns about security are greatly reduced. A private cloud offers nearly the same level of security that is available for other corporate systems. Likewise, regulatory compliance becomes a nonissue with a properly configured and secured private cloud environment.

HYBRID CLOUD

Hybrid clouds are where the greatest ambiguity about the nature of this particular beast lives (Fig. 4.3). Much has been written about it and there are many differing opinions. For this book, we define a hybrid cloud as one that enables the sharing of data between two or more clouds operated by different enterprises. This sharing could be between two public cloud SaaS applications operated by different companies and used by a third company (the customer). For example, the customer might want to share data between SalesForce and Marketo. More common is the **integration** of data between a public cloud application and a private cloud application. However, hybrid cloud is commonly viewed as a mix of public and private clouds.

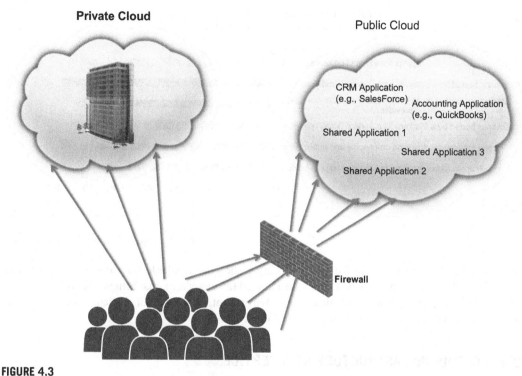

FIGURE 4.3

Hybrid cloud.

MANAGEMENT OF CLOUD APPLICATIONS

Managing applications in cloud environments brings a variety of challenges and those challenges vary, depending on the type of cloud environment. The difficulty in managing cloud-based applications depends largely on the type of cloud environment in which the application is running (Fig. 4.4). There are two sides to the management coin in a cloud environment: service provider and user. As we will see shortly, management can mean very different things for those two groups.

PRIVATE CLOUD

The simplest environment in which to manage an application is a private cloud. A private cloud is completely within the enterprise and so are any applications running in that cloud. IT (or its equivalent in a business unit) has complete control of all the hardware and software that is enabling the cloud. IT is able to install and use any management tools that it feels will be helpful in monitoring the environment or analyzing the data captured by the management tools. IT can modify the configuration of each of the cloud components to optimize the **performance** of an application. IT's ability to manage an application is limited only by budget and the availability of management tools. In short, IT is able to manage applications in a private cloud as completely and effectively as it can manage any other applications that it

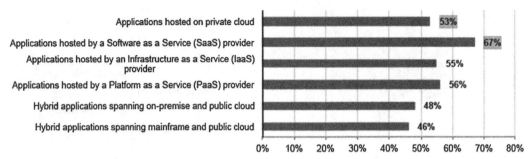

Which cloud application types is your company currently delivering as a production service?

FIGURE 4.4

Cloud deployments.

Figure 1, page 6, "Public Cloud Comes of Age".

runs in noncloud environments (a list of monitoring techniques available for cloud environments is shown in Fig. 4.5). Yes, if the private cloud is virtualized (as many are), that brings a set of challenges related to operating and managing the virtualized environment. Those are not challenges of application management and therefore not within the scope of this chapter.

PUBLIC CLOUD: INFRASTRUCTURE AS A SERVICE

The first step beyond the enterprise and a private cloud is IaaS. In the IaaS environment, application is relatively straightforward. The customer (i.e., usually the IT department) can use whatever management tools and strategies they wish (Fig. 4.6). They can install agents to monitor the applications and provide data to management tools. They can install application management tools on the IaaS server. Those tools can be accessed remotely and used to monitor and control the application(s) on that remote server. It is also possible to use remote tools to manage the application(s) running on the IaaS server. Of course, that is constrained by the security measures on the IaaS server and the terms of the license agreements for those management tools. In short, applications on an IaaS server can be managed as if that environment is just another corporate data center, at least to the extent that the service provider will allow.

The fact that an application in an IaaS environment happens to be remote is only a minor consideration. It does introduce the network as a factor that must be taken into account when assessing the application's performance. However, this is true with any application, whether that application is behind the corporate **firewall** or outside of it.

PUBLIC CLOUD: PLATFORM AS A SERVICE

When an application is moved into a PaaS environment, management of that application becomes more difficult. The customer's IT department no longer has complete control of the environment. It is the service provider's staff that will make and implement the decisions about the configuration of the environment in which the application will run. They will determine what security measures will be put in

Agent-based monitoring
Synthetic transactions
Endpoint (desktop, mobile device, etc.) monitoring
Real user (network-focused) monitoring (RUM)
Transaction tracing and "stitching" to deliver end-to-end execution visibility
Infrastructure instrumentation
Browser injection
Web server instrumentation
Java instrumentation
.NET instrumentation
Transaction tagging
Protocols such as WMI, SNMP, HTTP/S, etc.
Network flow tools
Third-party agents
Log files
Unstructured data
APIs (for public cloud platforms)
Automated discovery data
CMDB/CMS data/metadata

FIGURE 4.5

Cloud data collection techniques and data sources.

place (those measures may impact access to the application, or associated agents, by management tools). Some service providers offer some limited management information, but this is not a universal practice.

Unless the customer is able to negotiate an exception to the service provider's policy, the customer will not be able to install management software in the cloud environment. Furthermore, in most situations, the customer will not be able to use remote management tools to see through the firewall and monitor the application. If the service provider allows customers to install and run their own applications in the environment, then some management capability may be able to be included in the application (this approach is closer to IaaS than the usual PaaS offering).

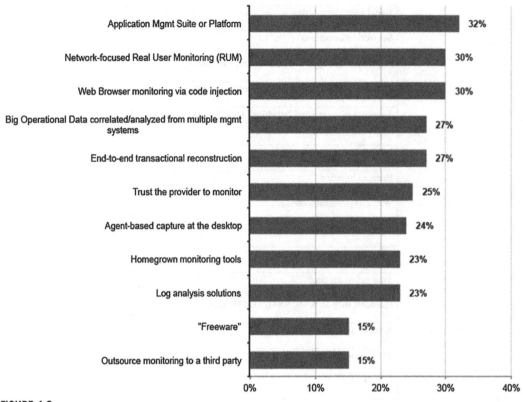

FIGURE 4.6

Approaches to managing application performance and availability in public clouds.

Public Cloud Comes of Age by EMA 2016.

The primary options are to use **synthetic transactions** and/or **real user monitoring (RUM)** to give an indication of performance and availability of the application. Either approach can be considered as approximating the **end-user experience (EUE)**. It provides a reasonable approximation of the end-to-end response time that is seen by a user.

Some products are specifically described as EUE. This approach inserts instrumentation (a network device or agent) on premise to track every interaction between the user and the service provider. The EUE solution "sees" when a transaction calls out to the cloud and when it receives data back. These EUE tools provide an overall metric on how long it took for the transaction to traverse the **wide area network (WAN)**, the Internet, the processing on the provider side, and the return trip. However, everything outside the organizational borders becomes a black box. So while the tool measures how long execution took outside the organizational borders, it is unable to tell you how long each segment took—or the specific performance on the PaaS side.

A synthetic transaction can give a reasonable estimate of end-to-end response time and a rough approximation of the availability of the application. RUM is a **passive monitoring** technology that records all user interactions with an application or a website. It provides information similar to what synthetic transactions provide, that is, availability and response time. Either approach will require the deployment of software and in the case of RUM, possibly hardware as well. It is possible to custom build these tools internally, however, most organizations opt to turn to commercial solutions to address these requirements.

However, when performance is degraded, neither synthetic transactions nor RUM can identify the source of the problem. They cannot determine if the problem is originating in the network, if there is an operating system problem, or if it originates in one or more of a myriad of other possible causes. At that point, the customer is primarily limited to contacting the service provider's support desk for help resolving the problem.

Some network providers are willing to give service-level guarantees (particularly to their largest clients). Those guarantees are typically structured around metrics for the performance and availability of the network. Some of the carriers will provide real-time access to data about the network. Others will only give monthly, or even quarterly, reports. The latter have almost no value in the management of PaaS-based applications.

The net result is that in a PaaS environment the customer has little information about the performance or availability of an application and no ability to make changes even if they did have that information. However, the information that the customer has is useful for holding a PaaS service provider accountable and being able to demonstrate that a problem exists.

PUBLIC CLOUD: SOFTWARE AS A SERVICE

There are thousands of SaaS applications. Therefore, we have to be careful in making sweeping generalizations because there are almost certainly exceptions to any statement that can be made about them. However, while accepting that there are exceptions, we need to take a look at management as it applies to SaaS applications. SaaS applications are useful, and usually cost-effective, solutions tailored to address specific needs. Their functionality tends to be fixed and relatively inflexible.

No real-time application management information is provided to the users (i.e., the customer) of SaaS applications (remember that there can be exceptions). Like users of a PaaS system, the users may be able to use synthetic transactions, EUE, or RUM technology to gauge the performance and availability of an application. Similarly, data from the network service provider may help to isolate performance issues. Ultimately, the data is useful only for convincing the service provider's service desk personnel that there is a problem and for evaluating whether or not service-level guarantees have been met.

The management of SaaS applications is the responsibility of the service provider's staff. They will perform all the management functions required for those applications. For those people, managing a SaaS application is no different than managing a private cloud application is for an IT department in an enterprise.

HYBRID CLOUD

In Dante's *Divine Comedy*, one of the characters comes upon a gate that is the entrance to Hell. Above the gate is written, "Abandon all hope, ye who enter here." Such a warning should be given to anyone contemplating the challenge of managing applications in a hybrid cloud environment. In truth, the situation is not entirely hopeless, but it is a daunting challenge. The management of applications in each of the parts of a hybrid cloud equation, separate from the other parts, is no different and no more difficult than managing those parts outside of a hybrid cloud environment. However, in the case of a hybrid cloud, those parts do not exist in isolation from each other and those parts do not have common ownership or singular, comprehensive, overarching control.

If a SaaS or PaaS application is one part of the equation for application management, it is effectively a black box. The customer's IT department has no control over the application and little or no insight into the workings of the application specifically, or the environment in general. The only semblance of control over a SaaS application is any action that the customer might coax from the service provider's staff.

The lack of management control in a simple SaaS or PaaS environment is enough of a challenge, but when it is joined with a private cloud environment or an IaaS environment to provide greater functionality through a hybrid cloud structure, the complexity soars. There used to be a saying among Central Office technicians in telephony companies: "The trouble is leaving here fine." In a hybrid cloud that combines SaaS or PaaS with IaaS or private cloud, the customer's IT staff responsible for managing those hybrid cloud applications is in the same position as those Central Office technicians. They know what is happening to the applications in the private cloud or IaaS. They have all the tools they need to evaluate and control those pieces. However, they cannot see what is happening in the PaaS or SaaS applications. Furthermore, it is very difficult for them to assess how the interactions between these applications may alter the behavior of each application.

In more sophisticated organizations, a hybrid cloud may not be made up of a single, static pair of applications. Instead, it may be a collection of applications running in a dozen or more clouds. The interactions between them can be dynamic and unpredictable, appearing and disappearing depending on the needs of the various organizations. Management tools, techniques, and data sources that are relevant for one part of a hybrid cloud may be totally irrelevant for another portion of that same hybrid cloud. A significant challenge is in recognizing when relationships appear and disappear. It is only with that awareness that management tools can attempt to apply the relevant management techniques and data collection to all parts of the hybrid cloud.

SUMMARY

The use of public and private cloud environments by organizations around the world continues to grow at a rapid pace and shows no signs of abating in the near future. The financial benefits of cloud computing will continue to drive its adoption. However, there is a tradeoff for those savings. In the IaaS and PaaS environments, the customers have the ability to monitor and control the environment and the applications running in it. Cloud computing brings unique challenges for managing the applications that run in those environments.

Application management in cloud environments is multifaceted. There are at least four types of cloud environments: private cloud, public cloud (SaaS), public cloud (PaaS), and public cloud (IaaS). In each of the public cloud environments there is a user (i.e., the customer's IT department) dimension to the question of application management. There is also a service provider aspect to application management. The capabilities and responsibilities are different in each instance. Unless the service provider offers some reporting, SaaS or PaaS environments are essentially black boxes. In IaaS and private cloud environments, the customer's IT department is responsible for the active management of the applications and is able to install the appropriate tools that allow them to do that.

	Manage Application Performance	Manage Application Availability	Monitor End User Experience
Private	Customer	Customer	Customer
SaaS	Service provider	Service provider	Customer
PaaS	Service provider	Service provider	Customer
IaaS	Customer	Customer	Customer

APPLICATION MANAGEMENT IN VIRTUALIZED SYSTEMS

5

When customers start using virtualization, they have a preliminary notion of what virtualization is. But, once they get in and start using it, they see it's like a Swiss army knife, and they can use it in many different ways.
Raghu Raghuram

A Day in the Life at Acme Manufacturing: A Little Cooperation Goes a Long Way!

*Meet Bruce. He is an IT manager at Acme Manufacturing. As part of Acme's program to encourage professional development of their employees, Bruce does some teaching at the local community college. Lately, he became aware of a plethora of **IT service management (ITSM)** jobs in the area and a shortage of IT service management student recruits. To respond to this shortage, he created a new course in ITSM for the upcoming semester. Bruce is excited about the employment opportunities that this type of course will offer to the community college students upon graduation. However, there's one big stumbling block: the community college does not have the funds to purchase the expensive ITSM software to offer the students the hands-on experience Bruce feels is critical to supplement the learning modules he developed. He wants to differentiate his students from those at nearby colleges and universities when they apply for their first ITSM job after graduation, and he knows that being software-proficient will set them apart from the rest.*

After a few sleepless nights he realizes that he might have the answer. In his job at Acme, Bruce uses a well-respected ITSM software package and Acme's IT organization recently completed a large server virtualization implementation. Bruce thinks it's time to set up a meeting with Amanda, his CIO.

Meet Amanda. She is CIO at Acme. She agrees to meet with Bruce, who arrives armed with recent statistics about the lack of ITSM college courses and the consequent lack of skilled ITSM student interns and college recruits. During the meeting, Amanda is impressed by the innovative approach Bruce is proposing. She agrees that partnering with the community college is an excellent idea and agrees to provide the resources that Bruce needs to create a virtual disk image by which the students can access the much-needed software. Amanda is very interested the outcome of Bruce's project and asks him to report back to her at the end of the semester.

Next, Bruce schedules a twice weekly one-hour time slot to access the ITSM software and registers the email address of each of student with Acme's IT services department. Once a virtual desktop is created for each of the students to log into at the specified times, the course is ready to go live.

Meet Kurt. He is a second-year student who is majoring in information systems. He has enrolled in Bruce's new ITSM course and at first, Kurt isn't sure whether this new course is right for him. Initially, he found the textbook material a little boring, but once he is exposed to the "really cool" virtualized desktop that he gets to use each week, Kurt is much more motivated and never misses a class! By the end of the semester, Kurt is pulling an "A" and is quick to tell others that he's really glad that he took the course. He also has an interview with Acme and is hoping that it will lead to his very first job in ITSM.

At the end of the course, Bruce submits his report to Amanda. Thanks to the power of virtualization and a little cooperation between practice and academia, he is proud to report that the partnership was a huge success. His students are proficient in using a well-respected ITSM software package, understand how ITSM works in a real-time environment, and have even learned a little about the benefits of working in a virtualized environment. And there's already a waiting list for the next offering of the course!

Amanda is excited, too. The partnership with the community college not only provided Acme with a pool of skilled ITSM students from which to recruit, like Kurt, but Amanda was also invited to sit on the college IS Board of Advisors. It's a position she's wanted for some time and she looks forward to identifying other opportunities for Acme to partner with the college.

INTRODUCTION TO VIRTUALIZATION

The concept of **virtualization** is not new, but it is revolutionizing the world of computing. First introduced in the mid-1970s when IBM began shipping virtualized mainframes, its purpose is to provide multiple **logical representations of resources** that allow a system to represent more resources than the actual **physical resources** available. For example, virtual memory allows a system to use more memory than is actually physically available.

In the 1990s, the concept of **virtual machines (VMs)** became mainstream with the introduction of X86 systems, which allow one physical machine to support one or more virtual machines. In some cases, 20 or more VMs could be hosted on one physical machine. This allowed for not only reduced hardware requirements and power and cooling needs, but also enabled and required a whole new way of managing systems.

Now, virtualization is the norm in today's business, thanks to the new opportunities that it created at every level of IT **application management**, from maintenance improvements to operational and capital savings. These savings often equate to 20–50% of the cost of servers, data center power, and personnel.

WHY VIRTUALIZE?

Before we begin exploring the different aspects of virtualization, it is useful to first understand why an organization would consider virtualization as an option to simplify its application management. We will begin by looking at the hardware on which **applications** exist. Most traditional servers are inherently inefficient. Typically, to ensure consistent **performance**, servers run at far less than full capacity of the peak application loads they are designed to handle; on average, they operate at only 10–15% capacity of their peak **application performance** requirements.

Next, the flexibility of applications must be considered. Having just one **operating system (OS)** on a server severely limits this flexibility, and there are also potential conflicts between applications running on the same server. To avoid this, server administrators must run each application on a separate server. This is not an efficient way to manage IT resources since this leads to not only substantial equipment costs, but also a considerable amount of funds being spent on power, cooling, storage, maintenance, and personnel. The good news is that there is a better way, and it is virtualization.

In a virtualized environment, each VM has its own operating system and application and, thanks to specialized software known as a **virtual machine manager (VMM)**, or **hypervisor,** each is totally unaware it is sharing hardware with other operating systems and applications (see Fig. 5.1).

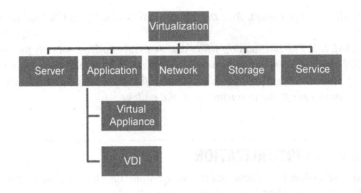

FIGURE 5.1

The many facets of virtualization.

Transforming physical servers into VMs addresses some of the sustainability concerns faced by many organizations by "greening" their data centers to achieve significant energy savings. Each individual VM instance is commonly referred to as a guest, and the computer that runs all the VMs is known as the host.

In this way, the world of virtualization significantly reduces operating costs and allows greater business agility and scaling, as well as better data protection and improved compliance with industry and corporate standards. This type of architecture equips application managers with new **management** techniques and tools that lead to increased flexibility and control, help reduce downtime, and promise better usage efficiencies not normally possible in a nonvirtualized environment. The following sections will cover the various facets of virtualization that enable these huge savings in **total cost of ownership**.

SERVER VIRTUALIZATION

The most common aspect of virtualization is server virtualization. Now considered a mainstream technology, server virtualization benefits organizations by allowing server consolidation. A single physical server allows support for multiple VMs, which in turn allow support for applications that normally require dedicated servers. In this way, resources can be shared on a single server. Ultimately, this practice reduces unnecessary server hardware costs. It is no wonder that recent estimates show that most organizations have virtualized over half of their production workloads to facilitate the mobility of applications and application systems. Fig. 5.2 shows how applications and their underlying operating systems in a virtualized environment are completely independent of the physical host machine. In their new **configuration**, a layer of specialized software known as the VMM or hypervisor creates a separation layer between the applications and the underlying hardware. The hypervisor provides an **abstraction software layer** to disconnect direct reliance of the applications on specific hardware capabilities and communicates instead with the generalized virtual hardware interface in the hypervisor. This allows applications to run on literally any hardware system that can run the same hypervisor.

A key benefit on the server side of applications is that new **virtual servers** can be activated in hours, if not minutes, to meet the need for new applications or applications that require additional capacity.

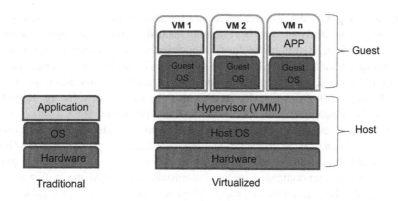

FIGURE 5.2

Comparison of traditional versus virtualized architectures.

Prior to virtualization, if a new application or an existing application needed more capacity, the only answer was to order new hardware and then physically install, test, and provision it. In some cases, this could take weeks or months. In a traditional IT architecture, it is not uncommon for an organization to be faced with the need to upgrade power requirements or build a new data center to meet their requirements. Neither option is easy, efficient, or inexpensive. With virtualized servers, these extreme measures are no longer necessary.

Applications that rely on specific hardware functions are less mobile than other applications that do not have hardware-specific feature dependencies. When applications need direct hardware access for performance reasons, those applications are also less portable. Virtualization can run most applications with little performance degradation, as if they were run natively on a server. However, it is best to avoid deploying applications with hardware-specific dependencies whenever possible.

Server and desktop virtualization also creates new ways to package, deploy, and manage applications. Single and multitier applications can be installed on a system with all of it dependent on libraries and **services**. A copy of that virtual disk image can then be saved as a file along with metadata about the image, which can be reused or cloned for future deployments.

Another advantage of virtualized servers is the ability to make a copy of the disk image of the system. This allows application managers to make a replica of a system, with all of its operating systems and application components that can be deployed when another VM instance is needed. These images may be in various formats, depending on the platform. For example, VMware uses virtual machine disk, Microsoft and others use virtual hard drive, and Amazon Cloud uses **Amazon Machine Image**.

A packaging format for these images called **open virtualization format** (**OVF**) was created to provide an industry standard to link to the VM image, along with **metadata** about the VM(s). For example, VMware packages their metadata in a VMX file that contains description and resources requirements for the disk image to be loaded and booted. In multitier applications, the metadata may include information about the machines like the sequence by which the machines should be started. Although these image formats are different, there are several tools that allow you to easily convert one format to another. And, although the conversion is not always perfect, it's close enough to get you going! In addition to the disk image format there is associated metadata (OVF will be covered in greater detail in Chapter 16).

Using metadata along with the disk images allows for a much quicker installation of new applications since disk images are distributed without running the install process and applications are often up and running in minutes instead of hours or days. Of course, there is a certain amount of configuration/customization that may need to be done before the application or application system is fully functional. This is normally done via some user prompts and configuration wizards. Many products today are delivered as VM images. This process also ensures that the necessary software dependencies were already installed at the appropriate level for the distributed application.

Virtualized server images are also used by **cloud** service providers to offer machine images or **templates**. These templates can provide prepackaged applications and services such as a web server, database server, or a load balancer. In this way, cloud server providers for either **public** or **private clouds** can offer their customers a comprehensive menu of preinstalled packaged application services for their use. Customers can also be assured that all the required components and dependencies were installed in the image. Templates also allow for version control of the applications and services. If and when newer versions of the software become available that are safer, faster, and provide the latest functions, templates also allow for control of end-of-life versions of the software.

APPLICATION VIRTUALIZATION

Application virtualization provides organizations with the best return on investment. Applications that are distributed across multiple **personal computers** present the single biggest problem for IT organizations. Preparing a complex application for deployment can take as much as 10 days; when there are hundreds of applications to manage, this can be a daunting task. As new versions of the application are released, the deployment process must be repeated ad nauseam. Instead of taking control of an application's Windows Installer-based installation, application virtualization grabs the running state and delivers it to each desktop. In essence, this means that applications no longer need to be installed because they can simply be copied. Any virtualized application will run on any version of Windows, so there is no need to revisit applications when they are moved or upgraded from one Windows version to another.

In addition to providing a single image that can be shared by many users, application virtualization also improves **patch management** of end-user applications and can eliminate the need for wasting hundreds, if not thousands, of hours upgrading systems.

A core concept of application virtualization is **application streaming**, or the ability to stream applications from a central point to multiple PCs. Similar to video or audio streaming, application streaming buffers content when an application is launched by a user and begins playing the selected content as soon as enough content is available. The rest of the application content is then delivered in the background. The beauty of application streaming is that the process is transparent to the end users.

Another concept that gained a lot of attention relative to virtualized applications is **ThinApp**. Developed by VMware, ThinApp encapsulates application files and registries into a single packet that can be easily deployed, managed, and updated independent of the underlying OS. With this approach, applications can be run on a physical PC, a shared network drive, a virtual desktop, or a USB stick without installing them on the local machine. This technique provides several features, including portability, reduced help desk costs, ease of updating, stronger endpoint **security**, and the ability to run multiple versions of the application on the same machine. This capability is now offered by a number of vendors and provides considerable cost savings, along with improved management and control.

All in all, virtualizing applications provides for greatly simplified application management by eliminating complex software deployment infrastructures and installation processes. It also provides an improved ability to customize individual user application delivery through a transparent **user experience**.

VIRTUAL APPLIANCES

One of the most efficient ways to deploy a server or test a server-based application is by using a **virtual appliance (VA)**. A VA fundamentally changes the way an application is delivered, configured, and managed. The VA is essentially a VM image (VMI), which is a large file that a VMM can use to create a VM that can be duplicated and moved between VMMs. In contrast to an application that is deployed in a nonvirtual environment, the focus of the VA is on the application. The VA includes a single application and its appropriate operating system, libraries, and services already configured and tuned for the specific application. This enables a user to simply download a single file to run an application. VAs can be open or closed. A **closed VA** is always packaged, distributed, maintained, updated, and managed as a single unit. An **open VA** allows customers to make modifications. Some examples of VAs include **WAN** optimization controllers, application delivery controllers, **firewalls**, performance monitoring solutions, enterprise applications, and web applications.

From a management perspective, there are a number of important benefits to be gained from using VAs. These include the following:

1. Significant reduction in application deployment time because the focus is on the application. The VMI incorporates everything necessary to run the application in a virtualized environment. It is configured and tuned for the specific application, streamlining its deployment.
2. Reduced resources required for maintenance. There are less services and drivers to maintain, fewer patches to keep the operating system up to date, less bandwidth, and less storage requirements.
3. Reduced cost of deploying a software-based VA compared to its nonvirtual, hardware-based counterpart.
4. Greater economies of scale when a VA is deployed to multiple individuals by eliminating the need to expend necessary costs to acquire additional hardware-based appliances.
5. Problem solutions associated with heterogenous hardware and operating systems by focusing on the application prepackaged with its single appropriately configured operating system.
6. Facilitated management of network applications by deploying and managing VAs at remote sites where there are limited resources.
7. Accelerated evaluation of new applications. Vendors offer a VA with a new application preinstalled on its appropriate operating system.

VIRTUAL DESKTOP INTERFACE

Another important aspect of application virtualization is the **virtual desktop interface** (**VDI**). Desktop virtualization focuses on centralizing the management of complete desktops or individual desktop applications. This centralization process simplifies management operations by allowing IT organizations to perform maintenance across various virtualized desktops. The two primary forms of desktop virtualization include client-side application/desktop and server-side application/desktop.

Client-side application virtualization focuses on allowing applications to be streamed on-demand from central servers by a client's device. The primary challenge of managing desktop virtualization is acquiring and maintaining optimal bandwidth to achieve a good user experience. Alternatively, in server-side virtualization, a client's device acts as a terminal that accesses an application or desktop hosted on a centralized server. This method can be achieved in one of two ways: a server-based computing or virtual desktop infrastructure (VDI).

While the cost of traditional PCs and storage has decreased, the operational cost of managing individual physical desktop computers increased due to rising labor costs and the escalating complexity associated with maintenance of individual physical PCs. Implementing VDIs reduces this total cost of ownership since users connect using just a keyboard, monitor, and mouse connected to the hosting virtual desktop server via PC over IP. Overall, the management of the physical PC lifecycle consumes a large amount of IT resources, whereas a VDI solution can shortcut and even eliminate many of these desktop management tasks, thus significantly reducing the associated operational costs. It also provides a much more streamlined application management approach by centralizing all management tasks. In a large company, these savings can be multiplied by hundreds or thousands of users, resulting in huge savings. In addition, a VDI greatly reduces security risks and the power and cooling requirements of the enterprise.

The virtualized desktop enables a broad range of **mobile devices** to allow users to launch their applications safely and securely on smartphones and tablets, and accommodates the seamless integration of cloud-based applications. Mobile and cloud-based applications are discussed further in Chapters 4 and 6.

NETWORK VIRTUALIZATION

To avoid the complexities of traditional network configuration and provisioning and fully realize the benefits of virtualization, a virtualized network must be used. Traditional networks simply cannot withstand the strain placed on them by the increasing demands of applications, servers, and the large bandwidth requirements of virtualization. With a virtualized network, the same agility, reduced costs, and business continuity that were enabled in the hardware/software environment by server virtualization can be realized.

In many organizations, nonvirtualized networks are still anchored to the hardware and their configurations are spread across multiple physical and virtual network devices. Despite IT's ability to deploy virtual applications within minutes, a network can delay their use for days or weeks. This growing demand to provide multiuser network services that enable each user to specify, deploy, and control their own virtual network presents a golden opportunity to revise network management strategies, making sure that the complexities and failings of the traditional network are not repeated in the virtual network. For example, the focus must be on required network functionality rather than on infrastructure configuration and control.

As with other virtualization offerings, the virtual layer must be decoupled from the infrastructure and be efficient, scalable, and highly available. It is also important to consider the dynamic nature of **virtualized data centers** where endpoints are created, deleted, and migrated. Some recommend the development of network blueprints to determine and verify the network functionality specifications and allow the complete application lifecycle to be managed independently of the endpoint lifecycle.

STORAGE VIRTUALIZATION

Legacy storage systems are ill-suited to meet today's business needs. Deployed in storage silos, these systems do not have the ability to fully address virtualization needs or to deliver economies of function and scale in modern data centers. To capture new data from various media sources, such as mobile, social media, and the cloud, IT managers need a storage architecture that is scalable, focuses on business-critical workloads, and offers lower storage total cost of ownership (TCO). To harness and manage all of this, new data managers are turning to storage virtualization strategies. These strategies enable them to save money on basic storage functions, apply those funds to new business-critical workloads, and take advantage of its capability to enhance data analytics functions by dynamically moving data from system to system.

Storage virtualization achieves these benefits by pooling physical storage from multiple network storage devices into what appears to be a single storage device that is managed from a central console. Converting to virtualized storage helps solve a number of storage-related problems such as improving capacity utilization to improve the 40–50% capacity utilization rates that are typical in most IT organizations. This benefit is amplified in situations where storage is mirrored to other sites. Storage virtualization can also facilitate disaster recovery efforts by replicating data without having to provide a matching host or disk at the disaster recovery site. It can also eliminate bottlenecks created by communication between agents on the application server and the backup server by taking a snapshot of a file system, thus eliminating the need for a backup window and simplifying the management of storage throughout the application management lifecycle. These snapshot capabilities provide online data copies that allow the system to roll back to a time before file corruption or loss occurred. Other benefits of virtualizing storage include:

- Faster data migration between heterogenous platforms
- Automatic capacity expansion
- Easier and safer application testing using a replicated data set
- Improved database performance by sharing an expensive solid-state disk
- Higher availability by separating the application from its data storage to insulate an application from its server failure

Storage virtualization also helps the storage administrator perform the tasks of backup, archiving, and recovery more easily and in less time by disguising the actual complexity of the **storage area network (SAN)**. Users simply implement virtualization through software or hybrid hardware/software appliances on different levels of its SAN.

SERVICE VIRTUALIZATION

The last piece of the virtualization collage is **service virtualization**. This facet of virtualization increases agility throughout the **software development lifecycle (SDLC)**, which allows for the testing of interconnected applications earlier in the development process, enables faster deployment of higher quality applications, and reduces project risk. It is particularly useful if there are complex applications with multiple dependencies. With its ability to simulate complex test environments, service virtualization is truly a game changer that drastically improves the way software can be managed throughout its lifecycle.

The goal of an IT manager is to deliver high quality, high performing applications on time and under budget. Service virtualization moves this goal closer to reality by reducing testing bottlenecks. It achieves this by emulating unavailable application components to allow end-to-end testing of the application as a whole. By using these **virtual services** instead of production services, testing can be done earlier and more frequently throughout the SDLC. These virtual components can be constructed by monitoring the network traffic of the service or by reading service specifications that describe the operations offered by a service, including the parameters and data outputs. In this way, service virtualization can dramatically alter the economics and flow of the entire application lifecycle.

Let's face it: most applications have "bugs" when they are released—it is a fact of life in the IT industry. However, the later in the application lifecycle that these defects are found, the more expensive they are to fix. By using service virtualization, organizations can identify problems and fix them with fewer consequences to timelines and budgets by testing frequently throughout the process. Service virtualization can also be used to fix defects. If a defect is found in testing, it can block the application from performing properly. However, service virtualization can be used to emulate its correct functionality so that further testing can proceed. It is best to begin using service virtualization incrementally to realize "quick wins," for example, virtualizing components that are the most stable and the most expensive to test. Next, ask these questions to determine the need for service virtualization:

- How much downtime does the development team experience during testing because they cannot access dependent system components?
- How many dollars does this downtime represent?
- How often is access to third-party interfaces needed prior to scheduling a test?
- What are the costs associated with gaining access to third-party interfaces?
- How many defects are typically found in the various stages of the SDLC?
- What is the cost of resolving these defects?
- What is the cost of customer dissatisfaction due to these defects?

Next, consider the costs that will be incurred to implement service virtualization, e.g., software licenses, implementation costs, and training costs to bring developers up to speed on the new tools. A comparison of need versus costs, particularly for those organizations that struggle with testing complex applications or are dependent on third-party services, can result in significant cost savings. It is easy to see why a growing number of organizations have made service virtualization a key part of their testing strategy throughout the application lifecycle.

VIRTUAL INTEGRATION

The most effective way to manage virtualization is to adopt an integrated, full-stack approach. This was initially addressed by the notion of **converged systems**, which emerged as a way to easily handle individual components of hardware setups. The range of hardware pieces controlled in a converged infrastructure generally consists of servers, networking equipment, and storage devices. A converged infrastructure can be likened to a number of components networked together topped by a management layer.

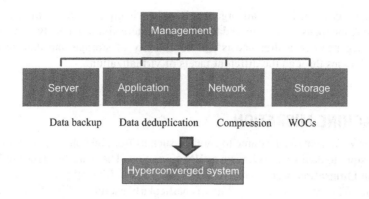

FIGURE 5.3

Virtualization integration through hyperconvergence.

However, greater efficiencies could be gained from streamlining IT architectures even more by integrating not only compute, storage, and management, but also compression, data deduplication, data backup, and WAN optimization through the higher concept of a **hyperconverged system** (see Fig. 5.3). Hyperconverged systems and converged systems are similar in many instances, but hyperconvergence increased the integration of IT resources to enable easier and more comprehensive management.

Hyperconverged systems rapidly gained momentum and acceptance as a way to address VM sprawl caused by incremental adoption of virtualized servers, applications, networks, and storage services. To simplify the operational issues related to this siloed approach to virtualization, a converged infrastructure evolved as multiple vendors combined their technologies into an integrated full stack containing servers, storage, and networking.

Hyperconverged systems advance the integration concept even further by combining the physical components of servers, storage, and networking into a single form-factor server that uses direct-attached storage in place of more expensive SAN-based storage. A natural progression in virtualizing IT could be to follow server virtualization with a hyperconverged approach as the standard for deploying new workloads. Hyperconverged systems can be delivered as **appliance-based systems** or software-only systems. Appliance-based systems are delivered as a VA that contains both hardware and software. Software-only systems are just that: software with no hardware. If an organization has a good relationship with its hardware vendor, a software-only system on existing hardware may be ideal. The downside is that diagnosing specific problems may be more difficult than if the hardware and software were deployed as a single unit.

The benefits of hyperconvergence include reduced operating costs and time to market, enhanced flexibility, and better application performance. For example, a hyperconverged system can be installed and spun up in less time than a large-scale virtual server solution. This is particularly appealing to smaller organizations that do not have experienced staff to carry out the installation. From a cost perspective, although hyperconverged systems are not significantly cheaper to deploy than a custom virtual server system, operating them definitely is. This is typically where significant cost savings can be realized. Managing a hyperconverged system is definitely easier thanks to vendors that improve monitoring functions to facilitate proactive support for their products. Whether organizations are just embarking on a virtualization exercise or have one well underway, hyperconvergence can help. For small organizations just beginning the virtualization journey, it represents an easy, inexpensive way to update all data centers simultaneously. For larger organizations, hyperconvergence can address costs and complexity of storage and data protection as the organization progresses through the different facets of virtualization.

VIRTUAL MACHINE MIGRATION

The movement of VMs from one resource to another, such as from one physical host to another physical host, or data store to data store, is known as VM migration. There are two types of VM migration: cold and live. **Cold migration** occurs when the VM is shut down. **Live migration** occurs while the VM is actually running. This amazing new capability is particularly useful if maintenance is required on the part of the physical infrastructure and the application running on that infrastructure is mission-critical. Before the availability of live migration applications, managers were stuck with the choice of either causing a planned outage, which in some global corporations is not always feasible, or waiting and not taking the system down, which risks an unplanned outage in the future. Needless to say, neither of these choices is optimal.

With live migration, a running system is copied to another system and when the last bits of the running system's state are copied, the switch is made and the new system becomes the active server. This process can take several minutes to complete, but is a great advantage over the two previous options.

Earlier versions of live migration were limited to moving VMs within the same data centers. That restriction was removed and it is now possible to perform live migrations between different data centers. This capability provides an entirely new set of options and availability, including the ability to move workloads from a data center that may be in the eye of a storm to another data center outside of the target area. Again, these application moves can be accomplished without any application outages. There are several products on the market today that provide some form of live migration. These products and platforms may have some guidelines and requirements to provide the capability. If an organization is considering live migration as an option, it is recommended to check with the virtualization software vendor to understand those requirements, particularly for the data center.

WORKLOAD BALANCING

Virtualized applications and servers provide a new level of mobility. Virtualized servers can be moved in a live migration mode as described earlier, or they can be moved in a stopped state. It is always good to remember that a physical server may have 20 or more virtual servers running on it. With live and static migrations, VMs may be moved to provide a workload balance. For the sake of example, let's say that a physical web services application server has 10 highly busy VMs running, and a physical line-of-business application server has little or no activity on the VM that it is hosting. In this case, it would make sense to move some of the workloads from the web services application server to the line-of-business server to balance the workload.

SCALING USING VIRTUAL SYSTEMS

One of the great things about virtualized systems is that it is not necessary to order lots of new hardware to gain increased capacity. Instead, a copy of the application server(s) can be made to easily and quickly deploy one or more additional servers. Cloning an existing VM saves time and reduces the amount of errors that may occur if each machine is created from scratch.

Those new machines can be spun up and—with the help of a load balancer—can quickly add capacity to an application. There are several tools and types of clones, but the basic idea is to create multiple instances of an application and then use some sort of load balancer to distribute the requests to a pool of servers. As there are different types of clones, there are also different types of load balancers. Some allow the selection algorithm criteria for the load balancer to be configured using a round robin approach to limit the time each process can run, or by sending the request to the server with the least number of current connections. Of course, it is important to make sure the parent of the clones was configured for optimum performance. Whatever inefficiencies were in the clone parent will be propagated to the child clones.

One other great advantage to scaling in this fashion is that when it is time to upgrade the server image, operating system, application software, or the configuration, it could be done to one server, then tested and then cloned again and replaced on the existing running images.

IMAGE CHECKPOINT AND ROLLBACK

Another nice facility provided by most virtualization vendors is the ability to create a checkpoint for a VM. This is a handy capability for developers when making changes to a VM, as it allows the developer to roll back the image to a previously known image without having to keep an entire copy of each image. A VMI can be several gigabytes in size, so creating a backup every time a change is made would require a lot of disk space. With check pointing, the system stores only the deltas of the change so it can roll back an image quickly and easily. This technique can also be used when making complex changes to a production server.

CHALLENGES OF MANAGING A VIRTUAL ENVIRONMENT

While virtualization solves some problems and offers amazing capabilities, it also intensifies some traditional application management challenges and creates several new ones.

SECURITY

Security concerns are consistently identified as one of the top five issues for senior-level IT managers and the security of virtualized servers, and infrastructure is high on their list of security concerns. Although a virtualized infrastructure is not inherently any less secure than that of a traditional infrastructure, it still has to be patched and maintained in the same way that a nonvirtual infrastructure does to keep abreast of potential vulnerabilities. As discussed earlier, virtualization adds an additional layer

(VMM or hypervisor) between the operating system and the applications to manage multiple VMs on a single host, and it is theoretically possible for hackers to attack the VMM specifically or hijack a VM and use it to attack other VMs. While there are security risks associated with the VMMs beyond accepting vendor patches and keeping VMMs maintained, these VMs are primarily reliant on vendor support to keep them secure. However, there are also a number of other server and network virtualization security issues that can and should be controlled by IT departments. Let's explore some of these virtualization security issues now to understand how they can be managed.

Host/platform configurations. In the case of virtual servers, configuration issues are magnified. The host platform can vary in the type of configuration options, depending on system architecture. To secure these systems, a number of best practice configurations can be implemented, such as setting file permissions, controlling users and groups, and synchronizing logs and times. To assist with this, a number of configuration guides are available free of charge from virtualization platform vendors, the Center for Internet Security, the National Security Agency, and the Defense Information Systems Agency.

VMM or hypervisor security. The VM manager is a piece of software. Since software is often released with "bugs" that need to be patched and maintained, it is important to maintain the latest service packs for both guests and hosts in a virtualized environment. This action is necessary to guard against any vulnerabilities and to apply the latest security roll-up patches if and when a virtual software vendor supplies them.

Least privilege controls. Creating separation of duties and providing the least amount of privilege necessary for users to perform their authorized tasks are basic tenets of information security that apply to both physical and virtual resources. For example, the director of marketing would not need access to a VM that runs a payroll application.

To address this issue, a system of checks and balances with processes to split functions and enforce dual controls for critical tasks must be put into place, and approval processes should be set up for creating new VMs and moving new applications to new VMs. Audit logs for VMs should be monitored for usage activity in the data center and on the endpoints. VMware monitoring tools that also monitor in nonvirtual environments to compare and report performance, per the least privileges policy, are also useful. Additionally, so are host-based firewalls and host intrusion prevention tools. To maximize the success of least privileges controls, it is important to involve all stakeholders in defining access levels and allocate access to specific roles, rather than individuals, and establish an annual review process to check that access levels remain consistent with business needs.

Failure to integrate into application lifecycle management. Managing vulnerabilities and patches across virtual systems can cause problems, and so can failing to conduct system integrity checks for a virtual system. However, with the appropriate combination of controls, you will be able to manage VM lifecycles more easily than their physical environment. An easy fix for this is to deploy appropriate tools that have these management capabilities. VMware vendors and third-party tools scan for weaknesses in VMs and work independently of and with the VMM.

Raising IT staff awareness. If IT staff do not know about an issue, they cannot manage it. Internal and external IT auditors need to be provided with a complete understanding of the virtualization infrastructure deployed, the data within the systems, and the policies that are put in place to govern the lifecycle of system instance creation, use, and end of lifecycle. Assessment of risk, compliance with relevant regulations, and even software licensing agreements are impacted when new VMs are dynamically deployed, temporarily retired, or eliminated. Traditional approaches to risk assessment and analysis, such as assessment questionnaires, may be inadequate in a virtual environment.

Risk must be assessed and analyzed at the onset of new virtualization projects, and risk management staff must be involved with changes in the virtualization infrastructure that may affect the level of risk. Educate risk management and compliance groups about virtualization capabilities and limitations, and consider involving compliance staff in critically shaping security policies for the virtual infrastructure in accordance with relevant regulations.

Traffic monitoring. One of the biggest security issues that may be faced in a virtualization environment is the lack of visibility into traffic among guests. Unlike the physical computing environment where a host platform has an internal virtual switch that each guest connects to, in the virtual environment, all VM traffic on a host is contained entirely within the host's virtual switching components. This severely compromises visibility and security. To get around this, mirror ports need to be created on the built-in Layer-2 switching controls that are provided by most virtualized solution vendors to monitor traffic.

Controlling user-installed VMs. Central IT staff may not recognize the existence of VMs on endpoint systems. Even if they do, there may not be any policies in place to control the use of these technologies by end users. Licensing and patching issues may also need to be resolved and appropriate policies instituted to address desktop applications on virtual endpoints that may be operated by unsophisticated users.

In anticipation of (or in response to) user-installed VMs, a new set of management capabilities should be created that allow IT desktop support, security operations, and help desk staff discover virtualization in use throughout the organization's endpoints, set and monitor policy, and gain visibility into the status of VMs running on desktop systems. An internal usage policy and network and endpoint security should be established that are VM-aware enough to locate and identify VMs and report them. To enable this visibility and control, endpoint security management needs to develop discovery protocols for virtual systems running on endpoints.

Lack of integration with existing tools and policies. Many common practices used in securing physical servers, such as hardware firewalls and intrusion sensors, either are not available or are extremely difficult to configure in virtual environments because the data is crisscrossing a system backplane, not an IP network. Unfortunately, hardware security tools that work in physical environments do not always work smoothly in a virtual environment. Instead, careful network configuration is required to help to avoid security issues related to VM failures, maintenance issues, and application removal. The good news is that security and network management vendors are moving to make their tools virtual-aware. To guard against some of these security issues, it is advisable to mirror standard security software including antimalware, host intrusion prevention, endpoint security software, and host firewalls on the VMs. Remember, a good number of traditional security and management vendors are adding functionality that addresses virtualized resources, so it is important to evaluate options for deploying system and file integrity tools, intrusion prevention systems, and firewalls as VAs with a vendor before purchasing new tools. Partnerships also enable maximum coverage at minimal cost.

DISASTER RECOVERY

It is necessary to have a disaster recovery plan to address a major outage in the data center. Before virtualization, applications were more hardware-dependent. Often, duplicate equipment would need to be purchased and staged in another location. Virtualization reduces the hardware dependencies for most applications and provides cost-effective disaster recovery site alternatives.

It is imperative for a good disaster recovery plan to be developed, regularly tested, and updated as new applications and technologies are deployed in the data center. Application managers need to ensure there is a plan in place and that mission-critical applications are part of the plan and tests. Virtualization greatly reduces the amount of work involved to make the backup and to activate it in the case of a disaster.

When any changes to the application systems and/or VMs are made, they need to be backed up and ready for deployment at the disaster recovery site. One of the challenges in restoring systems to a backup site is the time and effort involved in deploying and configuring data storage, networks, and correct versions of the machine images. A good disaster recovery plan and regular testing will greatly reduce the amount of downtime that may occur in the case of a disaster. In other scenarios, such as a data center in the path of a hurricane, the disaster recovery plan must be executed even though the data center is still functioning. In other scenarios such as an earthquake, there may not be time to prestage the disaster recovery site and the recovery could take more time.

The bottom line is that even though virtualized systems provide some handy ways to clone and move workloads, effective disaster recovery starts with good planning and requires constant testing and updating.

AVAILABILITY

Unlike traditional IT, virtualization relies on network connectivity and a centralized infrastructure in which numerous end users, from front-end connection brokers to back-end servers, share the same application and desktop delivery infrastructure. Consequently, while the failure of a physical desktop PC or application impacts only one user, a failure within the shared infrastructure of a virtual application and desktop deployment can impact the entire user population. To avoid this, the infrastructure design must protect against potential site-level outage failures, as well as individual component failures.

SCALABILITY

One of the main issues faced by application managers is VM sprawl, which can occur when administrators create VMs without regard for the resources the VMs consume or the possibility of overwhelming the host server's resources. The phenomenon of virtual sprawl introduces new management challenges as more and more VMs are created, and tracking VMs and their consumption of resources throughout their lifecycle become more difficult for the application manager. This issue is akin to discovering and monitoring applications in a traditional IT environment, but on a much larger scale. As systems can easily be created and cloned, the actual number of new servers, both virtual and physical, are constantly expanding. Therefore tracking, monitoring, and retiring servers is a constant challenge. The combined proliferation of virtualized servers, VMs, and **VLANs** places a significant strain on the manual processes used to manage physical servers and the supporting infrastructure.

To prevent VM sprawl, organizations should develop a **virtual machine lifecycle management (VMLM)** plan to empower administrators to oversee implementation, operation, delivery, and maintenance of all VMs throughout their entire lifecycle. A VMLM ensures accountability for the creation of each VM, monitoring throughout its lifecycle and systematic decommissioning at the end of its lifecycle.

PERFORMANCE MONITORING

Other traditional management challenges that are magnified in a virtual environment include **performance baselining**, **application profiling**, and response time analysis. All these activities are important because they help detect and resolve performance issues before they impact an organization's end users by providing a reference point to measure service quality and application delivery effectiveness. They also lead to an understanding of how critical applications are behaving. In a virtual environment, this becomes even more critical since the systems are less visible and are more difficult to track.

STORAGE ACCESS

While live VM migration can add significant value, it can be challenging to ensure that the VM retained the same level of storage access. Tracking the location of VMs and associated shifts in network traffic add even more complexity to the troubleshooting process and significantly complicate it.

LEGAL

Another important issue that requires close monitoring is tracking license entitlements for the ever-increasing number of servers and applications. Failure to do this can create a huge liability with fines and legal action if license entitlements are exceeded. Fortunately, there are a plethora of tools that can assist with managing virtualization deployments and the associated security risks.

SUMMARY

Virtualization adds a great deal of tools and capabilities as well as some unique challenges. Leveraging these technologies, taking advantage of new mobility, and scaling capabilities can improve application performance and uptime. Understanding this technology will help organizations be aware of some of the pitfalls to avoid. In the following chapters, we will build on the virtualization concepts as we take a look at **application lifecycle management** in **containerization** applications, cloud, mobile, web-based, componentized, and **agile** computing.

KEY TAKEAWAYS

- Virtualizing applications makes it easier to manage the application lifecycle while providing a transparent experience to end users.
- Virtualization overcomes the dependency on operating systems.
- Server virtualization addresses the gross underutilization of server capacity and enables IT managers to better manage their budget.
- VM sprawl can be controlled by implementing a VMLM plan.
- Virtualization has evolved from simple server virtualization to hyperconverged systems to streamline the process for companies of all sizes.
- Hyperconverged systems are useful to small organizations that are just embarking on their virtualization experience and to large organizations that are in the midst of virtualization, but are experiencing some issues.

MANAGEMENT OF MOBILE APPLICATIONS

6

We all know the future is mobile, right? And the iPhone and iPad are Perfect Expressions of Beauty, Ideal Combinations of Form and Function. Except they're Not.
John Battelle

As we grow up in more technology-enriched environments filled with laptops and smart phones, technology is not just becoming a part of our daily lives—it's becoming a part of each and every one of us.
Adora Svitak

As with any relatively recent technological development, terminology is still in flux. While the use and meanings of terms may evolve even before the ink is dry on the first printing of this book, it is important to clarify some common terms that are relevant to this chapter. However, to avoid confusion and ambiguity, we will begin with a review of widely used terminology.

Enterprise mobility management (EMM) reflects the global **management** of the mobile environment. It typically involves the combination of **mobile device management (MDM)**, **mobile application management (MAM)**, and **mobile security management (MSM)**. Fig. 6.1 illustrates the interrelationships of these pieces.

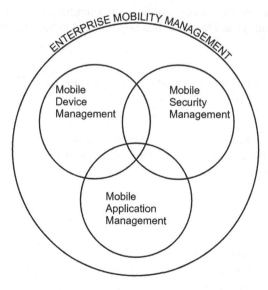

FIGURE 6.1

Enterprise mobility management.

Application Performance Management (APM) in the Digital Enterprise. http://dx.doi.org/10.1016/B978-0-12-804018-8.00006-1

The focus of MDM is the administration of the physical **mobile devices**. In particular, MDM is focused on making sure that the devices are configured and operating properly. MDM is also concerned with securing the devices and corporate data on those devices.

MAM is concerned with provisioning and controlling access to business **applications** running on mobile devices. It also provides controls at the application level that allow information technology (IT) to manage and secure application data.

The primary function of MSM is to control which applications and data users can access, download, or transmit and how those applications are permitted to be used. MSM profiles define privileges within the applications as well as access rights.

The security of MSM, MDM, and MAM will be addressed in Chapter 8.

MOBILE APPLICATIONS

The management of **mobile applications** is a complex and challenging issue. First, it is important to clarify exactly what is meant by "mobile applications." Applications themselves are not independently mobile. Applications reside and run on some type of computer. It does not matter if that computer is a **mainframe**, server, laptop, tablet, smartphone, or something else.

Without some kind of computer to run the program, an application is simply a set of coded instructions. Like a lightbulb without a source of electricity, its potential cannot be realized. If a computer is intended to be portable and is routinely moved from one location to another, then the applications that run on it are mobile. Of course, that begs the question of what is meant by "portable." Consider a rack-mounted server on an oil tanker that travels the globe. Does the movement of the ship mean that the server is portable? The answer is: "No!" This server may be administered locally or remotely and users may access applications running on it or elsewhere. However, the device itself is in a (relatively) fixed location. It is not designed to be carried to different locations on the ship or ashore.

> A mobile application (mobile app) is any application that runs on or is accessed from a device designed to be portable.

Mobile applications can be thought of as being characterized by the types of devices on which they run. There are three broad categories of mobile devices that will be considered in this chapter (Fig. 6.2):

- Laptop computers
- Tablets and smartphones
- Embedded devices

The embedded devices group includes a wide variety of devices ranging from handheld GPS units to smart cars, to portable gaming devices and many, many other devices. Each of those devices contains software that is more than some simple code burned permanently onto a chip.

FIGURE 6.2

The diverse world of mobile computing.

The primary focus of this chapter is applications that run on mobile devices—that is, laptops and handheld devices (tablets and smartphones). The applications may run entirely on the mobile device or be accessed from the mobile device, or it may be a combination of the two. The **Internet of Things (IoT)** includes a variety of applications running on a diverse assortment of devices, many of which are mobile. However, those applications will be addressed in Chapter 17.

For purposes of the discussion in this chapter, mobile applications must be manageable. That is, they must be:

- Addressable (i.e., can be communicated with)
- Configurable
- Updatable (e.g., a new version of the software installed)

BASIC MANAGEMENT OBJECTIVES

The objectives of **application management** were addressed in Chapter 3, but a quick review is in order. In simplest terms, the objective of application management is to ensure that the user can securely access the functionality and data provided by the applications whenever required at a level of **performance** that meet the user's needs. It is important to recognize that application management does not exist in isolation. System management is required to manage the performance and availability of the mobile device on which the application(s) run. Network management is necessary to allow the application to communicate with databases or applications located elsewhere. However, despite their importance, network management and system management are beyond the purview of this book.

Application management functions can be performed locally, on the mobile device, by the user. Consider one of your personal mobile devices. For the moment, we will use the example of a smartphone, although it could just as easily be a tablet or a laptop. You can go to the app store, purchase, download, install, and configure (i.e., adjust the settings) an incredible variety of applications. You can also configure the operating system (OS) or even download and install new versions of the **operating system** (it is important to remember that an OS is just another software element, albeit a special purpose one). You personally "monitor" the phone and any applications that you are using (or attempting to use). That is, you will be able to recognize if an app is available and working properly whenever you attempt to use it.

Alternatively, if the necessary management software is in place on the smartphone, and permissions granted, it is possible for an administrator to remotely perform some of the management tasks that can be done by a user. The smartphone managed by the administrator may be one issued by the company or a personal one authorized for business uses. Research has found that 78% of mobile devices (smartphones and tablets) and 46% of all laptops used to perform business tasks are employee owned.[1] In fact, depending on company policy, an administrator may have the authority to:

- Install (or update) applications
- Change the configurations of applications

---

[1]"Effective BYOD Management: Empowering a Mobile Workforce" Enterprise Management Associates, 2016.

Windows, MacOS, iOS, Android, etc.

FIGURE 6.3

Autonomous mobile computing.

- Grant or revoke access to applications or data
- Delete applications or data from the device
- Disable the device completely
- Monitor an application (i.e., availability and performance)
- Enforce security policies

LOCAL APPLICATIONS

In broad terms, there are three types of applications that may run on a mobile device. First, there are those that are strictly local applications (autonomous mobile computing), which means they do not require access to any resources other than those that may be found on that mobile device (or within a container on that device). For example, a spreadsheet on a laptop is a local application. Similarly, a notes application, an MP3 player, and a calculator on a smartphone or tablet are examples in those environments (Fig. 6.3).

REMOTE DATA

Second, there are applications that run on the mobile device but require access to data that is located somewhere else to provide the information or perform the function for which the applications were designed. In general, this means interfacing with an application on another computer to retrieve the required data. Once the data is retrieved, it may be stored and used later and analyzed in some manner. An eReader is a simple example of this type of application. The application user may use the local application to purchase and download a book. The book is stored on the device. The user can read the book later and even annotate it or bookmark it. A more sophisticated example is Microsoft Office 365. This application retrieves data required by the user from a server in the cloud. That data can then be reviewed or modified on the local device without maintaining the connection to the server. The next time the local application is able to connect to the host, the modified data will be uploaded.

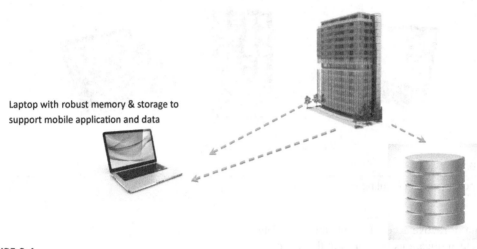

Laptop with robust memory & storage to support mobile application and data

FIGURE 6.4

Dependent mobile computing.

The concept represented by Fig. 6.4 (dependent mobile computing) is that a robust version of the application resides on the mobile device. In fact, in this case, most or all of the application functionality will reside on the mobile device and the host is accessed only to download or upload data. While not exclusive to laptop computers, that is the platform that is best suited to this model since the laptop will normally have much greater memory and storage available. Alternatively, a mobile device may have only minimal data and application functionality on the device itself. It then acts more in the role of providing a user interface and enabling access to full functionality and data on a remote system.

REMOTE FUNCTIONALITY

Whenever data reside on a mobile device, **security** must be given serious consideration. However, the level of security will be dependent on the sensitivity of the data. If the only data being stored are publicly available (e.g., statistics for the user's favorite sports team), then the need for security is minimal. Alternatively, if the data include confidential products plans or pricing strategy, then close attention must be given to securing the application and its data. Security for applications will be discussed in greater detail in Chapter 8.

The third category of mobile applications includes those that rely almost entirely on remote applications to provide the information or functionality required by the user. In this case, the mobile device is essentially acting as a smart terminal. There is an application resident on the mobile device; however, its roles are to enable secure access to the primary application and data residing on a remote server and to display the information supplied by that remote application. There are countless mobile applications that fall in this category—news service applications, travel applications, social media, weather forecasts, stock reports, and sites for rating restaurants, hotels, etc.

To greater and lesser extents, each of these types of applications can be found running on laptops, tablets, and smartphones. Tablets and smartphones tend to make greater use of the remote data and remote functionality types of applications. Laptops are very much a mixed bag. The primary type is determined by the nature of the work being done and the company's IT strategy. For example, at Enterprise Management Associates (EMA), the analysts use Microsoft Office extensively. In EMA's case, the policy for Microsoft Office is that each user has a copy of the software installed on his/her laptop (local application). They also use some SaaS applications (remote functionality).

APPLICATIONS ON LAPTOPS

The objectives and challenges of application management are largely the same, regardless of the type of device on which the applications run. However, the technologies, tools, and processes vary significantly from one environment to another. The vast majority of laptops are **personal computers** running some version of Windows and a much smaller number run MacOS.[2] There are still other operating systems for laptops, including Chrome OS, Linux, and Unix.

When an application runs on a laptop computer, most of the issues and solutions are very similar (or even identical) to those for applications running on desktop personal computers (PCs). However, there are some important differences.

First, in general, there are periods when a laptop computer is not connected to a network and therefore does not meet the first requirement for manageability: it is not addressable. It may simply be turned off or may be in a location where a network connection is not available or is not permitted. Without connectivity, remote management tasks cannot be performed until it is possible to once again communicate with the laptop.

Second, mobile devices and the applications that run on them are inherently less secure than their counterparts. Because the devices are small and portable, they are easy to conceal and that makes them more likely to be stolen. In fact, research by EMA found that one of every 12 mobile device users reported they had a device lost or stolen within the past year.[3] It also makes it easier for them to be lost. This is more likely when the device is taken outside of the company's facilities. However, even within the confines of an enterprise's premises, mobile devices can be lost, stolen, or damaged beyond repair (it is really impressive to see how much damage can be done to a laptop when it is run over by a forklift). That mobility greatly increases the likelihood that the laptop will end up in a place where it should not be; a place where bad things happen to good devices. An example of this is illustrated in Fig. 6.5 (That example happened recently to an EMA analyst's laptop with the unfortunate, predictable results.) Unfortunately, there is no way that administrators or management tools can prevent this from happening. Administrators can try to teach users how to treat a laptop, but as many comedians are quick to point out, there is no cure for stupid. Therefore, some users will learn and adapt how they protect their laptops, while others will not. This makes backup and security even more important than they are for non-mobile devices.

---

[2]Research conducted by EMA found: 90% Windows, 6% Macs, 3% Chromebooks, 1% Linux on business-used laptops. Ibid.
[3]Ibid.

FIGURE 6.5

Bad things can happen to good devices.

Third, when a mobile device is taken outside of the enterprise, it is also taken outside of the enterprise's **firewall**. That makes it much more vulnerable to attacks. This also raises the importance of having good security in place for every mobile device.

As long as the mobile devices are owned by the enterprise, it is easier for the organization to require access to exercise control over the device. The key word is "require." It is much harder to actually enforce those policies. Users are inclined to view the devices as their personal property. Unless there is management software in place to prevent or at least limit the possibility of policies being violated then is likely that some individuals will violate them. Therefore management software needs to be coupled with the promise of serious consequences for the employee if violations do occur (e.g., "… will be subject to disciplinary action up to and including dismissal"). Eventually, most users will violate policies. The most common policy violations are:

- Loading unauthorized applications (frequently games)
- Loading personal data (photos, documents, email, etc.)
- Disabling of security features
- Connecting to unsecured networks or websites
- Using USB drives to load data from outside of the corporate domains (a common way for the introduction of malware)[4]

However, when the device is the property of the employee, the difficulty increases significantly—and that is the world of **bring your own device (BYOD)**.

---

[4]50 percent of users who find a USB drive will plug it into their computer. http://www.theregister.co.uk/2016/04/11/half_plug_in_found_drives/.

TABLETS, SMARTPHONES, AND BYOD

The use of company-issued laptops was getting along fairly well. Yes, there were occasional problems, but generally things worked reasonably well. Then came the smartphone, which began in a seemingly innocuous way. In 2007, Apple introduced the iPhone. Employees started to buy them for their personal use. It took the tech-savvy ones about 30 seconds to realize that they could access their personal email from their phones. It was only a small step from that to wanting to be able to access their company email. Next came the call for access to other business applications. The inflection point for **mobile computing** happened in 2009. It was in that same timeframe that BYOD entered the picture (strictly speaking, devices used for BYOD do not have to be mobile, but the term is generally used to refer to mobile devices).

The basic premise of BYOD is that employees are allowed to use devices that they own to do some or all of their work. The impetus for BYOD came from two directions—employees and enterprises. Many employees had strong preferences regarding the type of mobile device they used. However, letting each employee specify and select the mobile devices that he or she would use promised to create a support nightmare. BYOD became the compromise solution. Employees are given the freedom to choose the device that they prefer but are responsible for providing the technical support for their device(s).

Organizations began to take an alternative approach to providing employees with laptops, phones, and tablets. Instead, they gave employees a sum of money with which to buy the appropriate piece of equipment. For example, they might give an employee an allowance of up to $500 for the purchase of a smartphone. The employee could purchase whichever brand he or she preferred and have it configured however they wish, as long as it met a set of minimum specifications defined by the company. If the employee wanted a smartphone that cost more than $500, the employee had to pay the amount in excess of the allowance.

In each case, in the world of BYOD (regardless of whether it is a laptop, tablet, or smartphone), the mobile device is the property of the employee. That ownership brings with it a new set of problems and challenges. However, the business must protect its interests. Therefore, if the device is going to be used to run business applications, the organization must establish a set of reasonable policies that must be followed if access to business applications and/or data is to be permitted (this will be addressed in Chapter 8).

Another difference in a BYOD environment is that the employee is "technical support" for that device and the applications that run on it (while not true in every instance, this is the norm for BYOD). This means that the employee is responsible for the installation, configuration, and performance of each application on that device. It is the employee's responsibility to ensure that personal applications running on the device do not conflict with the business applications.

On the other hand, it is the responsibility of the organization to grant or restrict access to business applications and data. A key question that must be addressed is whether to permit data to be downloaded to the device. The simplest and most secure answer is to not permit any data to be downloaded to any device. However, this approach does limit when business applications can be accessed, since it requires that the device is connected in order to use any remote data. This is a thorny question that any organization allowing mobile applications must address.

Certainly, some mobile applications reside completely on a mobile device. Perhaps they exist in total isolation from other applications, systems, and data. The more common types of mobile applications are ones that, at a minimum, access data that exists remotely. The entire application may reside on the mobile device and only the data is remote.

The other common scenario is one in which the mobile app is just a small fragment of software that runs on the mobile device and acts as an interface to the full application and data stores that exist elsewhere. In this scenario, while capable of much more, the mobile device is acting essentially as a thin client. The mobile app is simply acting as a means to provide access to the functionality of the remote application.

SECURITY IN BYOD[5]

The primary function of management solutions is to support BYOD and logically isolate business applications, data, and services (i.e., email, messaging, web browsing, etc.) from a user's nonbusiness resources (i.e., personal applications, email, games, and silly cat videos). In this way, the business IT operations can manage, secure, and restrict the enterprise resources without impacting or limiting any other device uses. Typically, profile-based policies are applied to a BYOD management solution allowing configuration and access rights for business resources to be customized for each individual user. While there are a number of resource isolation solutions on the market, they all principally fall into one of the following categories:

Desktop Virtualization
Arguably the first BYOD technology developed, desktop virtualization abstracts a user's workspace environment from the underlying device hardware and operating system. While there are many different types of desktop virtualization, the most commonly recognized is virtual desktop infrastructure (VDI), which remotely hosts a distinct workspace for each user on back office servers and displays them on any network-attached endpoint devices. The leading VDI technologies can be used on just about any endpoint device; however, since they are commonly implemented to be used on devices with larger screen sizes, they are most commonly used on desktop and laptop PCs.

Application Virtualization
Individual software components are hosted and run on enterprise servers but are displayed on user devices. To end users, a virtual application appears like any other local application on their device, but it is centrally maintained and restricted by the business. A particular advantage to this approach is that it allows application built on one platform to operate on any other. For instance, a Windows application can be accessed and used on an iPad or Android tablet.

Containerized Workspace
Containerization as a technology is an offshoot of virtualization with one principal difference, a container is completely self-contained and does not require the preinstallation of a hypervisor on the endpoint. While this simplifies the deployment process, it means any software must be designed for use specifically on the platform on which it will be run. For instance, a Windows application can only run on a Windows device and an iOS application can only run on an iOS device, etc. With this approach, an entire workspace environment—including all enterprise

---

[5]The BYOD Security section is taken from EMA Radar for Mobile Security Management (MSM), Enterprise Management Associates and is available at www.enterprisemanagement.com.

applications, data, and services—are available inside a single container. To access business resources, users simply open the container and use the isolated resources inside. Sometimes this method is referred to as a "duel persona" solution, although that term could reasonably also be applied to desktop virtualization.

Containerized Applications

Individual applications may be containerized rather than a whole desktop. Similar to application virtualization, end users are presented with business applications that appear on their devices just like any other local application, so there is no need to switch between a business environment and a personal environment.

App Wrapping

Rather than fully isolating an application, code can be added to an application that ensures it follows centrally-managed policies. There are two methods for accomplishing this. The most common method is for application developers to install hooks in their code that allow external management platforms to alter aspects of the application. Alternatively, a piece of software can be used that executes the application and effectively filters its use to limit its use or provide additional layers of authentication. While the latter approach can be effectively applied to any application (not just those supported by app developers), there are fewer application features than can be managed externally. For some time, app wrapping was generally preferred as the best approach to mobile app management; however, due to recent legal concerns over licensing altered software and a dwindling support from application developers who are not fond of maintaining hooks in their code for a variety of different management platforms, this approach has somewhat fallen out of favor.

Business-Dedicated Applications

Rather than relying on unsecure consumer applications, some organizations prefer to deploy business-dedicated applications that are designed to be inherently secure and may be managed from a centralized policy-based platform. For instance, a business-dedicated email package may be deployed that only allows messages to be sent from users to authorized personnel (limiting the distribution of sensitive information and files). Users would have a separate email solution for personal messages which has no access to business information. Similar software solution can be deployed for document editing, file sharing, web browsing, and remote access to business systems.

These approaches to BYOD management are not exclusive, and, in fact, most organizations that have adopted a BYOD platform employ more than one method. For instance, a virtual application can run on a virtual desktop or within a containerized workspace. Or another example might be using any business-dedicated applications that are available supplemented by app wrapping on any additionally required applications. Each organization is unique in its endpoint requirements, and care must be taken in deciding which approaches to use that will provide the best balance of accessibility with security in each particular use case.

SUMMARY

The first objective of mobile app management is to ensure that users are able to access the application functionality and the business data they require to do their jobs. Concurrent with providing that access, the other objective of application management is to protect corporate data and other assets.

KEY TAKEAWAYS

- Managing mobile applications consists of enabling users while protecting corporate assets.
- BYOD increases risk while shifting administrative responsibilities to the device's owners.
- Management of applications running on laptops can be very similar to managing applications on desktop PCs. However, the lack of persistent connectivity makes the management more difficult.
- Mobile computing has an inherently greater risk than computing done within the physical confines of the enterprise.

MANAGING WEB-BASED APPLICATIONS

7

First we thought the PC was a calculator. Then we found out how to turn numbers into letters with ASCII—and we thought it was a typewriter. Then we discovered graphics, and we thought it was a television. With the World Wide Web, we've realized it's a brochure.

Douglas Adams

People tend to think of the web as a way to get information or perhaps as a place to carry out ecommerce. But really, the web is about accessing applications. Think of each website as an application, and every single click, every single interaction with that site, is an opportunity to be on the very latest version of that application.

Marc Andreessen

A Day in the Life of Acme Manufacturing: Meeting Customer Needs.

    Meet Cassie. She is an executive relationship manager at Acme Manufacturing. Cassie's job is to sell Acme's products to a dozen or so very large customers, address their continuing needs, and maintain a good relationship with each customer so they can be used as references for other potential customers. To date, Acme has not had a web-based application that will enable Cassie and her counterparts at Acme to efficiently and effectively monitor customer interactions with Acme product development and support personnel. But as of today, things have changed. A team of Acme IT developers just released a sophisticated web-based application to make Cassie's life much easier and hopefully increase Acme's customer satisfaction ratings.

Application Performance Management (APM) in the Digital Enterprise. http://dx.doi.org/10.1016/B978-0-12-804018-8.00007-3

Using the web-based customer relationship management application, customers can now use their desktop or mobile devices to send any issues or concerns to product development and managed services and receive a quick response consistent with the service-level agreement (SLA) with Acme. Cassie will be kept in the loop so that she can monitor, control, and resolve any unanswered requests. The new application had only been in service a few days when Cassie really saw its value.

Meet Henry. Henry is the CEO of XYZ, Inc. Henry is a "problem customer" who has always taken up an inordinate amount of Cassie's time. Despite the fact that Henry's company, XYZ Inc., cannot afford many of Acme's premium managed services, Henry continually peppers Cassie with long drawn-out telephone queries to try to secure free demos and trial subscriptions to managed services that are clearly beyond the needs and financial reach of XYZ. He also continually harasses the Acme help desk. With the deployment of the customer relationship management application, all of Henry's interactions are systematically recorded and his pattern of unorthodox behavior is monitored. Now Cassie has the objective evidence she needs to bring the issue to the attention of her supervisor, Bryan. When Bryan steps in to put a stop to Henry's antics, Cassie is freed up to more effectively manage a greater number of Acme's more profitable customers and the help desk is grateful for her intervention.

Fast forward to the end of Acme's fiscal year, and it's clear that the web-based customer relationship application has enabled Cassie to achieve a much higher level of customer engagement overall and stay in much closer communication with Acme's product developers and managed services. On a recent survey of customer satisfaction, Cassie scored top marks for all her accounts, and levels of customer satisfaction with Acme and its products are at an all-time high.

INTRODUCTION TO WEB-BASED APPLICATIONS

Basically, a **web-based application** is a software program that is stored on a remote server and uses web technologies (e.g., Flash, Silverlight, JavaScript, HTML, CSS) and **web browsers** to deliver one or more functions for the end user over a network through a browser client. The varying levels of usefulness provided by websites have caused some debate as to what qualifies as a web application. The determining factor is whether the website provides a **service** or function. If it performs a task, no matter how insignificant, it is a web application and should be managed as such. A web application can be as simple as Google's search engine, the basic concept of which is to act as a phone directory to search names, locations, and numbers, or as complex as a word processor that enables users to store information and download the document to their personal hard drive. For example, the first mainstream web **applications** were relatively simple, but by the late 1990s there was a push toward more complex web applications, such as TurboTax, that are used by millions of Americans to prepare and file their income tax returns on the web.

It is useful, at this point, to distinguish between web-based applications and the cloud applications discussed in Chapter 4 (Fig. 7.1).

Although similar in many ways, there are some obvious differences between web-based applications and cloud applications that impact the style in which each is managed. While cloud applications can be construed as web applications in the sense that they can be used through web browsers, not all web applications qualify as cloud applications for the following reasons:

- Web Applications
  - Almost exclusively designed to be used from a web browser.

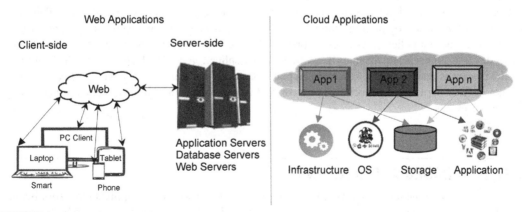

FIGURE 7.1

Comparison of web versus cloud.

- Typically use a mix of server-side script, such as ASP or PHP, and client-side script, such as HTML5 or JavaScript. The server-side script manages how the information is stored and retrieved while the client-side script manages the presentation of the information.
- The web browser (thin client) relies on the web server to provide its core functional **web services.**
- Exclusively web-based with limited options for consumer customization.
- Offer more limited functionality than **cloud** applications.
- Cloud Applications
  - Data are stored on a cloud or cloud-like infrastructure.
  - Data can be cached locally for full offline mode.
  - Support different use requirements, including data backup, data compression, and **security.**
  - Can be used from a web browser and/or customer-built apps installed on the web-connected devices, such as desktops and **mobile devices.**
  - Can be used to access a wider range of services, such as on-demand computing, storage, and application **development** platforms.
  - Depend on cloud technology but are available offline, if users choose.
  - Offer rich functionality and customization.
  - Support **virtualization.**

Web-based applications can be developed internally by an organization and then self-hosted, cloud-hosted, or provisioned as **software as a service (SaaS)**. Internally developed and hosted applications evolve from legacy applications with added web-based front ends to reduce the technical challenges of maintaining and supporting thick clients. This approach also accommodates endpoint evolutionary trends, including **mobile applications** and **bring your own device (BYOD)** policies.

As alternatives evolve with regard to where and how web-based applications are hosted, organizations are adding SaaS and cloud-hosted applications to their mix of web-based application offerings. SaaS is a particularly viable and popular alternative for those applications that need to be accessed by a mobile workforce. Similarly, where organizations experience variable levels of use and load, hosting applications in a third-party cloud either in whole or on a dynamic, as-needed basis is gaining in popularity.

Over the years, web-based applications have become more sophisticated and powerful thanks in large part to **AJAX**, a programming model used to create more responsive web applications such as Gmail and Yahoo mail clients. As a result, present-day web applications are better able to handle the day-to-day tasks of users and the lines between desktop applications and web applications have blurred.

Most recently, many existing web-based applications were recast into mobile web applications (i.e., Internet-enabled applications), such as Facebook and Google Maps, which have specific functionality for mobile devices.

WHY WEB-BASED APPLICATIONS?

It is difficult to imagine any organization existing today without web-based applications. An obvious advantage of web-based applications is that they are accessible from anywhere via a web browser. The main selling point of web applications is reduced support costs. Web applications eliminate the need to install software on a client, to routinely upgrade the software, and to maintain the client's **operating system**. To further reduce support costs, a web application can run on a PC or a Mac and on multiple browsers such Internet Explorer, Chrome, or Firefox. Consequently, web applications eliminate the need for developers to build a client for a specific type of computer or a specific operating system.

MANAGING WEB-BASED APPLICATIONS

Unlike **native applications** that are downloaded and installed on a specific device, web-based applications require a very different **management** approach to their development, accessibility, efficiency, and revenue-generation capabilities. The following sections discuss the different elements of **application lifecycle management** that specifically relate to the management of web-based applications.

HIRE CROSS-FUNCTIONAL PERSONNEL

The growing need for information technology (IT) to deliver web services, along with deploying and support infrastructure, has resulted in the need for processes and skills to be much more cross-functional. Traditionally, applications were the domain of the developers; however, as organizations move to web-based applications the line between **development and operations** blurs. Consequently, staffing, skills, and product requirements have changed drastically, resulting in a rise in IT support costs and a growing interest in best practices, such as the **IT Infrastructure Library** (**ITIL**) framework and the emergence of centers of excellence in large organizations.

To effectively manage this complex environment of web-based applications, it is also important to hire IT personnel with higher level cross-functional skills, such as knowing which server supports which application(s) or which database begins to underperform when it hits a given number of connections.

CAPITALIZE ON DATABASE DESIGN AND QUERY OPTIMIZATION

The database is the most important component of a web-based application. It is essential that web developers are familiar with these critical aspects in a web-based application. A high level of SQL knowledge is essential to optimizing and rewriting queries to save milliseconds on response time. Basic SQL queries can be problematic in the web-based production environment. Their fill-in-the-blank nature can cause problems since it will be the part of the web-based application that developers are least familiar with. Instead, they should be replaced with custom-created SQL queries that focus on the needs of the database being used by a specific web-based application. Another necessary skill is that of formulating contingencies about how the app can grow and the associated database problems that growth will create.

THINK LIKE A SERVER

Web-based applications are dependent on servers that can interpret code differently from the way it was written. When managing web-based applications, it is important to establish acceptable usage patterns, identify exceptions that may result in problems, and track and monitor all application activities to identify the way in which different resources are used.

CONSIDER THE SOURCE

Web-based applications are typically used through web browsers. Each browser is slightly different and displays web pages in different ways. As a result, programming of web-based applications needs to be specialized to accommodate the ways that browsers interact with different web languages, such as HTML, **XML**, Flash, Perl, ASP, and PHP. This variability in browsers, along with the likelihood of their use by potential users, must be considered when designing web-based applications. To address this issue and maximize exposure for a consumer-based application, open source code can be used to develop a web-based application.

SIMPLIFY DEVELOPMENT WITH WEB APPLICATION PROGRAMMING INTERFACES

Web **application programming interfaces (APIs)** are quickly becoming another critical web **application management** technique to assist developers in efficiently creating web applications. As public and private organizations are pressured to deliver products and services to more consumers as inexpensively and conveniently than ever before, organizations have no choice but to adapt or risk being left behind in the era of web APIs. APIs provide a framework that developers can use to quickly build web services or an application from multiple services to leverage, advertise, and combine corporate assets for widespread consumption. Using traditional **service-oriented architecture (SOA)**, organizations can create web services from diverse data sources, including databases and legacy systems, to extend strategic organizational assets such as product catalogs, phone listings, and order status data beyond conventional boundaries. **XML** or **JSON** formats provide internal and external developers with the ability to easily create readily accessible Web 2.0 applications. To create web applications that support a wide range of industry and **line of business** functions that lead to an increased share in new and existing markets, organizations need to develop a carefully constructed web API strategy. To achieve this, organizations should complete the following steps:

1. Develop a clear understanding of the underlying organizational objectives for creating web applications, such as:
   a. Rebrand the organization
   b. Educate customers about a new offering
   c. Explore new market channels to increase revenue
2. Choose which assets to expose and to whom
3. Determine Web API availability—internal developers only, or offer it for public consumption
4. Tap best developers to support organizational objectives through effective partnering
5. Understand legal implications of exposing organizational assets through a web API
6. Establish metrics to measure API success, such as tracking number of page visits or revenue generated

The world's largest API repository is the Programmable Web's API Directory (http://www.programmableweb.com/apis/directory), which currently lists approximately 15,000 public APIs that developers can use to build new products and business workflows. The repository is searchable by category and/or protocol/format.

DETERMINE BEST LEVEL OF TESTING

Getting a web-based application into use is sometimes far more important than spending an inordinate amount of time on testing. The goal is to test the application as much as possible without delaying its release. Testing can be accomplished by peer review, unit testing, ad-hoc testing, load testing, or **quality assurance** processes such as weekly reviews of error logs. Many development mistakes can be avoided by using a combination of these testing techniques. The more obscure mistakes can be left to the application users to report in real-time feedback. Take advantage of this commonly accepted, iterative process that emerged in the online software culture to manage the amount of testing that is performed in web-based application development.

PERFORM REAL-TIME MONITORING

In today's rapidly changing business landscape, IT managers and application developers are being called on to deliver web applications and web services without delay and maximize their end-user expectations by adeptly navigating the increased complexity and potential points of failure of their web applications. This requires organizations to perform **real-time monitoring** of the **user experience**, volume of traffic, and health and **performance** of web applications, including slow database queries. Fortunately, a number of vendors now offer tools (e.g., BMC's TrueSight App Visibility Manager) to accomplish these daunting tasks.

Another important aspect of a web-based application is its response time. If the application is well designed, elegantly coded, and technically correct but not fast enough, users will reject it. Solutions for these problems should include installing an accelerator on the servers and incorporating load testing to benchmark response times.

MEASURE APPLICATION PERFORMANCE

As web-based applications become an increasingly important component of conducting business, their performance becomes more tightly coupled with an organization's bottom line and ultimately its mission. Consequently, managing **application performance** is particularly essential in a web-based environment. However, the complexity of diverse, web-based application capabilities requires more than organizational knowledge and manual processes to ensure business continuity and organizational productivity.

For example, application performance differences of fractions of a second in online financial transactions can translate into losses of millions of dollars per hour in a large organization. Similarly, in the multibillion dollar online retail industry, a customer's perception of brand quality can adversely be affected by slow response times or a less than seamless online shopping experience.

Robust web-based **application performance management (APM)** is critical when delivering high-quality business services. Inefficiencies and points of failure in the communication, server, or data layers can lead to subpar performance or failure. Unfortunately, since these exhaustion points often are not discovered until user expectations are not met, **service-level agreement (SLA)** thresholds are missed and/or business is lost. Proactive monitoring of availability and performance is beneficial in these situations. This combination ensures that organizations consistently meet or exceed user expectations and enables companies to reap benefits of best practice implementation to successfully deliver against SLAs, lower overall resource costs, improve infrastructure utilization, and satisfying demanding customers.

APM tools such as New Relic, AppDynamics, Foglight, and BMC Software APM are particularly useful in addressing these complexities and mitigating risk to optimize costs, customer satisfaction, and retention, and in achieving a higher probability of meeting or exceeding service levels. In addition, the implementation of APMs frees up skilled personnel from lower level day-to-day support tasks to concentrate on developing new web-based applications to support higher level business goals and objectives.

CHALLENGES OF MANAGING WEB-BASED APPLICATIONS

While web-based applications offer higher levels of cost efficiency and flexibility, they also introduce new and unique visibility and control challenges.

REQUIRE A BILATERAL MANAGEMENT APPROACH

To meet performance and user experience expectations in addition to basic availability, IT teams must adopt a bilateral approach that combines performance visibility with proactive optimization technologies.

ABSENCE OF SOFTWARE DEVELOPMENT KITS

Another challenge is that while native applications have their own unique development process, web applications do not and **software development kits (SDKs)** that exist to provide developers with a suite of tools to efficiently develop native applications are not available to assist in the development of web-based applications.

API RELIABILITY

APIs, as discussed, are a mixed blessing when managing web-based applications. While APIs reduce development time and cost by allowing applications to share information, such as in Yelp where nearby restaurants can be displayed on a Google Map within Yelp, they have their drawbacks. For example, APIs can unexpectedly become unavailable when the companies that create them shut down their API services, restrict their accessibility, or go out of business, causing web applications to lose the services they depend on from the API.

SECURITY

Despite their many advantages, web-based applications raise a number of security concerns stemming from improper coding. A significant amount of confidential information is stolen every day from vulnerable web application servers that are publicly accessible and tied into backend database servers that store a wealth of corporate information. For example, an attacker can input an SQL query into the search field of a web form that can then be accepted by the web-based application and passed to the back-end database where read/write access is granted from the application to the database server. Then, the query is executed. This allows the attacker to view and/or delete the contents of the database. Another common security concern in web-based applications is **cross-site scripting (XSS)**, a common technique used by hackers to maliciously inject code into a legitimate web-based application to deceive users and redirect them toward phishing sites. Attackers do not directly target a user but instead exploit a vulnerability in a website or web-based application that the user visits to deliver a malicious script to the user's browser. A common example of this is when an attacker obtains the user's session cookie to impersonate that user.

The **Open Web Application Security Project (OWASP)** is a 501(c)(3) worldwide not-for-profit charitable organization dedicated to enabling organizations develop, purchase, and maintain applications that can be trusted. In its Top 10 project, OWASP raises awareness about web application security by identifying some of the most critical risks facing organizations (Table 7.1).

Table 7.1 OWASP Top 10 Web Application Security Issues

No.	Security Risk	Cause	Consequence
1	Injection	SQL, OS, and LDAP injection can occur when untrusted data is sent to an interpreter as part of a command or query.	Attackers' hostile data can trick the interpreter into executing unintended commands or accessing unauthorized data.
2	Cross-site scripting (XSS)	Application takes untrusted data and sends it to a web browser without proper validation.	Attacker can execute scripts in user's browser to hijack user session, deface website, or redirect user to phishing sites.
3	Broken authentication and session management	Functions related to authentication and session management are improperly implemented.	Attackers can compromise keys or session tokens, and exploit other implementation flaws to assume other users' identities.
4	Insecure direct object references	Developer exposes reference to an internal implementation file directory or database key.	Attackers can manipulate references to access unauthorized data.
5	Cross-site request forgery (CSRF)	Forces logged-on user's browser to send forged **HTTP** request, including session cookie and other automatically included authentication information.	Attacker forces user's browser to generate requests that vulnerable application recognizes as legitimate user requests.
6	Security misconfiguration	Many **configuration** settings are not shipped with secure defaults and settings are undefined.	Software, including all code libraries used by applications, are not kept up to date.
7	Insecure cryptographic storage	Sensitive data such as credit cards, SSNs, and authentication credentials are not properly encrypted or hashed.	Attackers may steal or modify weakly protected data to conduct identity theft, credit card fraud, and other crimes.
8	Failure to restrict URL access	Access-controlled checks are not performed each time protected links and buttons are accessed.	Attackers can forge URLs to access hidden pages.
9	Insufficient transport layer protection	Confidentiality and integrity of sensitive network traffic is not protected through authentication or **encryption**.	Applications support weak algorithms, use expired or invalid certifications, or use them incorrectly.
10	Invalidated redirects and forwards	Users are redirected or forwarded to other pages and websites. Untrusted data is used to determination the destination pages.	Attackers can redirect users to phishing or malware sites or use forwards to access unauthorized pages.

Adapted from OWASP (www.owasp.org/index.php/Top_10_2013-Top_10).

However, it is not sufficient to just be aware of potential risks or concentrate on preventative measures; it is also imperative that organizations understand how and why these security breaches occur. To guard against potential security breaches, organizations should conduct a thorough audit of their web applications on a regular basis, understand how web application attacks work, and consistently and faithfully apply the following principles:

- Appoint a visible executive advocate or management sponsor to encourage and demonstrate leadership backing to promote **collaboration** between business leaders, IT leaders, development, operations, and security teams.
- Integrate application security throughout the application development process and enforce key milestones.
- Raise awareness of sources of potential security flaws in developer and server administrator training.
- Develop a threat model so developers can anticipate authentication, encryption, data storage, and system **integration** security issues and design a secure application from the start.
- Employ manual static (**SAST**) and automated dynamic (**DAST**) application security testing tools to respectively spot check and repeatedly test the application's behavior. Cloud-based DAST tools are particularly useful because they can test large numbers of application in a short period of time without incurring the cost of setting up on-premises software.
- Use **web application firewalls (WAFs)** to block certain web application attacks like cross-site scripting. WAFs can also limit access from undesirable or suspicious networks, alter the way in which browsers and applications communicate, and protect an organization against vulnerabilities in third-party applications while vendors are working on fixes.
- Conduct a thorough audit of all web applications on a regular basis.

SUMMARY

Web-based applications have increasingly become a necessary part of conducting business. They enable organizations to significantly expand the geographical reach of their customer base and increase their market share. IT requirements for web-based applications are fewer than for native applications, and system-wide updates and patches are handled by the provider and implemented instantly. Add to this the **interoperability** and ease of use of web-based applications and it is clear to see that they are a powerful business tool.

Managing web-based applications requires a different approach to their development, accessibility, efficiency, and revenue-generation capabilities. The many facets of web application management that must be addressed span problem definitions, from operations and maintenance, with a particular emphasis on security in every phase of the system development lifecycle.

KEY TAKEAWAYS

- Organizations cannot effectively conduct business without one or more web-based applications.
- Web applications require a different application lifecycle management approach from the one required by native applications.

- Greater cross-functional skills are required to effectively develop, operate, and manage web-based applications.
- Website safety and security are crucial to establishing positive public perception and maintaining an organization's image, as well as managing potential financial and legal risks.
- The Open Web Application Security Project (OWASP) is a nonprofit organization dedicated to supporting and protecting organizations from web-based application security breaches.

Examples of vendors with products in this space:

Apica
AppDynamics
AppFirst
Appnomic
ASG
Aternity
BlazeMeter
BMC
CA Technologies
Dell Quest
Dyn
Dynatrace
EMC
ExtraHop
HP
IBM
Idera
ManageEngine
Nastel
NetScout
Netuitive
New Relic
Push Technology
Riverbed
SmartBear
SOASTA
Splunk
Stackify
Sumo Logic

APPLICATION MANAGEMENT SECURITY

8

I think computer viruses should count as life. I think it says something about human nature that the
only form of life we have created so far is purely destructive. We've created life in our own image.

Stephen Hawking

Security has too often been an afterthought. Organizations have traditionally perceived the threat level to be very low, akin to winning the Powerball lottery or being struck by lightning. Believing the risk to be so low made doing little or nothing seem like a reasonable course of action. Of course, we now know that it was not a wise choice, but many executives do not understand that. Then came one high profile incident after another. Today, the situation is changing (albeit slowly), and there is a new paradigm emerging, one that looks at an organization and says, "Assume that you have been breached or will be breached soon." This shift is leading many organizations to take more stringent security measures. In other cases, regulatory bodies are forcing tighter security on them.

Application security is not the same as securing a server, a router, database, etc., nor is it completely separate from securing those parts of the infrastructure where the **applications** are developed, tested, and run. Applications are different. They enforce security policies, are a trusted source of data, and provide trusted access to data. Applications hold the veritable "keys to the kingdom." Whoever controls or compromises an application has almost unlimited power relative to the domain of that application. Thus, it is imperative that robust security be in place for all of an organization's applications. Broadly, this issue can be divided into two areas: (1) design and develop and (2) deploy and run. This chapter is going to look at measures to protect the applications themselves.

APPLICATION DEVELOPMENT

When it comes to protecting or compromising applications, it is the people who develop and maintain applications who sit at the top of the pecking order. It is their responsibility to design and build applications that are secure. However, the first step in secure application **development** is to create an environment where applications can be developed securely.

What is a secure environment? It is one where reasonable measures are taken to guard against access to the development and test environments by unauthorized parties. Also, in those environments, access to code (whether in development or in production) is limited to individuals who are responsible for development or review of those applications.

In a perfect world, the systems where applications are developed would have no connectivity to anything outside of the secured environment. Unfortunately, in today's world that is not going to happen except for the most extreme cases (e.g., the most sensitive national security applications). Some programmers work from home. Others need to access code in middle of the night when there are problems in production. Also, it is generally desirable to be able to move application code from the development and test environments to a production environment by transmitting it electronically. Therefore, for these and other reasons, the total isolation of a development and test environment is simply not possible or at least not practical.

The security measures put in place for the design, development, and test environments need to be at least as stringent as, if not greater than, those for the production environments where those applications will run. The security measures are not limited to securing the system (server or mainframe) on which the application development takes place. That also includes any remote systems that may be used for development or to access the development and test environments. It must extend to each of the networks that connect to the application development and test environments. Code that is developed and stored on the application development and test environments must be secured. Generally, that will mean that the code will be encrypted. Similarly, any code that is stored on remote systems should be encrypted while at rest, as should the communications between the remote systems and the application development environment.

As noted earlier, the application developers (programmers) ultimately are the key to securely developing applications and to developing applications that are secure. Therefore, it is of utmost importance that the developers are vetted as much as possible. That last statement may bring a smile to the faces of some readers, for indeed the world of application development is filled with many "unique" individuals. Also, for decades, application development has been a space where there was a shortage of qualified personnel. Therefore, employers cannot always be as selective as they might like to be.

For decades, one of the authors (Sturm) has told audiences around the world that, "When it comes to money, sex, or power, trust no one." Application developers certainly have power and the potential for financial gain through the insertion of malicious code. We will leave it to the reader to decide whether sex is also part of the equation. However, it is clear that unless there are adequate safeguards in place, application developers have both the opportunity to introduce code that they can later exploit and some incentive to do so. This is not intended to suggest that all application developers are dishonest, for clearly not all are. However, in the case of application development, the law of large numbers definitely applies and there will be a few people who might succumb to temptation if they thought that they might not be detected. Therefore, maintaining a secure application development environment with adequate controls is essential.

Another important factor that warrants serious consideration is outsourcing, particularly when application development is outsourced to a company that develops the applications in another country (more so in some countries than others). The client company has control over who is actually writing the code. Also, the client cannot be certain that the development and test environments are adequately secured. Therefore, any code that is developed outside of the company must be analyzed thoroughly to ensure that there are not any backdoors or other weaknesses embedded for someone to exploit in the future. While this is true of applications that are developed in-house, it is much more important with applications that were developed by an outsourcer.

Once a secure environment is established and a team of developers hired, the next step in realizing application security is in the design of the applications. Security must be a priority when designing applications. In fact, security must be a priority throughout the application lifecycle beginning with requirements gathering and continuing through the design, development, testing (**quality assurance**), and deployment phases. It is essential that in the testing phase (perhaps as a separate step in the testing process) the security of the application is tested. It is interesting to note that the actual development phase (i.e., the coding of the application) is not where security is designed. That happens earlier. It is in development that the design is transformed into an executable program. Security for an application is created in the development phase only to the extent that the programmers adhere to the design. However, in the development phase, vulnerabilities can be introduced through errors or by a failure to adhere to the original design.

TOP 25 MOST DANGEROUS SOFTWARE ERRORS

Through a collaborative effort of SANS Institute/MITRE Corporation, many of the leading security experts around the world and with support from the U.S. Department of Homeland Security developed a concise list of the 25 most dangerous software errors, as listed in Tables 8.1, 8.2, and 8.3.

INSECURE INTERACTION BETWEEN COMPONENTS

These weaknesses are related to insecure ways in which data are sent and received between separate components, modules, programs, processes, threads, or systems.

Table 8.1 Interaction Between Components[a]

CWE ID	Name
CWE-89	Improper neutralization of special elements used in an SQL command ("SQL injection")
CWE-78	Improper neutralization of special elements used in an OS command ("OS command injection")
CWE-79	Improper neutralization of input during web page generation ("cross-site scripting")
CWE-434	Unrestricted upload of file with dangerous type
CWE-352	Cross-site request forgery (CSRF)
CWE-601	URL redirection to untrusted site ("open redirect")

[a]*2011 CWE/SANS "Top 25 Most Dangerous Software Errors" http://cwe.mitre.org/top25/.*

RISKY RESOURCE MANAGEMENT

The weaknesses in this category are related to ways in which software does not properly manage the creation, usage, transfer, or destruction of important system resources.

Table 8.2 Risky Resource Management[a]

CWE ID	Name
CWE-120	Buffer copy without checking size of input ("classic buffer overflow")
CWE-22	Improper limitation of a pathname to a restricted directory ("path traversal")
CWE-494	Download of code without integrity check
CWE-829	Inclusion of functionality from untrusted control sphere
CWE-676	Use of potentially dangerous function
CWE-131	Incorrect calculation of buffer size
CWE-134	Uncontrolled format string
CWE-190	Integer overflow or wraparound

[a]*2011 CWE/SANS "Top 25 Most Dangerous Software Errors" http://cwe.mitre.org/top25/.*

POROUS DEFENSES

The weaknesses in this category are related to defensive techniques that are often misused, abused, or just plain ignored.

Table 8.3 Porous Defenses[a]

CWE ID	Name
CWE-306	Missing authentication for critical function
CWE-862	Missing authorization
CWE-798	Use of hard-coded credentials
CWE-311	Missing encryption of sensitive data
CWE-807	Reliance on untrusted inputs in a security decision
CWE-250	Execution with unnecessary privileges
CWE-863	Incorrect authorization
CWE-732	Incorrect permission assignment for critical resource
CWE-327	Use of a broken or risky cryptographic algorithm
CWE-307	Improper restriction of excessive authentication attempts
CWE-759	Use of a one-way hash without a salt

[a]2011 CWE/SANS "Top 25 Most Dangerous Software Errors" http://cwe.mitre.org/top25/.

In addition to developing the list of most dangerous software errors, the team also developed a list of mitigations and general practices that can be used to defend against the consequences of those errors. That excellent work is included next and is set apart by being formatted in italics.

2011 CWE/SANS Top 25: Monster Mitigations
These mitigations will be effective in eliminating or reducing the severity of the Top 25. These mitigations will also address many weaknesses that are not even on the Top 25. If you adopt these mitigations, you are well on your way to making more secure software.
Monster Mitigation Index

ID	Name
M1	*Establish and maintain control over all of your inputs.*
M2	*Establish and maintain control over all of your outputs.*
M3	*Lock down your environment.*
M4	*Assume that external components can be subverted, and your code can be read by anyone.*
M5	*Use industry-accepted security features instead of inventing your own.*
GP1	*(general) Use libraries and frameworks that make it easier to avoid introducing weaknesses.*
GP2	*(general) Integrate security into the entire software development lifecycle.*
GP3	*(general) Use a broad mix of methods to comprehensively find and prevent weaknesses.*
GP4	*(general) Allow locked-down clients to interact with your software.*

Monster Mitigation Matrix

The following table maps CWEs to the recommended monster mitigations, along with a brief summary of the mitigation's effectiveness.

Effectiveness ratings include:

- **High**: *The mitigation has well-known, well-understood strengths and limitations; there is good coverage with respect to variations of the weakness.*
- **Moderate**: *The mitigation will prevent the weakness in multiple forms, but it does not have complete coverage of the weakness.*
- **Limited**: *The mitigation may be useful in limited circumstances, only be applicable to a subset of this weakness type, require extensive training/customization, or give limited visibility.*
- **Defense in Depth (DiD)**: *The mitigation may not necessarily prevent the weakness, but it may help to minimize the potential impact when an attacker exploits the weakness.*

  Within the matrix, the following mitigations are identified:
- *M1: Establish and maintain control over all of your inputs.*
- *M2: Establish and maintain control over all of your outputs.*
- *M3: Lock down your environment.*
- *M4: Assume that external components can be subverted, and your code can be read by anyone.*
- *M5: Use industry-accepted security features instead of inventing your own.*

  The following general practices are omitted from the matrix:
- *GP1: Use libraries and frameworks that make it easier to avoid introducing weaknesses.*
- *GP2: Integrate security into the entire software development lifecycle.*
- *GP3: Use a broad mix of methods to comprehensively find and prevent weaknesses.*
- *GP4: Allow locked-down clients to interact with your software.*

M1	M2	M3	M4	M5	CWE
High		DiD	Mod		CWE-22: Improper Limitation of a Pathname to a Restricted Directory ("Path Traversal")
Mod	High	DiD	Ltd		CWE-78: Improper Neutralization of Special Elements used in an OS Command ("OS Command Injection")
Mod	High		Ltd		CWE-79: Improper Neutralization of Input During Web Page Generation ("Cross-site Scripting")
Mod	High	DiD	Ltd		CWE-89: Improper Neutralization of Special Elements used in an SQL Command ("SQL Injection")
Mod		DiD	Ltd		CWE-120: Buffer Copy without Checking Size of Input ("Classic Buffer Overflow")
Mod		DiD	Ltd		CWE-131: Incorrect Calculation of Buffer Size
High		DiD	Mod		CWE-134: Uncontrolled Format String
Mod		DiD	Ltd		CWE-190: Integer Overflow or Wraparound
		High			CWE-250: Execution with Unnecessary Privileges
		Mod		Mod	CWE-306: Missing Authentication for Critical Function
				Mod	CWE-307: Improper Restriction of Excessive Authentication Attempts
		DiD			CWE-311: Missing Encryption of Sensitive Data
				High	CWE-327: Use of a Broken or Risky Cryptographic Algorithm
			Ltd		CWE-352: Cross-Site Request Forgery (CSRF)
Mod		DiD	Mod		CWE-434: Unrestricted Upload of File with Dangerous Type
		DiD			CWE-494: Download of Code Without Integrity Check

Continued

M1	M2	M3	M4	M5	CWE
Mod	Mod		Ltd		CWE-601: URL Redirection to Untrusted Site ("Open Redirect")
Mod	High	DiD			CWE-676: Use of Potentially Dangerous Function
	Ltd	DiD		Mod	CWE-732: Incorrect Permission Assignment for Critical Resource
				High	CWE-759: Use of a One-Way Hash without a Salt
		DiD	High	Mod	CWE-798: Use of Hard-coded Credentials
Mod		DiD	Mod	Mod	CWE-807: Reliance on Untrusted Inputs in a Security Decision
High		High	High		CWE-829: Inclusion of Functionality from Untrusted Control Sphere
DiD		Mod		Mod	CWE-862: Missing Authorization
		DiD		Mod	CWE-863: Incorrect Authorization

Mitigation Details

M1: Establish and maintain control over all of your inputs.

Target Audience: *Programmers.*

Associated CWEs:

CWE-20 Improper Input Validation

Improper input validation is the number one killer of healthy software, so you're just asking for trouble if you don't ensure that your input conforms to expectations. For example, an identifier that you expect to be numeric shouldn't ever contain letters. Nor should the price of a new car be allowed to be a dollar, not even in today's economy. Of course, applications often have more complex validation requirements than these simple examples. Incorrect input validation can lead to vulnerabilities when attackers can modify their inputs in unexpected ways. Many of today's most common vulnerabilities can be eliminated, or at least reduced, using proper input validation.

Use a standard input validation mechanism to validate all input for:

- *length*
- *type of input*
- *syntax*
- *missing or extra inputs*
- *consistency across related fields*
- *business rules*

As an example of business rule logic, "boat" may be syntactically valid because it only contains alphanumeric characters, but it is not valid if you are expecting color names such as "red" or "blue."

Where possible, use stringent whitelists that limit the character set based on the expected value of the parameter in the request. This can have indirect benefits, such as reducing or eliminating weaknesses that may exist elsewhere in the product.

Do not accept any inputs that violate these rules, or convert the inputs to safe values.

Understand all the potential areas where untrusted inputs can enter your software: parameters or arguments, cookies, anything read from the network, environment variables, reverse DNS lookups, query results, request headers, URL components, e-mail, files, databases, and any external systems that provide data to the application. Remember that such inputs may be obtained indirectly through API calls.

Be careful to properly decode the inputs and convert them to your internal representation before performing validation.

Applicable Top 25 CWEs:

CWE-120, CWE-129, CWE-131, CWE-134, CWE-190, CWE-209, CWE-22, CWE-285, CWE-306, CWE-311, CWE-327, CWE-352, CWE-362, CWE-434, CWE-494, CWE-601, CWE-676, CWE-732, CWE-754, CWE-770, CWE-78, CWE-79, CWE-798, CWE-805, CWE-807, CWE-829, CWE-862, CWE-89, CWE-98.

M2: Establish and maintain control over all of your outputs.

Target Audience: *Programmers, Designers*

Associated CWEs:

CWE-116 Improper Encoding or Escaping of Output

Computers have a strange habit of doing what you say, not what you mean. Insufficient output encoding is the often-ignored sibling to improper input validation, but it is at the root of most injection-based attacks, which are all the rage these days. An attacker can modify the commands that you intend to send to other components, possibly leading to a complete compromise of your application - not to mention exposing the other components to exploits that the attacker would not be able to launch directly. This turns "do what I mean" into "do what the attacker says." When your program generates outputs to other components in the form of structured messages such as queries or requests, it needs to separate control information and metadata from the actual data. This is easy to forget, because many paradigms carry data and commands bundled together in the same stream, with only a few special characters enforcing the boundaries. An example is Web 2.0 and other frameworks that work by blurring these lines. This further exposes them to attack.

If available, use structured mechanisms that automatically enforce the separation between data and code. These mechanisms may be able to provide the relevant quoting, encoding, and validation automatically, instead of relying on the developer to provide this capability at every point where output is generated.

For example, stored procedures can enforce database query structure and reduce the likelihood of SQL injection.

Understand the context in which your data will be used and the encoding that will be expected. This is especially important when transmitting data between different components, or when generating outputs that can contain multiple encodings at the same time, such as web pages or multi-part mail messages. Study all expected communication protocols and data representations to determine the required encoding strategies.

Applicable Top 25 CWEs:

CWE-120, CWE-129, CWE-131, CWE-190, CWE-209, CWE-22, CWE-285, CWE-306, CWE-311, CWE-327, CWE-352, CWE-362, CWE-434, CWE-494, CWE-601, CWE-676, CWE-732, CWE-754, CWE-770, CWE-78, CWE-79, CWE-798, CWE-805, CWE-807, CWE-89, CWE-98.

M3: Lock down your environment.

Target Audience: Project Managers, Designers

Associated CWEs:

CWE-250 Execution with Unnecessary Privileges

It's an unfortunate fact of life: weaknesses happen, even with your best efforts. By using defense in depth, you can limit the scope and severity of a successful attack against an unexpected weakness, sometimes even reducing the problems to an occasional annoyance. The core aspect of defense in depth is to avoid dependence on a single feature, solution, mitigation or barrier (e.g., firewall) to provide all the security. Locking down your environment helps to achieve this.

Run your software in a restricted environment, using available security features to limit the scope of what your software can do to its host systems and adjacent networks. Even if an attacker manages to find and exploit a vulnerability, an environmental lockdown can limit what the attacker can do, reducing the overall severity of the problem and making the attacker work harder. In some cases, the lockdown may prevent the problem from becoming a vulnerability in the first place.

Some of the aspects of environment lockdown are:

- Run as an unprivileged user. Run your software with the lowest privileges possible. Even if your software is compromised via a weakness that you were not aware of, it will make it more difficult for an attacker to cause further damage. Spider Man, the well-known comic superhero, lives by the motto "With great power comes great responsibility." Your software may need special privileges to perform certain operations, but wielding those privileges longer than necessary can be extremely risky. When running with extra privileges, your application has access to resources that the application's user can't directly reach. For example, you might intentionally launch a separate program, and that program allows its user to specify a file to open; this feature is frequently present in help utilities or editors. The user can access unauthorized files through the launched program, thanks to those extra privileges. Command execution can happen in a similar fashion. Even if you don't launch other programs, additional vulnerabilities in your software could have more serious consequences than if it were running at a lower privilege level.

- Consider disabling verbose error messages for messages that are displayed to users without special privileges. If you use chatty error messages, then they could disclose secrets to any attacker who dares to misuse your software. The secrets could cover a wide range of valuable data, including personally identifiable information (PII), authentication credentials, and server configuration. Sometimes, they might seem like harmless secrets that are convenient for your

Continued

users and admins, such as the full installation path of your software. Even these little secrets can greatly simplify a more concerted attack that yields much bigger rewards, which is done in real-world attacks all the time. This is a concern whether you send temporary error messages back to the user or if you permanently record them in a log file.

- *Wherever possible, if you must third-party libraries, use best-of-breed libraries with an established record of good security.*
- *Build or compile your code using security-related options. For example, some compilers provide built-in protection against buffer overflows.*
- *Use operating system and hardware features, when available, that limit the impact of a successful attack. For example, some chips, OS features, and libraries make it more difficult to exploit buffer overflows. Some OS configurations allow you to specify quotas for disk usage, CPU, memory, open files, and others.*
- *Use virtualization, sandboxes, jails, or similar technologies that limit access to the environment. Even if an attacker completely compromises your software, the damage to the rest of the environment may be minimized. For example, an application may intend to write to files within a limited subdirectory, but path traversal weaknesses typically allow an attacker to navigate outside of the directory and through the entire file system.*
- *Consider adopting secure configurations using security benchmarks or hardening guides such as the Federal Desktop Core Configuration (FDCC).*
- *Use vulnerability scanners and regularly apply security patches to ensure that your system does not have any known vulnerabilities. Even if your application does not have any obvious problems, an attacker may be able to compromise the application by attacking the system itself.*

Applicable Top 25 CWEs:
CWE-120, CWE-129, CWE-131, CWE-134, CWE-190, CWE-209, CWE-22, CWE-250, CWE-285, CWE-306, CWE-311, CWE-327, CWE-352, CWE-362, CWE-434, CWE-494, CWE-601, CWE-676, CWE-732, CWE-754, CWE-770, CWE-78, CWE-79, CWE-798, CWE-805, CWE-807, CWE-829, CWE-862, CWE-863, CWE-89, CWE-98.

M4: Assume that external components can be subverted, and your code can be read by anyone.
Target Audience: *Project Managers, Programmers, Designers*
Associated CWEs:

CWE-602 Client-Side Enforcement of Server-Side Security
CWE-649 Reliance on Obfuscation or Encryption of Security-Relevant Inputs without Integrity Checking
CWE-656 Reliance on Security Through Obscurity
If it's out of your hands, it's out of your control.

When it comes to security, your code operates in a hostile environment. Attackers can analyze your software - even if it's obfuscated - and figure out what's going on. They can modify external components to ignore security controls. They can try any type of attack against every component in the system. If your code is distributed to your consumers, even better - they can run your software and attack it in their own environment, forever, without you ever knowing about it.

Many developers assume that their compiled code, or custom protocols, cannot be figured out by attackers. However, modern reverse engineering techniques are very mature, and hackers can figure out the inner workings of software quickly, even with proprietary protocols, lack of access to specifications, and no source code. When software's protection mechanisms rely on this secrecy for protection, those mechanisms can often be defeated. You might try to encrypt your own code, but even so, it's a stalling tactic in most environments.

You also can't trust a client to perform security checks on behalf of your server, even if you wrote the client yourself. Remember that underneath that fancy GUI, it's just code. Attackers can reverse engineer your client and write their own custom clients that leave out certain inconvenient features like all those pesky security controls. The consequences will vary depending on what your security checks are protecting, but some of the more common targets are authentication, authorization, and input validation. If you've implemented security in your servers, then you need to make sure that you're not solely relying on the clients to enforce that security.

Applicable Top 25 CWEs:
CWE-120, CWE-129, CWE-131, CWE-134, CWE-190, CWE-209, CWE-22, CWE-285, CWE-306, CWE-311, CWE-327, CWE-352, CWE-362, CWE-434, CWE-494, CWE-601, CWE-732, CWE-754, CWE-770, CWE-78, CWE-79, CWE-798, CWE-805, CWE-807, CWE-829, CWE-89, CWE-98.

M5: Use industry-accepted security features instead of inventing your own.
Target Audience: *Project Managers, Designers, Programmers*
Associated CWEs:

CWE-693 Protection Mechanism Failure.

You might be tempted to create your own security algorithms, but seriously, this is tough to do correctly. You might think you created a brand-new algorithm that nobody will figure out, but it's more likely that you're reinventing a wheel that falls off just before the parade is about to start.

This applies to features including cryptography, authentication, authorization, randomness, session management, logging, and others.

- Investigate which of the security algorithms available to you is the strongest for cryptography, authentication, and authorization, and use it by default. Use well-vetted, industry-standard algorithms that are currently considered to be strong by experts in the field, and select well-tested implementations. Stay away from proprietary and secret algorithms. Note that the number of key bits often isn't a reliable indication; when in doubt, seek advice.
- Use languages, libraries, or frameworks that make it easier to use these features.
- When you use industry-approved techniques, you need to use them correctly. Don't cut corners by skipping resource-intensive steps (CWE-325). These steps are often essential for preventing common attacks.

Applicable Top 25 CWEs:
CWE-120, CWE-129, CWE-131, CWE-190, CWE-209, CWE-22, CWE-285, CWE-306, CWE-307, CWE-311, CWE-327, CWE-352, CWE-362, CWE-434, CWE-494, CWE-601, CWE-732, CWE-754, CWE-759, CWE-770, CWE-78, CWE-79, CWE-798, CWE-805, CWE-807, CWE-862, CWE-863, CWE-89, CWE-98.

GP1: Use libraries and frameworks that make it easier to avoid introducing weaknesses.
Target Audience: *Project Managers, Designers, Programmers*
In recent years, various frameworks and libraries have been developed that make it easier for you to introduce security features and avoid accidentally introducing weaknesses. Use of solid, security-relevant libraries may save development effort and establish a well-understood level of security. If a security problem is found, the fix might be local to the library, instead of requiring wholesale changes throughout the code.

Ultimately, you may choose to develop your own custom frameworks or libraries; but in the meantime, there are some resources available to give you a head start. Options range from safe string handling libraries for C/C++ code, parameterized query mechanisms such as those available for SQL, input validation frameworks such as Struts, API schemes such as ESAPI, and so on.

While it is often advocated that you could choose a safer language, this is rarely feasible in the middle of an ongoing project. In addition, each language has features that could be misused in ways that introduce weaknesses. Finally, as seen in the "Weaknesses by Language" focus profile, very few weaknesses are language-specific - i.e., most weaknesses apply to a broad array of languages.

GP2: Integrate security into the entire software development lifecycle.
Target Audience: *Project Managers*
The Top 25 is only the first step on the road to more secure software. Weaknesses and vulnerabilities can only be avoided when secure development practices are integrated into all phases of the software lifecycle, including (but not limited to) requirements and specification, design and architecture, implementation, build, testing, deployment, operation, and maintenance. Creating a software security group (SSG) may be the most critical step.

Projects such as BSIMM, SAFECode, and OpenSAMM can help you understand what leading organizations are doing for secure development.

GP3: Use a broad mix of methods to comprehensively find and prevent weaknesses.
Target Audience: *Project Managers*
There is no single tool, technique, or process that will guarantee that your software is secure. Each approach has its own strengths and limitations, so an appropriate combination will improve your security posture beyond any single technique.

Continued

Approaches include, but are not limited to:

- *Automated static code analysis: whether for source code or binary code. Modern automated static code analysis can provide extensive code coverage, with high hit rates for certain types of weaknesses, especially for implementation errors. However, in some contexts, these techniques can report a large number of issues that a developer may not wish to address. They also have difficulty with various design-level problems, which often require human analysis to recognize.*
- *Manual static code analysis: Can be useful for finding subtle errors and design flaws, and for giving an overall assessment of development practices. Useful for detecting business logic flaws. However, it can be expensive to conduct, code coverage is a challenge, and it may not catch all attack vectors.*
- *Automated dynamic code analysis: fuzzers, scanners. These can find some issues that are difficult to detect with static analysis, such as environmental problems, and generate a large number of inputs or interactions that can find subtle flaws that may be missed by static analysis. However, code coverage is a problem.*
- *Manual dynamic code analysis ("pen testing," etc.): This can be effective for identifying flaws in business logic, for quickly finding certain types of issues that are not easy to automate, and for understanding the overall security posture of the software.*
- *Threat modeling: these are useful for finding problems before any code is developed. While techniques are still under development, currently this approach is difficult to teach, available tools have limited power, and it benefits significantly from expert participation.*
- *Application firewalls and external monitoring/control frameworks (web application firewalls, proxies, IPS, Struts, etc.): using application firewalls and similar mechanisms may be appropriate for protecting software that is known to contain weaknesses, but cannot be modified. They may also be useful for preventing attacks against latent weaknesses that have not yet been discovered yet. However, deployment could affect legitimate functionality, customization may be needed, and not all attacks can be automatically detected or prevented.*
- *Education and training: Appropriate training will help programmers avoid introducing errors into code in the first place, reducing downstream costs. However, training itself may be expensive, face cultural challenges for adoption, and require updates as the software and detection methods evolve.*
- *Architecture and design reviews: these can be important for detecting problems that would be too difficult, time-consuming, or expensive to fix after the product has been deployed. They may require expert-level effort.*
- *Coding standards: following appropriate coding standards can reduce the number of weaknesses that are introduced into code, which may save on maintenance costs. However, these are difficult to integrate into existing projects, especially large ones.*

Additional methods and practices are provided in the Software Security Framework (SSF), which is associated with BSIMM.

GP4: Allow locked-down clients to interact with your software.
Target Audience: *Project Managers, Designers, Programmers*
If a user has a locked-down client that does not support all the features used by your application, consider allowing that user some access, instead of completely denying access, which may force the user to degrade the client's security stance. This may help protect users and slow the propagation of malware. For example, in a web environment, some users may have Javascript or browser plug-ins disabled, and requiring these features exposes them to attacks from other web sites.[1]

[1]2011 CWE/SANS "Top 25: Monster Mitigations" http://cwe.mitre.org/top25/mitigations.html.

SECURING APPLICATIONS IN PRODUCTION

The key to securing applications in a production environment lies in implementing a thorough, unified, multilayered approach to security for the environment [often referred to as "**defense in depth**" (DiD)]. That begins with making the production environment physically secure. Physical security is achieved by placing servers in a protected computer room with controlled access.

The next step is to establish **perimeter security**. That begins with putting in place **firewalls** for the production environment. Also, personal firewalls should be installed in client computers that are used

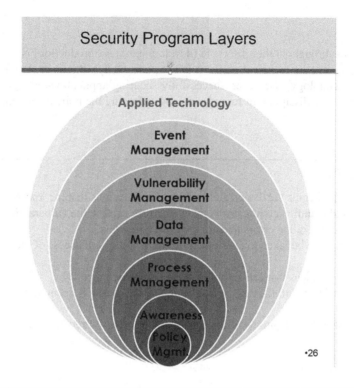

FIGURE 8.1

Defense in depth (DiD).

outside of the organization's secure facilities. Regularly scan for intrusion using **intrusion detection (IDS)**, **intrusion prevention (IPS)**, or **next generation firewalls (NGFWs)** that include such functionality. Other techniques might also be used (e.g., SSL and SSH interception, website filtering, **QoS/bandwidth management**, and antivirus inspection) (Fig. 8.1).

The development, test, and production environments must be in sync in terms of **operating system** version levels, patch levels, etc. This seems obvious but every year there are numerous breaches that result because the production environment is not at the same level as the other environments.

Additional measures that can be taken to ensure the security of applications in the production environment include access control, enforcement of strong and regularly changed **passwords**, **encryption** of application code when at rest, and of data and of network traffic.

Characteristics of very strong passwords:
Passwords must be 15 characters and contain at least three of the following four items:
> uppercase letter
> lowercase letter
> number
> special character
> Expire after 30–60 days.
> Passwords cannot be reused for at least 1 year.
Cannot contain any information that can be associated with the user (user's name, name of family members, dates, etc.)
Cannot contain easily guessable passwords (e.g, "password," "1234567890," etc.)

SUMMARY

Securing applications throughout their lifecycle (development, test, production) is an essential part of **application management**. In technical terms, it is not particularly difficult to do (at least within the limits of available technology). However, successfully securing applications is highly dependent on organization and personal discipline in formulating and enforcing the policies that make that security possible.

KEY TAKEAWAYS

- Application security begins the design and coding of applications that incorporate security best practices and avoid common coding errors that can create exploitable vulnerabilities.
- There are 25 common coding errors that are the most egregious.
- There are steps that can be taken to eliminate or minimize the seriousness of those common errors.
- There are general practices that can be put in place to improve security.
- The production environment, the test environment, and the production environments must be synchronized.
- The best way to secure applications is through a unified, multilayered approach that is described as DiD.

DISTRIBUTED AND COMPONENTIZED APPLICATIONS

9

All things are difficult before they are easy.
Chinese proverb

INTRODUCTION

The growth of distributed **applications**—which can include everything from **web services** and **service-oriented architecture (SOA)** services to applications leveraging **application programming interface (API)** connections—introduces organizational, technical, and governance challenges. The applications themselves run across silos, and the skills and tools required to manage them are far more cross-functional than those required to support, for example, Microsoft Word running on a desktop.

Payment processing, airline reservations, and high-speed trading are examples of large-scale componentized applications. In each, transactions execute across front-end systems of engagement and back-end systems of record. They may traverse a variety of databases, along with **content delivery networks (CDNs)**, web infrastructure, and devices. In many cases, these transactions also execute across third-party systems such as those provided by payment card providers, brokerage networks, and credit reporting agencies.

While a desktop application is encapsulated on a single device, componentized applications are almost unimaginable in their complexity. They can run across thousands of devices and hundreds of diverse platforms and code bases, traverse the Internet, and access data from the data centers of partners or suppliers. At the same time, these are among the most business-critical applications on the planet, with exceedingly high requirements for performance and availability. The question is, how does this combination of complexity and business criticality impact **application management**?

The intent of this chapter is to provide a background and foundation for the following three chapters:

- Chapter 10 covers "**DevOps** and **Continuous Delivery**." DevOps provides the cross-functional **management** capabilities that are fundamental foundations for application support. DevOps also provides a dynamic core supporting continuous delivery, the processes relating to delivering new software into production on an ongoing basis.
- Chapter 11, titled "**Application Programming Interfaces** and **Connected Systems**," details the management challenges relating to providing and consuming APIs and to delivering **container-based microservices**.
- Chapter 12 on "**Application Performance Management** and User Experience Management" covers the gamut of **application performance management (APM)** and **user experience management (UEM)** solution types and use cases.

This chapter and the next three discuss and elaborate on the theme of managing complex applications, each providing specific detail about the process- and tools-related aspects of a particular dimension of application delivery.

While distributed and **component-based applications** present a wide variety of challenges to virtually every information technology (IT) department, they also compose the majority of applications supporting virtually every mid-sized to enterprise-sized company. Developing an understanding of the elements that go into managing these types of applications is a necessary foundation for successful tools planning.

APPLICATION DIVERSITY

Although the consumer user typically thinks of an "application" as a mobile app or a mail program such as Microsoft Outlook, the majority of the applications running in today's mid-sized and enterprise-sized data centers are far more complex and less straightforward in function. Fig. 9.1 shows the wide diversity of component-based and **integrated applications** delivered by today's companies. It also shows that a large percentage of companies are running these types of applications.

As Fig. 9.1 also shows, many of these application types interoperate with other systems. Web services, typically understood to be **representational state transfer (REST)**- or **simple object access protocol (SOAP)**-based services, run in about 50% of companies. **Integrations** with mainframes—typically via APIs or web services—are the second most common type of integration. **Enterprise**

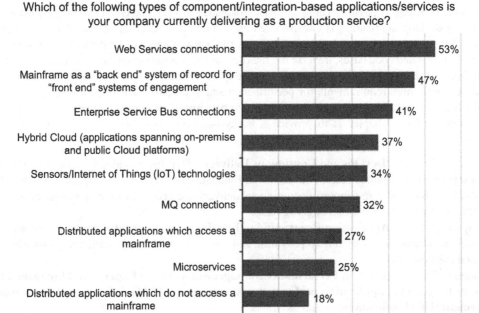

Which of the following types of component/integration-based applications/services is your company currently delivering as a production service?

- Web Services connections — 53%
- Mainframe as a "back end" system of record for "front end" systems of engagement — 47%
- Enterprise Service Bus connections — 41%
- Hybrid Cloud (applications spanning on-premise and public Cloud platforms) — 37%
- Sensors/Internet of Things (IoT) technologies — 34%
- MQ connections — 32%
- Distributed applications which access a mainframe — 27%
- Microservices — 25%
- Distributed applications which do not access a mainframe — 18%

FIGURE 9.1

Integration technologies used for production service delivery.

service bus (ESB) connections, which are typically used to integrate internally hosted applications, run in about 40% of companies.

Even a "simple" banking app running on a mobile phone may be supported by a wireless network, web-related applications and servers, mainframe systems of record, databases, and a host of other infrastructure elements. While a user views an app as an icon on a phone, IT support teams view the same app as a transaction executing across a wide array of complex infrastructure. A glitch at any point in the execution chain impacts the end user in the form of slow performance or even an outright failure to execute.

The transactions spawned by these applications execute across software and data scattered across a broad array of diverse platforms. They often run across distributed servers running on heterogenous platforms, **operating systems**, and programming languages. They may access code from multiple applications and data from multiple databases. They are highly network-centric and may even execute in part in the **cloud** or on other systems external to the corporate **firewall**, such as partner or supplier systems.

And while many of these applications are built on traditional platforms, new application **development** often focuses on technologies such as APIs, containers, and even **Internet of Things (IoT)** applications. Modern development teams are using **agile** development practices. This, in turn, has led to the growth of continuous delivery as the primary methodology for delivering new software applications, features, and functions.

Fig. 9.2 shows the types of applications most frequently delivered via continuous delivery practices—basically the "new" application types that are now being deployed to production. One takeaway

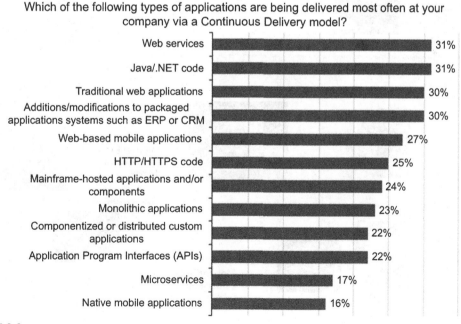

FIGURE 9.2

Application types most frequently developed/delivered via continuous delivery practices.

from this graphic is that, of the types of applications that are currently in development, almost all can be considered "distributed." With the exception of "native mobile" and "monolithic applications," every application type in this chart can legitimately bear this description.

In short, managing the heterogeneity underlying today's enterprise applications presents significant challenges in the areas of staffing, tooling, performance, and availability. Windows, mainframe applications, and databases coexist with .NET, Java, and COBOL components, and this diversity creates risk. Each platform is typically supported by its own team of specialists relying on siloed management tools. Few companies have accurate, comprehensive **topology** models of composite applications and fewer still have the "industrial-strength" APM solutions necessary to automate the support process to any meaningful degree.

THE EVOLUTION OF APPLICATION COMPLEXITY

Much of this complexity evolved over time. Fig. 9.3 shows the evolution of technology and application architectures since the introduction of **client/server architectures** in the mid-1990s. In the "distributed era" users accessed applications that were generally delivered by private data centers.

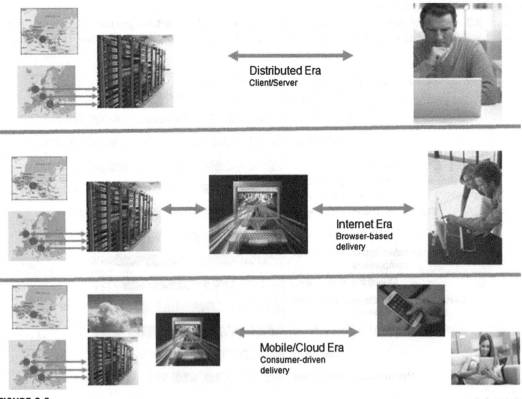

FIGURE 9.3

Evolution of distributed computing.

As the Internet matured and companies began delivering web applications to employees and customers in the "Internet era," web-enabled applications became the norm. Finally, the "mobile/cloud era" depicts the age in which "consumers" became "end users," when Internet-connected applications became ubiquitous, and when companies of every size were scrambling to web-enable traditional applications and consumer-enable new ones. This is also the era in which transactions routinely exit private data centers and execute, at least in part, in the cloud or on third party systems.

It is interesting to note that each era includes additional elements and more connection points than the preceding one. It is also interesting to note that the promise of the Internet to connect "anything to anything" was indeed achieved. Consumers empowered by easy access to the Internet and a host of high-performing **mobile devices** ushered in the "era of the consumer user." As a result, both on-premises and cloud-hosted applications not only became increasingly complex, but also became increasingly business-critical revenue drivers.

At the same time, while users expect to access applications as easily on tablets and phones as they do on laptops, they have also become accustomed to the sub-second performance that was the norm during the distributed and early Internet eras. And while IT professionals understand that it is reasonable to assume that a transaction traversing multiple geographic locations takes longer to execute than one that is direct-connected to a backend system, users do not see it that way. They have no knowledge of application architectures or locations or network speeds, but rather judge application performance from the perspective of their own subjective experience. These realities—combined with the dollar value attached to virtually every "consumer user" in this mobile era—are key reasons for the growth of both APM and UEM solutions.

Applications built over SOA and/or container-based microservices usher in a new concept in application delivery. SOA components and microservices are developed as "building blocks." They provide examples of services (versus applications) that are built by orchestrating the execution of multiple software components; further, these components can be internal or external to a company.

These componentized services introduce an additional concept into the "distributed" definition, which is the concept of integrations. SOA components can be connected via ESBs, SOAP, or REST. Over the past 5 years, SOA architectures became the norm for both new and refactored applications. They have become increasingly important for restructuring and modernizing traditional application portfolios or, at the other end of the spectrum, acting as the predominant structural platform for new software services. While approximately 60% of companies indicate that they are at some stage of SOA adoption, to some degree many still rely on homegrown management products to manage these complex, componentized services.

By definition, microservices, the latest generation of component-based services, are virtually always connected via APIs. Today, microservices hosted in containers such as **Docker** are adapting the orchestration concept to a new breed of uber-connected, uber-integrated services.[1] Again, this new functionality requires updates adding API and container visibility on the part of APM vendors.

---

[1]Chapter 11, titled "Application Programming Interfaces and Connected Systems," describes API and container concepts in detail.

HETEROGENEITY, SCALE, AND INTEGRATIONS: THE "LOOSE CANNONS" OF APPLICATION PERFORMANCE

Three primary characteristics make "complex applications" complex: heterogeneity, scale, and integration. Each element adds unique challenges to the task of application support.

HETEROGENEITY

Supporting heterogenous applications and platforms requires both tools and in-house skills addressing each silo platform. For example, when applications are running on Windows, Linux, and z/OS as examples of diverse operating systems, an IT organization must invest in personnel and tools capable of supporting each of these areas of expertise.

It is important to bear in mind that the new technologies introduced in each of the different eras did not replace existing systems. Instead, each technology was added to the growing inventory of hardware and software that already existed in virtually every enterprise data center.

Today, most larger companies are supporting modern applications and infrastructure alongside applications running on traditional platforms and using older protocols. "Don't fix what ain't broke" may be the golden rule of IT, and many IT professionals report that their data centers contain older devices that are still running—even though nobody can remember which applications or users they actually support.

One reason for this is that both applications and data have become valuable business assets performing critical business functions. The 15-year-old server sitting in the corner may well contain data or spreadsheets used by the CFO for financial or compliance-related reporting.

There is often business risk associated with retiring old infrastructure and introducing new hardware and software into production. Most enterprise IT organizations learned over time that it is far less risky to continue to build on proven systems than it is to retire those systems and modernize via hardware purchases and software rewrites. A great deal of traditional mainframe software, for example, was componentized and deployed first as SOA services, then "wrapped" in web services protocols such as SOAP and REST. These practices extend the functional lifetime of software assets, while also modernizing them for access by APIs, ESBs, and similar integration technologies.

SCALE

Scale is another growing problem compounding the challenges associated with application delivery. And because both heterogeneity and complexity are two key factors driving scale, this factor is very difficult to mitigate. Scale is an issue for a variety of reasons. However, the primary reason is based on a simple equation:

More Components = More Potential Failure Points.

Today's IT organizations, particularly those in enterprise-sized companies and telecommunications carrier environments, are managing a level of scale that can be difficult to conceptualize for users whose experience is limited to laptops and mobile devices. A single **mobile application** may be supported by hundreds or thousands of hardware and software elements. And that is just one of the hundreds of applications running in the average enterprise-sized company. EMA's latest research found that most mid-sized companies are running between 50 and 100 production applications—and that approximately 10% (typically larger companies) are running more than 1000.

The impact of **virtualization** and, more recently, container-based microservices is another element of scale. In either type of environment, particularly when such technologies are hosted on cloud-based **infrastructure as a service (IaaS)**, scaling becomes a relatively simple matter of duplicating a container, a **virtual machine**, or a server cluster. So from the APM and UEM perspectives, this means that while the number of elements supporting the application can scale very rapidly to meet performance demands, the complexity underlying the application scales in equal proportion. This adds to the uncertainties relating to application topologies that increase the difficulties associated with application support and particularly with root-cause analysis.

Further, many companies actively using IaaS for day-to-day production purposes rely on this elastic infrastructure to scale on demand at the cluster level versus the server level. This means that instead of scaling one server at a time, they may well be deploying 50 or 100 servers at a time. Using "prescale clustering," IT specialists calculate the number of **virtual servers** necessary to support a given number of users. In extreme scaling situations, such as those that retailers encounter on Black Friday, cloud-based servers can then be provisioned as blocks or clusters supporting an additional 1000 to 3000 users. While this type of provisioning can obviously solve immediate problems related to overutilization, it again makes the troubleshooting/root-cause analysis process far more difficult— when problems occur, there are simply far more places to look.

Similarly, in environments such as those characteristic of dynamic scaling or VMware VMotions, servers are provisioned and workloads moved in real time. If a given user is experiencing an application-related problem, it can be extremely difficult to determine which server or class of servers is the culprit.

INTEGRATION

Integration presents unique challenges related to connections between diverse systems. Often, the systems are so different that they have virtually no common features. **Hybrid cloud** is a contemporary example of a complex integration challenge that quickly becomes a concern for nearly every company leveraging **public cloud** to deliver a production service.

Integration points create additional support challenges because each integration point is also a potential point of failure. At the same time, for many application types integration technologies have become the critical glue supporting end-to-end execution.

Web service, ESB, and API connections are all widely used for application and/or data integration. Mobile and containerized applications in particular have ushered in the era of the API, with API-based connectivity being the primary interaction method for container-based microservices. APIs have also become the preferred way of integrating mobile applications with the back-end applications supporting them.

The support problem lies in the fact that monitoring the quality of the end **user experience** relies on the ability of the support tools to monitor the transaction, versus simply the underlying infrastructure. Since this cannot be done at the silo level, this means that monitoring integrations—in context to transaction execution—has become a critical element of both APM and UEM solutions.

APM FOR COMPLEX APPLICATIONS, IN A NUTSHELL

Many IT organizations lack the tools-based visibility, access, and control necessary to manage these complex applications. Without these three capabilities, root-cause analysis and problem resolution become trial-and-error efforts versus relatively simple repair processes.

If visibility, access, and/or control is lacking—as is often the case when components are hosted in the public cloud or by third parties—troubleshooting becomes correspondingly difficult. Keeping in mind the fact that application execution takes a horizontal path *across* hardware and software silos, the following capabilities (which most IT organizations still lack) are prerequisites for automating application management:

- The ability to keep track of the path of each transaction, even in cloud-based or load-balanced environments. This is particularly critical for transactions in which a single error in availability or timing can result in enormous monetary losses, such as with banking transactions.
- The ability to track changing topologies across dynamically changing cloud scale-ups, vMotions, and **software-defined networking.**
- The ability to track topologies across both internal systems, which can be instrumented, and external systems run by cloud providers, partners, or suppliers, which cannot be instrumented.

APM solutions deliver varying levels of insight into application performance from a variety of perspectives, depending on the product. And almost none of the solutions available today cover all three elements detailed in the preceding list. Part of the reason is because, with public cloud IaaS and SaaS in particular, much of the instrumentation necessary for end-to-end transaction visibility is, as yet, not available. APM solutions will become increasingly robust as the data sources underlying execution become increasingly instrumented.

A few specific examples of common instrumentation gaps include:

- Visibility into API performance
- Visibility into dynamic, cluster-based scaling
- Instrumentation of **SaaS/PaaS** performance that is accessible to APM solutions via API
- Visibility into dynamic definitions and changes within **software-defined networks (SDNs)**

That being said, there are multiple high-quality UEM products in today's marketplace supporting one of the most important types of visibility: the ability to see application performance from the end user perspective. In addition, industry-leading APM solutions support comprehensive, machine-generated topologies, sophisticated root-cause analysis across complex applications, and visibility to **API gateways** and similar integration solutions. These topologies deliver the end-to-end views of application and transaction flows that are essential to both APM and UEM.

Developing this end-to-end perspective is not simply a matter of monitoring infrastructure. Often, silo tools indicate that all databases and servers are performing well—yet users still report performance problems. APM tools fill in the gaps—the linkages and relationships between silos—that infrastructure-focused tools miss. By detecting consolidated performance information from the user viewpoint and by relating this information to performance of the underlying silo technology, APM tools support IT organizations in the day-to-day tasks of performance and availability management, root-cause analysis, and problem resolution.

How would you characterize your company's existing application support process?

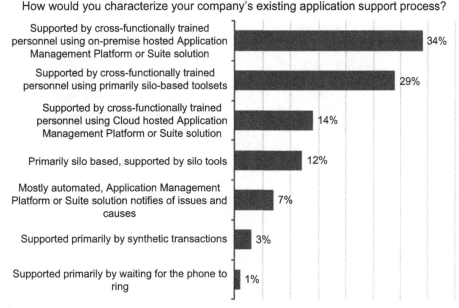

Supported by cross-functionally trained personnel using on-premise hosted Application Management Platform or Suite solution	34%
Supported by cross-functionally trained personnel using primarily silo-based toolsets	29%
Supported by cross-functionally trained personnel using Cloud hosted Application Management Platform or Suite solution	14%
Primarily silo based, supported by silo tools	12%
Mostly automated, Application Management Platform or Suite solution notifies of issues and causes	7%
Supported primarily by synthetic transactions	3%
Supported primarily by waiting for the phone to ring	1%

FIGURE 9.4

While most companies support applications with cross-functional teams, fewer than 60% are currently using APM-specific tooling.

In terms of tools, as Fig. 9.4 reveals, fewer than 10% of companies have "mostly automated" application support processes. Nearly 50% are using a combination of "cross-functional teams" and application management platforms or suites. However, that means more than 40% are still trying to manage applications with silo tools and IT personnel who may or may not be application conversant, despite the growing complexity of the applications, transactions, and services running in the average data center.

There are a number of reasons for this. Traditionally, APM platforms are expensive to purchase and deploy. Application-focused skills have been lacking, and the great majority of companies were still holding out hope that they could somehow manage applications at the silo level. Today, the cost and complexity of such tools have diminished as leading enterprise management vendors invested heavily in improvements aimed at making APM tools easier to deploy and use. In addition, multiple SaaS-based APM solutions have now come to market, eliminating the requirement for a massive up-front investment and for ongoing management of the management tools themselves.

"REAL WORLD" APM

As a final example of what the end-to-end big picture actually looks like, Fig. 9.5 shows a topology map for a relatively simple Java-based application. The map was autogenerated by AppDynamics, a leading APM solution that automates monitoring and root-cause analysis for complex application environments.

Application complexity is exploding

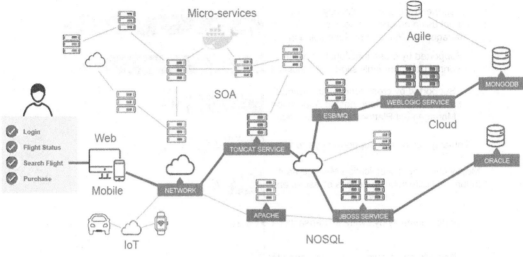

FIGURE 9.5

Automated topology map generated by AppDynamics Platform.

© 2016 AppDynamics, Inc., courtesy of AppDynamics.

Agents installed on key nodes gather metrics, which are then relayed to a central **analytics** system. In much the same way as a human brain gathers sensory information from a wide variety of sources and makes near instantaneous decisions based on that input, AppDynamics (and similar APM solutions delivered by vendors such as IBM, CA Technologies, BMC, and Dynatrace, etc.) gathers metrics from multiple infrastructure sources and centrally consolidates them into a real-time model of application execution.

This state-of-the-art solution and others like it are now available to IT organizations seeking to automate the extremely complex tasks of topology mapping, troubleshooting, and root-cause analysis.

THE ROLE OF ANALYTICS

Leading-edge application management vendors are well aware that tiered, distributed, and dynamic applications have become too complex for technicians to track and manage manually. IT support teams require automation capable of predicting the impact of change, tracking capacity utilization and trends, and supporting troubleshooting of incidents and problems. Analytics provide the basis for each of these functions.

Analytics have always been a hallmark of the enterprise management space, virtually since the introduction of the first network-focused solutions. These early tools still encountered the requirement to correlate a host of metrics and notifications to a single probable root cause. This early form of "analytics" set the stage for today's analytics processes, which embody extremely high levels of industry knowledge and expertise. Today's tools can assimilate metrics from a wide variety of sources and still perform the cognitive-esque processes associated with root-cause determination. Analytics processes also assist in **topology modeling**, end-to-end transaction recognition, predictive support activities, and "self-learning" of execution environments.

In addition, APM solutions must not only analyze the metrics from underlying infrastructure supporting the application but also do so in context with the application or transaction running horizontally across the infrastructure. From this perspective, instrumenting the silo layer is just a starting point. The real difficulties lie in tracing transactions *across* the infrastructure, keeping track of dynamic infrastructure and path changes, and doing all of these things in the context of application performance and availability.

The term "Big Operational Data" is used to refer to the sea of metrics being generated by application ecosystems. Data sources include management protocols such as **SNMP** and **WMI**, log files generated by web and Java servers, and proprietary agents installed on devices and supporting systems. In fact, virtually every hardware or software component underlying application execution becomes a source of Big Operational Data input to APM analytics. Due to the wide availability of execution-related metrics, differentiation in the application management space is based primarily on differentiation in the analytics versus differentiation in the metrics themselves.

Leading APM vendors have all developed proprietary algorithms and heuristics aimed at self-learning the environment surrounding the application, topology modeling for the components supporting the application, and **transaction tracing** for tracking transactions as they traverse variable paths across the execution environment. The ultimate purpose of these analytics is to deliver the visibility and control necessary to automate the process of managing applications in dynamic, high-scale environments.

In today's leading edge APM solutions, analytics pull together the complete execution picture, often in near-real time. Application-focused algorithms "understand" how silo performance contributes to end-to-end performance and how the various devices and the software running on them support complex, component-based applications.

SUMMARY

The costs associated with IT have always been viewed as high but were traditionally considered to be a "cost of doing business," similar to utility costs. However, now that technology is the raw material that constitutes a *product*—as it is for social media firms, online services, and other consumer-accessible businesses—the IT functions suddenly become mission critical. At this point, IT budgets start to be viewed as critical investments supporting business growth versus simple overhead.

At the same time, this new emphasis changed the role of IT by adding a new level of responsibility. IT organizations are now key contributors to the business bottom line. This elevation also brings with it a heightened emphasis on accelerating delivery of new services, along with new requirements for improvements in availability, uptime, and performance.

Modern IT services deliver substantial business value. At the same time, they also magnify IT's support burden. Progress is never free, and in the case of SOA and distributed applications, the business reaps the benefit while IT pays the price. In lieu of automation, IT turns to manual support processes to keep pace. The result is clearly illustrated by a discussion between an EMA analyst and a mid-level manager in the healthcare industry. The support team's manager described spending 30 hours on a root-cause analysis conference call while team members worked to troubleshoot and resolve an application-related problem. Clearly, efforts of this magnitude eat away at IT budgets and are unacceptable to businesses focused on IT services as sources of revenue. High-quality APM solutions can eliminate the need for calls of this nature.

KEY TAKEAWAYS

- The definition of the word "application" is exceedingly broad and defined differently in a wide variety of contexts. Often, the only thing "applications" have in common is the fact that they are created from software code and designed to perform a discrete task or set of tasks.
- Complex, component-based applications comprise the majority of "applications" supporting virtually every enterprise-sized company. At the same time, their diversity, scale, and complexity make them very difficult to support.
- Heterogeneity, complexity (i.e., multiple moving parts), and scale are key support challenges in managing "modern" applications.
- Topology models relating transaction execution to underlying infrastructure can dramatically simplify troubleshooting and root-cause analysis. Lack of such a model means IT support teams are "flying blind" in terms of application support.
- Although supported by multiple infrastructure and software elements, component-based applications cannot be managed at the silo level; managing such applications requires visibility to end-to-end execution *in context to* underlying technical elements.
- Approximately 40% of companies are still trying to manage applications with silo tools; this becomes untenable as complexity of the underlying infrastructure scales out.

Examples of vendors with products in this space:

Apica
AppDynamics
AppFirst
ASG
Appnomic
Aternity
BlazeMeter
BMC
CA Technologies
Dynatrace
Dell Quest
EMC
ExtraHop
HP
IBM
Idera
ManageEngine
Nastel

New Relic
NetScout
Netuitive
Oracle
Push Technology
Riverbed
SmartBear
SOASTA
Splunk
Stackify
Sumo Logic

DEVOPS AND CONTINUOUS DELIVERY

I've been studying high-performing IT organizations since 1999. What I've noticed is that there was this downward spiral that happens in almost every IT organization. It led to more fragile applications in production, longer deployment times, building up of technical debt, and the business goes slower and slower. I think one of the reasons that I cared so much about this is that it led to preordained failure. Where people felt, especially downstream (operations, test, security), trapped in a system where we were powerless to change the outcomes. No matter what we did, failure has been preordained. I think the way out of the downward spiral is what organizations like Google, Amazon, Twitter, LinkedIn, and GitHub are doing. These organizations are doing tens, hundreds, or even thousands of deploys a day. And this in a world where most of us are stuck with one deploy every nine months with catastrophic outcomes.

Gene Kim, coauthor of The Phoenix Project: A Novel About IT, DevOps, and Helping Your Business Win and the upcoming DevOps Handbook.

INTRODUCTION

Software drives business and today, businesses have a "need for speed." The speed of a proprietary trading system gives a financial services firm a split second cost advantage over competitors. Routing algorithms enable a package delivery firm to deliver faster and increase revenue by shaving fuel costs. A social media firm can continuously tweak its website to engage visitors longer and sell more add-on services—and it is always a race to translate new ideas into code faster than competitors.

In each of these examples, software correlates directly with revenue. And in each of these companies, **Development** and **Operations** teams are under the gun to deliver software faster, more efficiently, and at higher levels of quality. Today, IT is finally being perceived as a revenue producer versus simply a cost center, and virtually every IT organization has the opportunity to directly impact business success. Far from being "the guys in the back room who run the financial system," as they used to be viewed, IT professionals are now responsible for architecting, building, and delivering one of the most valuable assets of any company—software.

However, taking advantage of this opportunity requires the ability to accelerate the delivery of infrastructure and **applications**. People, processes, and tools all impact the delivery, and to some degree flexibility and risk tolerance are part of the picture as well.

Traditionally, IT Operations teams in particular had a vested interest in maintaining the status quo; change has long been the enemy because modifications to IT systems often caused production problems. IT organizations in general still walk a tightrope, balancing business demands for new services with the hard realities of day-to-day production support.

Application Performance Management (APM) in the Digital Enterprise. http://dx.doi.org/10.1016/B978-0-12-804018-8.00010-3

In psychology, an approach/avoidance conflict[1] arises when no choice is the perfect choice—in other words, every option generates both positive and negative results. "Can't win" situations result in high levels of inertia combined with high levels of stress. Yet modern IT organizations are confronted with the ultimate in dueling objectives: to keep production systems running flawlessly while absorbing constant and ever-increasing levels of potentially disruptive change.

Within this fast-moving and competitive business scenario, **DevOps** and **continuous delivery** are agents of change. When done in a disciplined manner, both can significantly reduce the risks associated with high rates of change while directly benefitting bottom line revenue. In an atmosphere of seemingly irreconcilable differences between the static and dynamic forces impacting every IT organization, both DevOps and continuous delivery are gaining traction.

Particularly when the two are viewed as linked versus disconnected processes, they have the potential not only to reconcile these opposing forces/outcomes, but also to fulfill the IT-driven business objectives so coveted in today's corporate environments.

AGILE DEVELOPMENT

To fully understand the emergence and value proposition of DevOps and continuous delivery, it is first necessary to understand the impact of **agile** practices on application lifecycle **management** and application delivery in general. Agile practices were designed, in part, to reduce the risks of the "catastrophic outcomes" Gene Kim describes in his quote at the beginning of this chapter. **Independent software vendors (ISVs)** of enterprise software such as **enterprise resource planning (ERP)** or **customer relationship management (CRM)** systems traditionally required between 9 and 18 months to develop a full software release. "Waterfall methodologies" delivered hundreds or thousands of features and packages in enormous bundles that could require weeks or months for customers to install. On the customer side, a tremendous amount of prep work went into the deployment of these packages and, once installed, the impact to production was often catastrophic.[2] In many cases, this meant that customers simply did not upgrade and remained on old software releases for years. This remains a persistent problem for virtually every ISV developing and delivering on-premise software.

Over time, agile development practices replaced waterfall methodologies as the new de facto standard for software development. The resulting software is more frequently useful and less frequently catastrophic than traditional software packages often were. There are multiple definitions of agile, but the key ideas listed in Table 10.1 seem to resonate across methodologies and practitioners.

As an example of an early application of agile practices, a well-known enterprise management ISV[3] began using agile techniques in 2006 to rearchitect and rewrite the products in its **business service management (BSM)** portfolio. The resulting products are simpler to deploy and manage, easier to

---

[1]Elements of stress introduced by social psychologist Kurt Lewin. Essentially, approach/avoidance conflicts are those choices in which the end result has both positive and negative characteristics.

[2]In fact, IT organizations still cite packaged applications as being more challenging to manage than even in-house developed custom software. *Automating for Digital Transformation: Tools-Driven DevOps and Continuous Software Delivery in the Enterprise.* Available at: www.emausa.com.

[3]BMC Software is headquartered in Houston, Texas.

> **Table 10.1 Characteristics of Agile Practices**
>
> **Key Tenets of Agile Practices**
>
> Development of software in small increments via multiple iterative and incremental cycles
>
> Flexibility to adapt and evolve requirements throughout the development cycle
>
> Collaborative approach in which small teams (typically no more than 10 engineers) work closely together and meet frequently (typically for 15–20 minutes daily)
>
> Continuous testing and ongoing integration of newly developed code
>
> Stakeholder (such as customers or line of business project sponsors) involvement throughout the delivery process
>
> Frequent software delivery, with stakeholder acceptance and signoff at project milestones

integrate to third-party vendor solutions, and easier to use than previous software versions. Delivery performance in terms of breadth of capability and time-to-market were also exceptional.

As a result of this initial success, the vendor was able to deliver new software to market two to three times faster than the industry norm, producing product releases in 4–5 month cycles, versus industry averages of 12–13 months for comparable releases.

Today, virtually every major ISV develops software in this way. For the vendor, not only is software delivered more quickly, but customers are more satisfied with the resulting product. It more often hits the mark because it is delivered within months of customer requests, versus the years required with traditional development methodologies. The collaborative, iterative nature of agile development practices means that customers have a far greater likelihood of getting features they actually want and need. In addition, delivery of smaller software packages makes the upgrade process less risky—customers can install new vendor releases in hours versus weeks or months.

Agile development has become the norm in enterprise IT as well, with more than 90% of companies leveraging agile techniques for at least some software projects. Going beyond software, however, it is also interesting to consider the applicability of agile practices to other areas of the business. From a big-picture perspective, the same techniques that can transform software development—historically a difficult and risky activity—can potentially empower other collaborative efforts within the business as well.

DEVOPS: "IT TAKES A VILLAGE"
INTRODUCTION

The adoption of agile techniques undoubtedly yields benefits, but it also has a dark side. As agile life-cycles accelerated, continuous delivery became the norm, increasing rates of production change and often adversely impacting production environments. Instead of deploying software once every 9 months, IT Operations teams were confronted with the need to deploy more frequently. Today, leading-edge companies are deploying small software packages hundreds or thousands of times per week; deploying monthly or more often is the industry norm.

To back up a bit, **change management** has always been an industrywide problem. For example, in 2007 most companies were still releasing software to production very slowly via waterfall development practices. Still, consulting teams reported extremely high rates of adverse impact from routine production changes, depending on the maturity of a given company and its change management processes. Highly mature companies—those with structured, governed change control methodologies—reported that changes drove between 25% and 30% of production incidents.[4] Less mature companies—those with more of a Wild West approach to service management—reported that changes drove between 75% and 80% of production incidents.

Fast forward to 2016, an era in which some companies are making code changes thousands of times per week, and it is not surprising to see that the job of IT (delivering high-quality business applications) has become exponentially more difficult. Not only is software being delivered faster, software components are running on far more diverse infrastructure. A single transaction can span multiple languages and platforms, and the software elements themselves are becoming more granular. In this complex environment, the entire span of **application management** activities has become significantly more complex. At the same time, software applications must be designed, developed, deployed, architected, and monitored via an ongoing, never-ending lifecycle.

When issues occur, each issue must be traced to its root cause before it can be fixed. And while problem management and incident management were the traditional realm of IT service management practices, the reality is that modern applications are far too complicated to be supported by a single individual or silo team. In other words, "it takes a village" to support today's complex applications, and the name of that village is DevOps.

As agile became a mainstream standard practice for software delivery, DevOps became a standard term within the IT lexicon—and DevOps teams assumed a great deal of importance in terms of overall software quality. While there are as many definitions of the term as there are industry experts, a simple stripped-down definition is as follows: DevOps is a collaborative, team-based approach to software delivery leveraging specialists with cross-functional development and operations skills to address application-related issues.

Today, more than 80% of companies have such teams in place. Companies vary in terms of which stages of the lifecycle these teams support—in about 15% of companies they support the entire lifecycle, to a greater or lesser degree. In larger companies these are dedicated teams, while at smaller companies they are often composed of ad hoc groups of IT specialists skilled in some aspect of application support. The names of these teams also vary from company to company. They are known as DevOps teams in about 25% of companies, Application Management teams in about 30%, and Infrastructure Services in about 20%.

Regardless, the teams are virtually always composed of senior IT specialists who are experienced in multiple software and infrastructure disciplines. At minimum, these teams typically include personnel with development and coding skills, as well as experts in network, systems, database, **integration**, and similar related areas. Their role is to span the technical silos, which, of necessity, exist within virtually every IT organization of size, and elevate the support function to an application versus infrastructure focus. In other words, they take a top-down approach to the support function—supporting applications from an end-to-end standpoint—versus a bottom-up, infrastructure-centric approach.

By collaborating and pooling their skills, these teams are empowered to support complex deployments, to deploy appropriate monitoring, and to troubleshoot the complex issues that arise in modern production environments. Collectively, they are far more efficient and powerful than would be the case if each worked separately at the silo level.

---

[4]All research numbers quoted in this chapter are from survey-based research conducted by Enterprise Management Associates.

IMPLEMENTATION

Although there are as many proposed approaches to DevOps as there are DevOps practitioners, Enterprise Management Associates (EMA) experts believe that the best approach is to apply cross-functional practices across the application lifecycle, if at all possible. It is also the case that automation is a key enabler for cross-functional support. Automating across the lifecycle while supporting automation with cross-functional skills and practices enables IT organizations to adopt a more nimble and iterative approach to application design, development, delivery, and support.

This view of DevOps also actively involves business stakeholders just as agile development practices do. **Line of business (LOB)** involvement helps ensure that the product delivered meets the needs of the business and that any requirements and modifications are incorporated into the software at the earliest possible stage in the lifecycle. Research demonstrates that software is far easier and cheaper to fix at earlier stages of the lifecycle than it is at later stages.

There are other factors driving the expansion of DevOps practices to a more lifecycle–centric approach. They include the following:

1. Iterative development impacting the entire lifecycle (not just deployment): The broad adoption of agile methodologies in the enterprise means that the deployment stage transitioned from being a point-in-time turnover of responsibilities to an ongoing process. Both Development and Operations are feeling the impact of this transition. Development must find ways to build and test code incrementally and iteratively, and Operations must find ways to engineer production environments capable of absorbing high rates of change. Neither group can do this without the skills of the other.

2. Abstraction of applications from hardware impedes manageability: **Cloud**, mobile, **sensor systems**, **virtualization**, and **containers** are freeing applications from the bonds of the physical data center. While moving applications and/or application components to the cloud and to consumers, retail facilities, and even train tracks can provide significant business benefits, the abstraction introduced by off-premise hosting of any sort makes applications more complex to manage, govern, and troubleshoot. When applications or their components are externally hosted, IT loses the visibility and control necessary to effectively monitor and manage the ecosystem. At the same time, IT still has responsibility for all aspects of application delivery including performance, availability, and troubleshooting. This means that **performance management** must often be done at the network level, since the network is the one common factor across these diverse components.

3. Application heterogeneity: From multibrand server farms to server clusters, load balancers, web servers, and heterogeneous databases, even applications hosted 100% on premise are so complex that supporting them requires a broad arsenal of skills. This is true across the entire six-stage application lifecycle, making it imperative that DevOps is approached as a lifecycle versus a point-in-time handoff.

4. Automated deployment: With the growth of highly virtualized environments deployed as both **private cloud** and public **infrastructure as a service**, software deployment is becoming increasingly **automated** and **metadata**-driven. However, as functionality previously supported by runbooks and manual job submissions is automated, the primary role of IT—to deliver quality applications to the business—remains the same. Many CIOs are seeking new and better ways to deliver on this mandate, and DevOps supported by automation is a proven approach for doing so.

5. Increased focus on LOB as part of the application lifecycle: A key element of agile method-ologies is the involvement of LOB throughout the application lifecycle. From requirements to iterative checkpoints to acceptance testing, business stakeholders are more involved than ever before. Traditional development practices virtually ignore this group, which is becoming increasingly indispensable to customer satisfaction and project success. The DevOps lifecycle, shown in Fig. 10.1, includes LOB as a third stakeholder that assumes key leadership roles at given stages of the lifecycle.

DEVOPS ACROSS THE LIFECYCLE

The lifecycle model shown in Fig. 10.1 has two notable differences compared to DevOps models addressing a subset of the application lifecycle. Not only are DevOps concepts extended across the lifecycle, but Development, Operations, and business stakeholders are involved at every stage. This model of DevOps addresses the complexities associated with supporting today's dynamically changing and business-critical software ecosystems.

While all three stakeholder roles work together to some degree at each stage, the lead role(s) (under-lined in the diagram) change at each stage based on changing deliverables and objectives. Collaboration takes the form of cross-functional cooperative efforts, and leadership handoffs replace a full-fledged

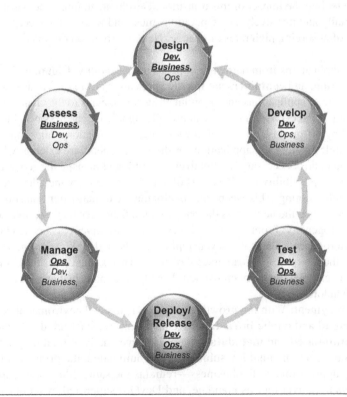

FIGURE 10.1

DevOps across the application lifecycle.

relinquishment of responsibility as software progresses through the stages. In addition, via automation, each stage of the lifecycle ideally shares relevant data with the previous and following stages, as depicted via the gray arrows between the stages.

In this model, the DevOps interactions at each stage are as follows:

1. Assess: Input from business stakeholders (for new services) and **service-level agreement** assessments (for existing services) is used to determine priorities for new business services and desired modifications to existing ones. Development and Operations stay in the loop because such improvements require new code, modified code, and changes to operational infrastructure.

2. Design: Development and Business take the lead in this stage, with Operations available to provide input as needed. Development has primary responsibility for incorporating requirements into a software design. Business has responsibility for educating Development about specific requirements, as well as for reviewing and signing off on the design. The role of Operations during this stage is to evaluate anticipated impact on production systems and assess any requirements for infrastructure acquisitions and/or enhancements.

3. Develop: Development is the lead during this stage and is ultimately responsible for building software that meets the needs of the business. Particularly in agile shops, business stakeholders perform functional reviews and sign off on application functionality on an iterative and ongoing basis. Operations is brought in as needed to support development teams in building development and testing environments and/or to be advised of infrastructure **configurations** and anticipated delivery timeframes.

4. Test: Development [including **quality assurance (QA)**] and operations are the leads during this stage, as final preparations are made for unit testing, integration testing, and release to production. While Development and QA teams perform unit and integration testing, Operations participates in integration and load testing to assess operational readiness. Acceptance testing becomes a critical role for business stakeholders, and all three groups must collaborate to agree on a final go-live plan.

5. Deploy/Release: This is the traditional DevOps handoff stage, but in this scenario, the handoff is a change in lead roles versus a turnover of responsibility. Development and Operations (or DevOps) teams lead this stage, while business stakeholders conduct final user acceptance processes.

6. Manage: During this stage, infrastructure, systems, and application management tools monitor production environments and applications. **Service-level management (SLM)**, performance and availability management, troubleshooting/root-cause analysis, and **capacity management** solutions all monitor and measure **application performance** as part of ongoing assessments. The resulting metrics can then be iteratively pumped back into the Assess stage (Stage 1) to ensure that the current state of an application is known and monitored in preparation for any modifications that may occur over time. In addition, DevOps teams are typically responsible for monitoring, managing, and troubleshooting the overall health of the application, and for working with Ops to see that production issues are fixed.

DEVOPS TOOLING: BRIDGING DIVERSE TASKS, GROUPS, AND SKILLS

EMA research has shown that, for applications written in-house, Development or DevOps groups remain in the loop in terms of application support for the life of the application. This is particularly true for custom applications written in-house versus packaged applications purchased from an external vendor. Cross-functional collaboration becomes critical because this is where applications actually touch end users and impact the business.

At the same time, production application quality depends on far more than manual support or efficient code. Approaching DevOps as a lifecycle has significant implications in terms of tool design, choices, and options. As DevOps progresses from being a point-in-time handoff to an ongoing process of creating, deploying, and supporting business software assets, tools become a primary factor unifying lifecycle stages, roles, and leadership changes.

The tooling implications are significant and center on several key areas:

- Integration: Approaching DevOps as a lifecycle requires information sharing across discrete lifecycle stages and toolsets. Tools **interoperability** is a unifying force across diverse teams, skills, technology languages, and methodologies. Modern applications don't exist as siloed entities. Instead, they exist as distributed ecosystems that execute across a host of technology elements, all of which must efficiently interoperate for an end-to-end application to become a reality. In the same way, tools must support the fact that technology silos and lifecycle stages don't live in a stand-alone world. They are a product of a multistage lifecycle continuum and an end-to-end execution environment. While each stage brings with it specialized toolsets to support its own internal lifecycle, these tools must also interoperate to support seamless collaboration across stages.

- Workflow: As applications themselves become increasingly complex, building, deploying, and managing them becomes more complex as well. Workflow management is essential to governance and traceability, particularly since most IT processes combine human and automated tasks. One of the biggest challenges facing today's technology teams is managing the orchestration of complex, multistep processes in context with manual tasks, automated steps, and reviews/approvals. This is particularly true for cases in which multiple projects, tasks, or deliverables have dependencies on others, and where multiple projects (and deployments) are being completed in parallel. In such environments, the sheer effort of keeping track of bottlenecks, work queues, point-in-time responsibilities, and similar factors can be gargantuan. This, combined with the touch points across stages that lifecycle DevOps entails, makes **application lifecycle management (ALM)**, **workflow automation**, **release automation**, and **business process automation** tools essential elements for large-scale automation of the application lifecycle.

- Cross–lifecycle Service Quality Supported by Tooling: Research studies have repeatedly found that the best way to reduce the cost of supporting applications is to find and fix flaws early in the lifecycle. A famous **National Institute of Standards and Technology (NIST)** study found that if it costs x to fix an application problem during the design stage, making the same fix during production will cost between $470x$ and $880x$. If the fix requires an engineering change, the cost could be as high as $2900x$.[5] The clear implication is that testing early, often, and iteratively is a far more cost-effective strategy than waiting to find problems in production. In terms of DevOps, this means moving application viability testing to a point far earlier in the lifecycle

---

[5]The Economic Impacts of Inadequate Infrastructure for Software Testing, www.nist.gov/director/planning/upload/report 02-3.pdf.

(often referred to as "shifting left"). It also reinforces the value proposition of application performance management (APM) and **user experience management (UEM)** tools. Such tools can be used during preproduction (as well as during production) to enable IT specialists to better understand the projected impact of a software release once it hits production.

Service virtualization solutions are important to this process as well. These are a new class of tools supporting integration testing, which has traditionally been shortchanged. Traditionally, integration testing was done by either testing against stub programs, essentially dummy programs leading nowhere, or testing against expensive duplicates of production environments. While the latter was preferable, high costs limited access by developers and testers and therefore the frequency of test runs. For example, one CA Technologies (www.ca.com) customer was interviewed as part of a case study profiling the vendor's service virtualization solution. The client had already installed two integration testing environments at a cost of $4.5 million apiece. However, software releases were still being held up because testers and developers had to schedule testing time in advance, and available time slots were rapidly filled.

Faced with the prospect of building a third testing environment, the company sought alternatives and discovered that using service virtualization products, developers and testers could test as often as necessary against virtual models that realistically mimicked interactions with production systems. Software delivery times were accelerated and there was no longer a need for an additional $4.5 million testing environment.

Budget, Staffing, and Quality Efficiencies: Tools that enable data sharing across the lifecycle not only extend the value proposition of tools investments, they also empower technical personnel to move beyond the boundaries of their own skill sets. It is unreasonable to expect that developers will be operations experts, that operations personnel will be **security** experts, or security experts will understand how to install an **operating system** on a mainframe. As an alternative, integrated toolsets and workflow automation allow IT specialists to effectively collaborate with a common language and view of software ecosystems.

There are a number of tools-related capabilities that contribute to these positive outcomes. One is that IT specialists should be able to see the impact of their own silo on the quality of the application as a whole. Another is that IT specialists should be capable of collaborating in such a way that they can rapidly solve application-related problems in complex ecosystems. Finally, and potentially most important, is that tools should be unifying forces across silos instead of roadblocks to cross-functional collaboration.

CONTINUOUS DELIVERY
INTRODUCTION

Both agile development practices and DevOps have become essential elements contributing to the rise of continuous delivery. The value to the business is that good ideas can be translated into software much faster than was possible in the past with traditional delivery models. The term itself can be misleading, however, as "continuous delivery" also means different things in different contexts. At its most generic, the term encompasses an iterative and ongoing cycle of development, testing, and delivery of software to a targeted destination. The destination could be a production environment, a staging environment, or a software product package. Regardless of the target, the goal is to accelerate the delivery of software functions and capabilities to support the business need for agile decision-making.

Although continuous delivery is often considered to be primarily an IT-related initiative, the primary drivers for continuous delivery are business- and customer-related. Businesses need new products and **services** to remain competitive, and customers expect to be able to interact with a company in efficient, seamless ways. In other words, from the business perspective, continuous delivery is no longer simply nice to have. It is a must-have for **digital transformation** as companies bank their futures on accelerating the speed at which new products are delivered to the marketplace.

IMPLEMENTATION

From the lifecycle perspective, DevOps and continuous delivery are intimately intertwined (see Fig. 10.2). Software components are developed via iterative stages, with each stage of the lifecycle having a specific purpose and its own inputs and outputs. Continuous delivery requires that each stage of the lifecycle be accelerated and optimized since a primary goal is to deliver software to the business as rapidly as possible.

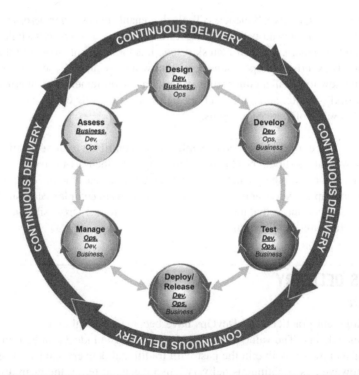

FIGURE 10.2

DevOps as a framework for continuous delivery.

Since each stage (and the artifacts generated at that stage) supports the next, DevOps practices can be viewed as a framework and foundation for accelerating continuous delivery. In effect, applying DevOps principles across the lifecycle paves the way for efficient delivery of application code. DevOps practices support staffing efficiencies necessary to free up both Development and Operations groups to actually work on new products. As the lifecycle is automated, software delivery naturally accelerates. Finally, automated processes produce more predictable results than manual ones, an outcome that also frees up Development and Operations staff from spending excessive amounts of time (and budget) on production support.

There is an old adage in the software development world that delivering high-quality software requires three key ingredients at optimal levels: time, budget, and skilled personnel. Reductions in budget or personnel extend timeframes, while reductions in timeframes require additional budget and personnel. That model can be reversed with the addition of two new ingredients: automation and the "grease" of DevOps practices. DevOps reduces the friction associated with the people- and process-related aspects of software delivery.

Governable, repeatable processes across the lifecycle support a factory approach much like Henry Ford's assembly line, which accelerated the process of building automobiles. Ford changed the way people worked, with each person performing a very limited number of tasks very efficiently, and therefore very quickly. He changed industrial production processes forever, and many other industries followed.

In the real world, IT organizations are, in fact, delivering software functionality faster than ever before. Almost 20% are delivering new code daily or even more frequently. However, it is not the case that delivery timeframes somehow magically become shorter. Accelerating software delivery requires acceleration of each stage of the underlying lifecycle. This can be done, in part, by reducing the volume of code contained in each release and by optimizing processes underlying the lifecycle.

CONTINUOUS DELIVERY TOOLING: ACCELERATION VIA AUTOMATION

As is the case with DevOps, automation is also a facilitator for continuous delivery. It is, in fact, the essential core for delivering on the continuous delivery vision, as it supports iteration within each stage of the lifecycle as well as the handshakes and artifact handoffs that must occur between the stages. In this scenario, each stage is appropriately instrumented and automated, and the artifacts generated at each stage are shared with the next. Requirements generated during the design stage, for example, will need to be available in subsequent stages to support development, testing, and service-level measurements. This underlines the importance of solutions that act as integration hubs supporting cross-tool, cross-stage data sharing.

As an example, Fig. 10.3, courtesy of CloudBees (www.cloudbees.com), shows the Jenkins ecosystem, which includes plugins to more than 1000 third-party solutions. These plugins allow Jenkins to act as an integration hub, supporting tasks at multiple lifecycle stages. Given the fact that today's software lifecycles heavily rely on cross-tool data sharing, these plugins are one reason for the success of Jenkins as a "continuous integration" platform: it provides a way for multiple tools to share information with one another across the lifecycle.

Another key value-add of high-quality enterprise management products is innate product intelligence. Imbued with industry-leading expertise in one or more key areas, modern toolsets are more than capable of executing skilled but repetitive tasks typically performed manually. From this perspective,

FIGURE 10.3

Jenkins as a hub for the DevOps/continuous delivery ecosystem.

tools investments extend IT budgets by enabling IT specialists to work smarter. They are also one of the best ways for IT organizations to accelerate continuous delivery by institutionalizing repeatable, governable processes without increasing headcount.

Since we are essentially talking about tools and practices that span the entire application lifecycle, there are other product types that should be part of the discussion as well.

- Collaboration tools are essential accelerators for requirements assessment, software design, and virtually every task executed by DevOps teams. Most IT practitioners indicate they currently lack a way to collaborate with peers and believe that such tools would make them more effective in terms of delivering software services to the business.
- Service virtualization and automated environment provisioning (release automation) are accelerators for QA testing, software deployment, and release management.
- Configuration, change, performance, and availability management tools reduce the manpower required to maintain the status quo in production application environments, freeing up personnel to more effectively address the needs of the business.
- Release automation tools govern, orchestrate, and apply software releases. They automate workflows as well as the provisioning and configuration tasks underlying software deployment at scale.

While they can definitely reduce the personnel needs associated with software deployments and delivery, their greater value lies in the fact that they make outcomes more predictable. The repetitive manual tasks underlying deployment of software releases are error prone and lack an audit trail. Every action performed by release automation tools is logged and the tools themselves ensure that deployments are always performed in the correct order and on the correct artifacts. Deployment becomes more predictable, and adverse impact to production is minimized.

DEVOPS AND CONTINUOUS DELIVERY

Today, many companies are utilizing both DevOps and continuous delivery and finding that both approaches are revenue drivers. Together, they can be a powerful combination. Industry research has found strong correlations between the frequency of code delivery and revenue growth. Even stronger correlations were made between the quality of a company's interactions between Development and Operations and revenue growth. Research findings also reveal the revenue-related negative impacts of failure to evolve the software delivery process to meet the changing needs of a business.

However, there are multiple implications to accelerated software delivery, both positive and negative. While it can have a profoundly positive business impact, it also significantly compounds the difficulties associated with day-to-day management of production environments. For example, the research also indicates that the number one bottleneck hampering efforts to accelerate the continuous delivery pipeline relates to the adverse impact of constant change on production environments.

It is also interesting to note that while the primary benefits of continuous delivery are business-related, the negative impacts are felt primarily by IT. More than 50% of companies engaged in continuous delivery indicate that Operations is spending more time managing production environments and nearly 50% say that Development is spending more time supporting production. Forty-five percent say service levels have degraded, and more than 35% cite an increase in the number of performance and availability problems.[6]

So, while the positive side of continuous delivery lies in the potential for business growth, the negative side can mean a decrease in service quality or increased costs related to managing production. In short, increased frequency of code delivery too often equates to production environments that are far more dynamic and far less stable due to constant and relentless changes to production.

Strong DevOps practices and teams supporting continuous delivery can mitigate adverse production impact while maximizing the value proposition to the business bottom line. The research also shows that automation supporting continuous delivery in particular can reduce and essentially eliminate adverse production impact over time, as the process becomes increasingly automated and "cookie cutter."

SUMMARY

There appears to be a dichotomy at present between the organizational imperative of accelerating software delivery and the potential costs of doing so. What continuous delivery has done, in effect, is massively increase the rate of change to production environments, often with adverse results. However, both production issues and costs can be mitigated by well-chosen tools, and this is another argument for application-related automation. ALM, testing tools, release automation, change management, and **APM** platforms/suites all become valuable assets that reinforce an organization's commitment to accelerating the lifecycle.

Automation has always been one of the best ways to ensure application quality, and this is particularly true today. Automating personnel-intensive tasks (such as manipulating test data, building test

---

[6]All statements and figures in this section are from survey-based research conducted by Enterprise Management Associates.

environments, executing QA tests, deploying software packages, and troubleshooting production issues) minimizes the possibility for the human error inherent in multistep processes. It also supports "build once, run many" scenarios in which automated processes can be controlled by standardized tools with repositories, policies, **templates**, and similar organizational assets designed to promote and enforce QA.

We as an industry are nearing a point where the absence of enterprise management automation could well mean the demise of a business. We have already seen this in the security arena, and the rise of continuous delivery brings the message home to application support teams as well. It's very difficult to continuously deliver software when an organization lacks adequate release management tooling or when Development and Operations teams are consumed with production support issues.

It is also the case that manual support processes have now run out of runway; automated management toolsets have become a necessity for those companies seeking to deploy and support applications at speed and scale.

KEY TAKEAWAYS

- DevOps and continuous delivery are separate but related IT practices that are neither institutionalized by standards nor uniformly defined and understood.
- When approached as a collaborative initiative spanning the lifecycle, strong DevOps practices act as a hub supporting accelerated continuous delivery.
- While often considered to be an IT-related initiative, continuous delivery is being driven primarily by business and customer demand.
- Both the quality of a company's DevOps interactions and the speed of continuous delivery correlate strongly with double-digit year-over-year revenue growth on the business side.
- While continuous delivery can yield compelling business benefits, it increases the load on IT organizations tasked with managing the impact of ongoing change on production execution environments.
- Tooling supporting DevOps and continuous delivery should be both lifecycle focused and siloed. In other words, information created in silo tools should be integrated for reporting purposes and shared across stages to facilitate a common knowledge platform and collaborative practices. Investment objectives should focus on enabling collaboration, facilitating complex workflows combining manual and automated tasks, dashboard building, and integrating diverse tools within and across lifecycle stages.

Examples of vendors with products in this space:

Appvance
BMC
CA Technologies
Chef
CollabNet
CloudBees
Compuware
Dell

HP
IBM
New Relic
NRG Global
OutSystems
Klocwork
Parasoft
Perforce
PuppetLabs
Riverbed
SaltStack
Serena
Tasktop

APPLICATION PROGRAMMING INTERFACES AND CONNECTED SYSTEMS

11

Today, everything is connected to everything.
IT Manager, Global Bank

INTRODUCTION

In an industry that is hungry for business agility, the growth of the **application programming interface (API)** Economy promises to enable companies to accelerate delivery of new software supporting new lines of business. Today, for example, consumers have unprecedented power in determining the fate of a business. Failure to deliver in terms of application features and quality is no longer simply a matter of losing a single customer. With the rise of social media, one customer's perception can also quickly influence the perceptions of other potential customers and, in doing so, influence their buying habits.

Software-driven businesses, consumer-facing **applications**, **public cloud**, and mobile applications are all driving growth in API usage, as are social media platforms and **Internet of Things (IoT)**. In short, APIs have become a mainstay supporting business agility and high-velocity business growth. APIs are code sequences that expose data [typically via **representational state transfer (REST)**] or functionality [typically via **simple object access protocol (SOAP)**] for use by an internal or external system. APIs enable diverse software systems to interact with one another to share data, **services**, or functionality. Standards-based in the current era, they offer a shortcut methodology for connecting heterogenous systems via a simpler mechanism than that provided by previous **integration** technologies such as electronic data interchange (EDI).

Before APIs, connecting an internal data center–based application to a supplier or partner application required a custom project and weeks or months of effort. Today, the delay introduced by a similarly lengthy development process is not well tolerated by **line of business** leaders seeking rapid transformation of ideas into action. Businesses seek agility, and APIs offer a way to make brittle organizational borders more flexible.

Despite all the current hype around APIs, they are not a freshly minted miracle technology that was purpose-built to support mobile, **cloud**, and IoT. APIs have been around since the 1990s; however, the API technologies of older generations were not necessarily pretty. They consisted of custom-written, code-enabled "plumbing," with each API purpose-built to support a specific application-to-application connection. Each new integration required an arduous analysis, design, and coding effort, which made **interoperability** a luxury versus the commodity it is today.

The growth of standards during the early part of the 21st century provided a foundation for the growth of API usage and resulting API Economy. The interoperability delivered by standards such as

REST and hypertext transfer protocol/secure (HTTP/S) provides a common technology framework for companies that are, or want to become, more flexible and agile in their digital interactions.

This evolution has made API creation and delivery far more efficient. Virtually every company is now playing by the same rules, utilizing REST-based APIs to communicate over standard HTTP/S protocols that use the same HTTP language (GET, POST, PUT, DELETE, etc.) as **web browsers**. Now supported by standards and built over familiar interaction patterns, modern APIs are easier to build and simpler to maintain and run than their predecessors.

THE ROLE OF TOOLS IN THE API ECONOMY

Most companies start out as API consumers. That is, they access APIs provided by other organizations, typically on a very small scale. For example, many **software as a service** and **infrastructure as a service** vendors offer APIs that can be used by customers to access **management** data, application data, or performance/availability statistics. These types of APIs can offer an opportunity for companies to test the waters of API usage before attempting to utilize an unfamiliar technology for delivery of production-grade business applications. Over time, many companies become API providers as well. These companies create APIs that provide access to their own data or functions. Typically serviced and managed by **API gateway** solutions, provider APIs offer easy access to data and/or functionality to internal and external stakeholders alike.

So how and where do tools fit into this picture? Participating in the API Economy does not stop with providing or consuming APIs. **Security**, access, metering, chargeback, and other API-related functions become increasingly relevant as usage increases. As the number of API provider and/or consumer connections grows, as more users and applications connect, and as new API versions are created and deployed, the API Economy begins to look more like a maze to be navigated than a straightforward way to flexibly extend organizational borders.

Tools help mitigate this complexity by addressing key functional questions. Providers, for example, often find themselves asking:

- How can our organization synchronize API development with traditional application development lifecycles since the two are often linked?
- How can we secure API usage to ensure that sensitive data is protected?
- How can we track usage of for-pay services to correctly bill for access?
- How can we track usage growth and the impact of that growth on back-end systems for capacity planning purposes?
- How do we ensure that only authorized users and applications connect to our systems?

Consumers ask:

- How do we find out about new APIs offered by our vendors and partners, and how do we then go about accessing them?
- How do we know when the APIs our systems are accessing are changed or modified by the provider?
- We have hundreds of applications that access APIs—and some of them interact with one another. When one such application fails, how can we determine what changed, what's wrong, and how to fix it?

- How do we ensure that only authorized users can access for-pay external services so our usage fees don't skyrocket?

In other words, most companies find that API usage requires similar governance and management capabilities as those required for delivering any other type of software application. They also find that active participation in the API Economy, from a production standpoint, eventually requires investments in automation. In short, these types of questions can only be addressed by tools that are purpose-built to support API delivery and consumption.

THE ROLE OF THE APPLICATION PROGRAMMING INTERFACE GATEWAY

As Fig. 11.1 shows, the vast majority of providers and consumers are using commercial, API-specific management solutions such as API gateways to secure and govern API delivery and/or consumption. Such solutions have value for both API providers and consumers, and are essential elements of overall management of API-connected applications.

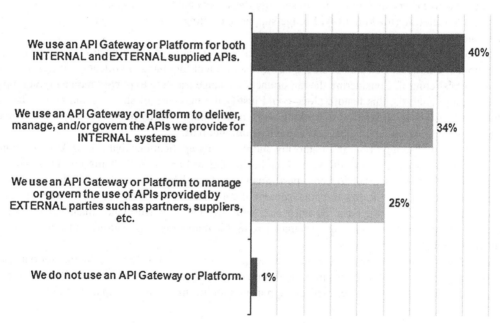

Which statement best describes how your company manages APIs?

We use an API Gateway or Platform for both INTERNAL and EXTERNAL supplied APIs. **40%**

We use an API Gateway or Platform to deliver, manage, and/or govern the APIs we provide for INTERNAL systems **34%**

We use an API Gateway or Platform to manage or govern the use of APIs provided by EXTERNAL parties such as partners, suppliers, etc. **25%**

We do not use an API Gateway or Platform. **1%**

FIGURE 11.1

Application programming interface (API) gateways are used by a majority of both API consumers and providers to manage and govern API connections.

Table 11.1 Examples of Application Programming Interface Gateway Functions[a]

Integrations: Typically integrate with third-party tools supporting multiple additional functions. Integrations with identity management solutions, for example, support authentication and authorization of message traffic. Other examples of integration may include lightweight directory access protocol, Microsoft Active Directory, etc.

Performance optimization: Via offloading traffic from application servers to XML acceleration function on gateway, scaling gateway instances.

REST support: Facilitates exposure of data as provider APIs.

SOAP support: Facilitates exposure of operations and functions as provider APIs.

Reporting: Auditing and reporting on usage to address operational and compliance requirements.

Management: Supports troubleshooting and root-cause analysis by identifying failure points in multiservice transactions and generating alerts.

Traffic monitoring and management: Protects services from traffic spikes via traffic throttling, limits clients to agreed service consumption levels, supports chargeback.

Security-related functions: Identity mediation across multiple identity platforms, governance and metering of API usage, service virtualization designed to shield endpoint services from direct access.

API, *application programming interface;* REST, *representational state transfer;* SOAP, *simple object access protocol.*
[a]*Prospective customers should check specification sheets and vendor descriptions to verify functions supported by specific products.*

As Table 11.1 shows, API gateways[1] have multiple functions including access control, delivering visibility of active users, and mitigation of security risks. Depending on the vendor, API gateways may also provide metering (tracking of API usage supporting billing and/or chargeback), monitoring, and other functions.

In short, API gateways have become the tool of choice for managing all aspects of API delivery and consumption. On the API consumer side, gateways are critical for change notification, usage monitoring, and access control. Considering the importance of change tracking to **performance management** and root-cause analysis, this feature alone could justify the purchase of such a solution. On the API provider side, gateways are critical to tracking users, maintaining security of back-end systems, managing user identity and authentication, and **capacity management**.

Gateways are also important in monitoring and managing applications that access APIs. As standalone solutions, they provide visibility into the health and welfare of APIs being provided and consumed. They also deliver a window into performance and availability of API connections that many companies utilize for monitoring and management of connected applications. However when management data from API gateways can be integrated with application performance management (APM) solutions, IT support teams have an automated basis for managing applications and transactions in context to the APIs they may be accessing.

Increasingly, leading-edge APM solutions[2] are now connecting to gateway solutions for data integration purposes. These connections inject real-time data on API connections into the APM solution for analysis and correlation with other metrics supporting monitoring of end-to-end execution.

---

[1]More information on how API gateways work is available at http://stackoverflow.com/questions/11331386/how-do-api-gateways-work.
[2]Prospective customers should check specification sheets and vendor descriptions to verify functions supported by specific products.

While most companies today are monitoring API connections from the single point of the gateway, integrations between API gateway monitoring functions and traditional APM platform/suite solutions support true performance management of API-connected applications. These integrations provide a foundation for detecting and resolving issues that may occur within applications/transactions accessing APIs.

EXAMPLE API USE CASE: MICROSERVICES AND APPLICATION PROGRAMMING INTERFACES

Microservices are a good example of state-of-the-art applications with API dependencies. From the business enablement perspective, microservice architectures speed time-to-market for new functions and features, as the componentized form factor enables a building block approach to application/service creation. From the IT perspective, they enable responsive scaling based on load. From the development perspective, they fit well into **agile** development practices and are faster to develop and modify than the monolithic enterprise applications running in many companies.

Often associated with **containerization** using platforms such as **Docker**, **container-based microservices** are portable in the sense that they are capable of running on any server that supports Docker—today usually a Linux-based server. In microservice architectures, monolithic applications are broken into small services (or, alternatively, new code is developed as small services), with each microservice performing a specific set of tasks and running as its own process (see Fig. 11.2).

Often touted as a new architectural model ideally suited for the agile business, software components in the form of microservices can then be strung together (orchestrated) via APIs. Orchestrated services then execute as work streams in much the same way as traditional transactions and applications typically function (see Fig. 11.3).

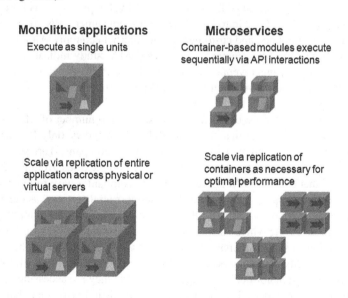

FIGURE 11.2

Microservice architectures enable responsive scaling based on load. They can also speed delivery of new services and expedite time-to-market for new functions and features.

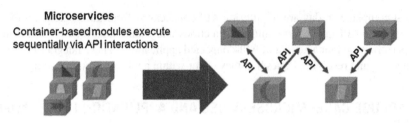

Microservices
Container-based modules execute
sequentially via API interactions

FIGURE 11.3

Microservices are orchestrated into applications/transactions via application programming interface connections.

With all their benefits, the success of microservice delivery hinges on the performance of the APIs connecting them. The microservices architecture replaces monolithic (or distributed) application delivery with hundreds or potentially thousands of API-based connections. From this perspective, performance and/or availability issues are bound to happen; the only question is when. These challenges highlight the need for integrated, production-grade gateway and APM solutions capable of supporting execution of API-connected services.

APPLICATION PROGRAMMING INTERFACE CONSUMER USAGE IN THE ENTERPRISE

This section and the following section address use cases and value propositions for consumer and provider APIs, respectively. In broad use in today's companies, consumer APIs are essential elements for interacting with partners, suppliers, and customers in the Internet economy. Almost 50% of companies surveyed in a recent Enterprise Management Associates (EMA) study indicated that **consumer APIs** were critical elements supporting revenue generation. These API connections drive inventory and ordering, sales fulfillment, financial reconciliation, and similar functions that are critical to the day-to-day business.

The research also shows that most companies use a substantial number of APIs. Very few API consumer companies are accessing fewer than ten—and as Fig. 11.4 shows, only 10% are in this category. Most are consuming between 11 and 50, and 10% (mostly large companies) are accessing 100 or more.

These numbers are important because they highlight the complexities, from an APM standpoint, of managing applications that connect to APIs. Relatively few companies have full visibility to the dependencies between production applications and the APIs supporting them. And as the number of APIs in use continues to escalate, it becomes increasingly difficult to keep track of API topologies—in essence, which applications are accessing which APIs. In lieu of tools capable of providing visibility into these interrelationships, the business risks increase with each new API rolled into production usage.

In the same way, visibility to change becomes of primary importance. Fig. 11.5 shows the ways in which API users are most often notified of changes to the APIs they are accessing. Since APIs directly connect the user to an API provider's back-end system, it stands to reason that changes to that system (such as database schema changes) may well impact the operation of APIs. And while API providers know when the API or the structure behind it changes, API consumers often have no way of knowing about the change until the application accessing the API stops functioning.

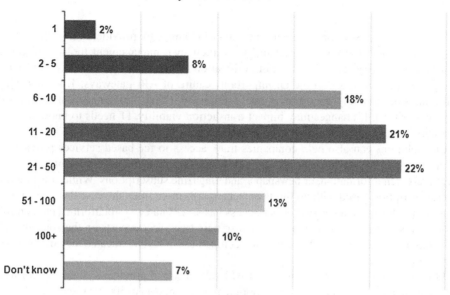

FIGURE 11.4

Most commonly, companies have between 11 and 50 consumer application programming interfaces in use.

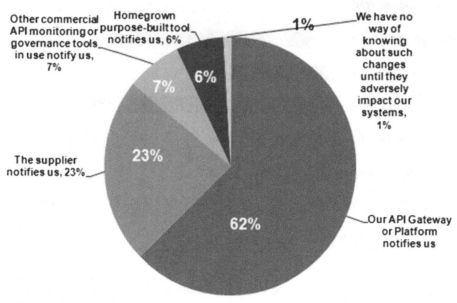

FIGURE 11.5

Application programming interface (API) providers notify consumers of their API of version changes only 23% of the time.

As Fig. 11.5 shows, API consumers are notified of changes by providers only about 25% of the time. Most often, they find out about changes via their own management tools—specifically API gateways—rather than receiving any type of notification from the provider. This is a primary reason why change notification has become an important feature of API gateways. Knowing when APIs change becomes increasingly important as the functionality of the API connection becomes increasingly business critical. If changes may impact transaction viability, IT needs to know if and when a change occurs.

Gateway solutions can also help companies track access to fee-based services provided via API connections. For-pay APIs provide access to paid services, such as financial information (e.g., Dun & Bradstreet), research information, or newspaper and magazine subscriptions. While consumption models can be subscription-based with no limits on access, it is more often the case that consumers access these types of platforms on a per-seat or per-access basis. API gateways/platforms help control access to such platforms on the provider side and can also help track access costs on the consumer side. Per EMA research, more than 60% of API consumer companies surveyed indicated they use their gateways for this purpose.

Fig. 11.6 illustrates the growing volume of API calls made to provider systems by consumer systems. Most companies consuming APIs reported making between 500,000 and 1 million calls to

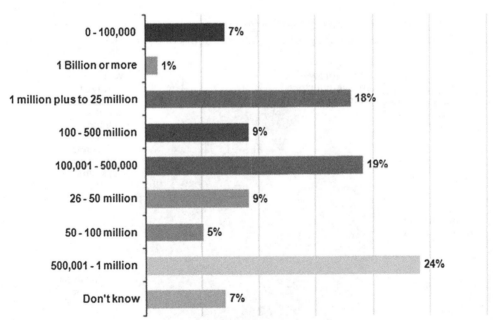

Approximately how many transactions per month currently access Consumer APIs?

Category	Percentage
0 - 100,000	7%
1 Billion or more	1%
1 million plus to 25 million	18%
100 - 500 million	9%
100,001 - 500,000	19%
26 - 50 million	9%
50 - 100 million	5%
500,001 - 1 million	24%
Don't know	7%

FIGURE 11.6

Most often, between 500,000 and 1 million transactions per month access (external) consumer application programming interfaces.

external APIs every month. However, more than 40% of the companies surveyed by EMA report 1 million or more calls per month. Furthermore, almost 80% report these numbers to be rising, most often by about 20% per month.

These numbers illustrate the facts that API usage is growing and that APIs continue to be increasingly important foundational enablers for eBusiness interactions.

APPLICATION PROGRAMMING INTERFACE PROVIDER USAGE IN THE ENTERPRISE

API providers expose data or functionality for consumption by internal or external entities. Provider APIs are critical or very important to the business at 95% of companies surveyed. Fig. 11.7 shows the types of entities that most often access provider APIs. Customers, suppliers, and partners make up the top three, while internal applications are the primary consumers more than 30% of the time (in this use case, APIs are often used to facilitate internal development by exposing frequently used data or code for easy access by new or existing applications. APIs are also often used to provide mobile access allowing internal users to access internally-delivered applications).

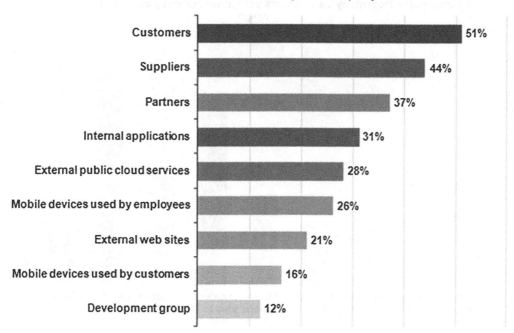

Which types of entities are the primary types connecting TO your applications or services via the Provider APIs your company delivers?

FIGURE 11.7

Customers, suppliers, and partners are the most frequent users of provider application programming interfaces.

Although Fig. 11.7 does not show the targets for these API requests, research points to database connections as the most common points of exposure with mainframes as the second most common targets. This is consistent with reports by IBM and other large vendors, which found that access by **mobile devices**, in particular, is driving increased usage of API connections to back-end mainframe systems. Banks, for example, are refactoring traditional mainframe applications into components and/ or microservices capable of handling a single request/response. As consumers increasingly access banking applications from mobile devices, hardware and software that were originally designed for batch processes become far more interactive. This tends to tax computing resources in ways not originally anticipated by designers.

It is also true that the vast majority of providers are not simply supporting a single API. Providers most commonly build and support 21 to 50 APIs; 10% host more than 100. These findings reinforce the need for security and governance support as well as the importance of ongoing capacity management–related measurements and capacity planning.

Fig. 11.8 shows IT professionals' estimates of the volume of transactions accessing the APIs provided by their companies. The numbers are enormous and getting larger by the month. Companies reporting between 100,000 and 1 million transactions per month account for almost 45% of the total. As would be expected, however, this number varies by company size. For example, the 500,000 to 1 million numbers are far more common for small and medium-sized companies. The largest set of

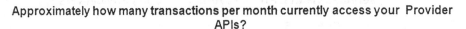

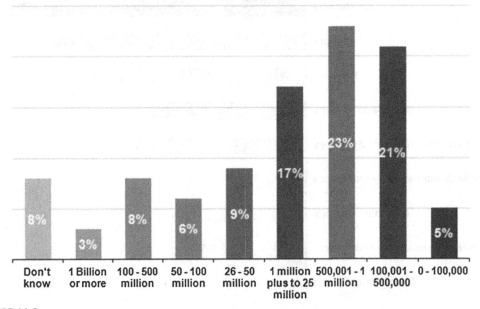

FIGURE 11.8

Most often, a company's provider application programming interfaces are accessed 100,000 to 1 million times per month.

companies, those with 10,000+ employees, most commonly report between 100 and 500 million API accesses monthly; no small companies and very few medium-sized companies experience these volumes.

Providers also often report that once APIs are exposed and become popular, usage growth can mushroom exponentially. Approximately 85% of respondents say traffic volumes are increasing over time. As Fig. 11.9 shows, the most frequently reported growth rate is between 10% and 20% per month.

For capacity planning purposes in the average data center, 20% growth per month is almost unheard of. When API growth percentages are viewed in light of their likely impact on back-end hardware and software infrastructure (including databases, applications, and servers), they reinforce the need for automation supporting performance, availability, and system usage. Visibility to transaction growth is an essential element of capacity planning. And tools capable of monitoring the performance and capacity impacts resulting from such growth are essential to providing a high-quality **user experience** of API-connected applications.

Fig. 11.10 reveals the most common challenges related to API delivery. Traffic volumes top the list by a significant margin, followed by security and identity management concerns. As APIs become increasingly popular with partners, suppliers, and customers, impacts on capacity are apparently as much of a concern as security. In fact, the two appear to be of approximately equal criticality, as there is not enough of a statistical difference between them to categorically declare either as the top issue.

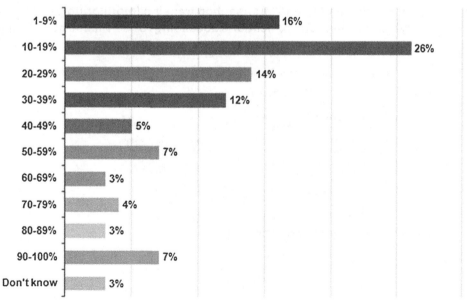

What is the approximate percentage monthly increase in transactions accessing your API platform?

FIGURE 11.9

Monthly transaction growth rates most commonly fall in the 10–19% range.

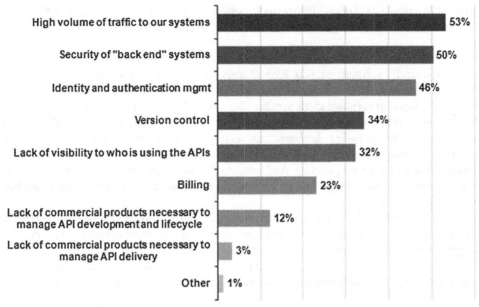

FIGURE 11.10

Traffic volumes, security-related factors are top challenges of application programming interface delivery.

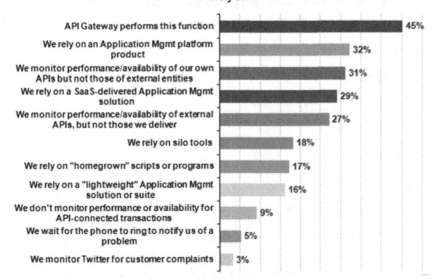

FIGURE 11.11

API gateways are more often used to track performance and availability than application management platforms.

Finally, as Fig. 11.11 shows, a majority of companies monitor performance and availability of applications accessing APIs from the perspective of the gateway. Although this is a good starting point, it is essentially a silo solution to a far broader and more complex problem.

API-connected applications, like any other tiered, distributed applications, have hundreds or thousands of potential failure points. From this perspective, simply monitoring the gateway is akin to monitoring servers, networks, or databases in isolation. In the end, APM platforms should have mechanisms for incorporating gateway data into **analytics**, correlations, and dashboards. Lacking this single point of visibility and control of application execution (versus silo performance), full automation of the end-to-end monitoring/management function remains a fruitless quest.

SUMMARY

APIs can provide a wide variety of business benefits. They can enable a company to become more efficient in delivering new products and services. They allow for a simpler way to integrate compared to the custom integrations and complicated middleware of the past. They enable businesses to become more agile and flexible in their interactions with customers, partners, and suppliers. They support modernization, enabling companies to very quickly adapt to changing technology, application architectures, and business requirements.

However, failure to plan for the realities of API delivery and consumption can be a fatal mistake. Applications relying on APIs for day-to-day execution are obviously business critical and often generate revenue. From this perspective, performance and availability management at multiple levels is an essential element in API delivery as well as API consumption. Gateway solutions support both API providers and consumers.

Chief concerns of providers include traffic volumes, availability, metering (usage of for-pay services), access control, security of back-end systems, and capacity impacts. While most of these functions can be provided by a gateway, the capacity planning function would typically be supported instead by an APM solution in context to data shared by the gateway. This adds visibility to the infrastructure elements impacted by API access and provides a common data and management platform for problem determination and future capacity planning.

Chief concerns of consumers include API change tracking, user authorization to utilize for-pay services, API up-time, and end-to-end performance of applications accessing APIs. Again, the first three are typically provided by the gateway, while end-to-end performance is usually the role of the APM solution. It is also important to recognize the fact that, in many cases, APM solutions will be (or should be) capable of analyzing data provided by external integrations with API gateways. In this case, the analytics supporting the APM solution will correlate both APM-related and gateway-related metrics in context with one another. This is the ideal solution for end-to-end management functionality, as it helps pinpoint the likely source of performance bottlenecks or availability failures.

KEY TAKEAWAYS

- APIs are critical software elements supporting data and/or functionality interchange between diverse entities. They are also utilized for standardizing data access within a software engineering organization to facilitate faster software development.
- The API Economy is well named, since APIs are deemed to be critical or very important to business as usual in the majority of companies surveyed.

- The rise of standards such as REST and HTTP significantly expanded the API Economy because of the ease of use they provide. Today's APIs can be developed and consumed faster and far more easily than was true of the custom-written integrations of past eras.
- API gateways are the universal standard for API delivery and consumption, providing both the real-time link supporting API usage and a host of governance, control, and management functions.
- API gateways are also commonly used for monitoring and managing API performance and availability, for both provider and consumer APIs. However, without information sharing between API gateways and APM platforms, management via the gateway simply creates another functional silo within IT. As with any type of application and **transaction management** function, silo metrics provide the raw material for system management functions (as opposed to **application management** functions). Analytics are the secret sauce that consolidates metrics from multiple sources to provide an end-to-end view of **application performance** and availability.

Examples of vendors with products in this space:

3Scale
Actian
Adeptia
Akana
Apigee
Attunity
CA Technologies
Dell Boomi
IBM
Informatica
Intuit
Jitterbit
Liaison Hubspan
Mashery
MuleSoft
Oracle
Parasoft
Scribe SW
SmartBear
SnapLogic
Software AG
Tibco

APPLICATION PERFORMANCE MANAGEMENT AND USER EXPERIENCE MANAGEMENT

When you see something that is technically sweet, you go ahead and do it and you argue about what to do about it only after you have had your technical success. That is the way it was with the atom bomb.

J. Robert Oppenheimer

INTRODUCTION

Modern distributed **applications** are the most complex example of business applications on the planet. They can be supported by hundreds or thousands of hardware and software subcomponents and are heavily network-dependent for performance and availability. In managing these applications, it is easy to lose sight of the forest and focus on the trees. In this case, the forest consists of business- and user-facing applications, while the trees are the underlying hardware and software infrastructure silos. Visibility to both, plus **analytics** capable of correlating the two in context to the end-to-end transaction, are the most important elements of application performance management (APM).

However, all too often, complex applications are deployed first and application management is an afterthought.

Traditionally, applications were supported with a combination of silo monitoring and tribal knowledge—knowledge built from the experience of the hands-on specialists supporting a company's enterprise applications. Now, however, in virtually every company and industry the number of enterprise applications[1] is growing. Only 30% of IT organizations are supporting 10 or fewer such applications, 25% are supporting between 11 and 50, and 15% support more than 150. The sheer volume and complexity of applications deployed in the average company have outstripped IT's ability to rely on human skills and knowledge alone to support them.

The industry solves the problem of complexity, in part, by breaking the IT ecosystem (and IT support) into consumable chunks or silos, with each technology team covering a small subset of an increasingly broad technology panorama. The net result is that most IT practitioners—and most **management** tools—tend to focus on a discrete subset of an ever-expanding application fabric.

The problem is that applications (not simply infrastructure) are the core supporting digital **services** generating billions of dollars annually in revenue. From this perspective, all the infrastructure and the billions of dollars expended annually on enterprise hardware and software boil down to one endgame: IT exists to meet a business need, not simply to create code, manage databases, provision servers, or

---

[1]An enterprise application is defined by EMA for APM purposes as "a complex, distributed application used company-wide" (versus a desktop or mobile application). A single enterprise application may well span multiple platforms, including mainframes and/or cloud services. APM investments capable of covering complex, business critical use cases such as these—encompassing tiered, hybrid, and componentized application architectures—are very likely to support less complex application types as well.

configure networks. Meeting that business need requires **application management**, not simply infrastructure management. Traditional enterprise management products, many of which have domain-focused roots, are still adapting to this reality, with a strong focus on silo management. And though management products that address databases, networks, and servers are still a part of the big picture, the picture itself is also far bigger than it was in the past.

This chapter focuses on the big picture—the enterprise applications executing on top of the silos. It details techniques, capabilities, and products required to evolve from silo-based to application-focused monitoring and management. APM and user experience management (UEM) are the two primary product types in this class. If applications are the new *lingua franca* enabling businesses to digitally communicate with customers, partners, and providers, these types of solutions provide IT organizations with the tools they need to effectively fulfill the service provider role.

APPLICATION PERFORMANCE MANAGEMENT: MULTIDIMENSIONAL VISIBILITY TO APPLICATION EXECUTION

APM requires visibility not only to underlying silos, but also to the executing transactions, applications, and/or services running atop the silos.

Managing applications versus simply monitoring applications requires automation supporting two primary functions:

- Monitoring and optimizing performance of the end-to-end application or transaction
- Troubleshooting and root cause analysis of performance or availability issues

While the majority of UEM solutions have functionality supporting the first, true **APM** solutions can do both. From this perspective, one key differentiator between the two product types is breadth of visibility. While UEM solutions can watch end-to-end execution, APM solutions can also see the interrelationships between the executing transaction/application and the supporting hardware, software, and other infrastructure elements. For the APM and UEM buyer, the line separating the two types of products is often blurred. For example, some UEM solutions do have the ability to correlate performance to underlying root cause to a degree, and many have features that APM products lack, such as specific visibility to end user actions. Likewise, leading APM solutions also encompass a level of UEM functionality, most notably the ability to trace transactions across the execution stream.

However, for the purposes of this book, which essentially focuses on capabilities versus specific products or vendors, keeping the two goals of performance management and problem resolution in mind provides a starting point for understanding the breadth of the APM challenge. Creating a management fabric sufficient for supporting automated troubleshooting and root cause analysis across complex application systems requires multidimensional visibility to the entire application ecosystem, and, often, the contributions of multiple product families.

Capabilities such as those characteristic of **configuration** and **metadata** repositories, **application discovery/dependency mapping** solutions, middleware monitoring, and code analytics offerings automate the process of detecting and modeling relationships among applications and infrastructure elements across the IT ecosystem—in effect, modeling an application execution fabric. Without such a comprehensive, multidimensional approach, activities like **change management** and root-cause analysis become increasingly problematic. In lieu of automation, they rely on human expertise, domain specialists, and tribal knowledge, all of which tend to be siloed, fragmentary, and inconclusive.

Increasingly, however, a new class of APM products targeting both application experts and, often, **line of business** application owners as well is emerging. The overarching role of these tools is to develop a comprehensive understanding of the forest in context with the trees—in other words, to build visibility to the interrelationships and dependencies supporting an application across both vertical infrastructure and horizontally flowing execution paths. This integrated view—or **topology model**—is an essential basis for root-cause analysis. Otherwise, application troubleshooting is essentially a matter of trial and error.

ANALYTICS

Any discussion of APM must start with a discussion of the role of analytics in supporting the APM function. Analytics are the core differentiators for vendors of APM and UEM solutions. Although the remainder of this chapter details the product types and instrumentation points supporting APM and UEM disciplines, the true "secret sauce" of any such solution lies in the heuristics, algorithms, and analyses conceived by the computer scientists creating the product.

Hardware and software systems generate execution metrics that can be gathered and analyzed for insights into system health. The same generic metrics and execution data are available to virtually every management solution and vendor. The true differentiators of a given product lie in two areas:

- Its ability to generate unique information from the data available to it, whether this is via standard metrics or proprietary metric generators such as software agents installed on the system
- Its inherent ability to analyze this information in a unique way to draw conclusions relevant to the process of application support

Enterprise Management Associates (EMA) calls these capabilities **Advanced IT Analytics (AIA)** and defines AIA as having the following three characteristics:

- AIA should be cross-domain and not restricted to just silos such as network, systems, application, database, or even business outcomes.
- AIA should assimilate many different data sources whether from third-party monitoring tools, unstructured log files, protocol-rich data sources, or ideally, all of the above.
- Over and above this data, AIA requires the application of advanced heuristics, such as machine learning, advanced correlation, anomaly detection, or predictive trending.[2]

State-of-the-art APM capabilities supplied by top vendors include ongoing self-learning of environmental norms, proactive notification when key metrics indicate an impending issue, and real-time topology modeling supporting troubleshooting/root cause analysis.

All of these capabilities, but particularly the analytics supporting them, are implemented differently by every vendor and are almost always patented. The most sophisticated APM solutions can also link tiny changes and glitches in execution to failures occurring minutes or hours later. These so-called rolling failures are extremely difficult to detect via manual analysis since the root cause of an issue and its

---

[2]Enterprise Management Associates, *Advanced IT Analytics: A Look at Real Adoptions in the Real World.* Available for download at www.enterprisemanagement.com.

manifestation may occur far apart in time. Sophisticated analytics solutions, however, can detect the fact that a given event or series of events has, in the past, set the ball rolling by initiating a chain of events that eventually results in a performance problem or service interruption.

The data and metrics collected at instrumentation points across the application ecosystem are essential to performance monitoring and root cause analysis. However, analytics capable of transforming data and metrics into an application-focused report or dashboard[3] are what separates actual application monitoring from relatively simple silo monitoring. Analytics add the context necessary to understand the role of each moving part in the end-to-end execution environment, a viewpoint that is absolutely critical for rapid—and eventually automated—problem determination and resolution. Without this context, these solutions would simply be operational data stores versus true tools capable of insight into application ecosystems.

APPLICATION PERFORMANCE MANAGEMENT AND USER EXPERIENCE MANAGEMENT, COMPARED AND CONTRASTED

There are a wide variety of tools supporting these processes. Some classes of application-facing tools monitor execution from the perspective of the servers running the software. Some quantify performance from the perspective of the end user (**user experience**) by monitoring web server interactions, monitoring the endpoint (desktop, **mobile device**, etc.), or running **synthetic transactions**. Some tools monitor performance from the perspective of the connective tissue supporting the application—message queues, **enterprise service buses (ESBs)**, or **application programming interface (API)** gateways. Some combine all of the above in large-scale suite or platform products that are designed to automate virtually every monitoring/management aspect of a large-scale data center. What these tools all have in common is the ability to analyze and report on at least one essential dimension or element of the end-to-end application.

While APM and UEM are certainly related, they are significantly different in terms of the types of information they provide. There are multiple areas of overlap:

- Both provide a quantification or approximation of **application performance**.
- Both provide insights on availability.
- Both focus on monitoring/measuring an end-to-end, cross-silo service versus a simple server, database, or network link.

In comparing the two product categories, APM solutions are more comprehensive in their technology coverage and richer in their analytical capabilities. UEM solutions, in contrast, typically focus on quantifying the user experience from a particular perspective—a single slice of the user experience, such as the network, the web server, or the transaction. They provide an automated approach to approximating application performance as experienced by end users.

APM solutions gather and analyze metrics from a wide range of viewpoints across the application ecosystem. They quantify performance from the perspective of the ecosystem versus the perspective of

---

[3]For the purposes of this chapter, the terms "applications" and "transactions" are used interchangeably since the key point is to describe products capable of creating an end-to-end (multidimensional) versus silo (vertical) perspective on the data center and ecosystem.

the user; for example, an organization's data center or a consumer cloud service that a given APM solution is monitoring. Because of their insights into execution, their unique value proposition lies in their ability to support troubleshooting—detecting and pinpointing the source of a performance or availability problem to automate the process of root cause analysis. In other words, while both APM and UEM tools can be used to detect performance or availability issues, APM solutions are purpose-built to support root-cause analysis as well.

UEM solutions, as the name implies, quantify performance as experienced by a user. While the user is typically considered to be a person sitting at a keyboard, in the case of machine-to-machine interactions, the user could just as easily be another device. Although UEM solutions focus on top-level, end-to-end performance versus troubleshooting or root-cause analysis, the types of information they do provide is extremely valuable. Often, UEM solutions are used as the proverbial "canaries in a coal mine," early warning systems for impending problems.

They also focus on viewpoints that APM solutions often lack—notably functions such as endpoint monitoring (in which agents are installed on a desktop or mobile device) and browser injection (in which a small monitoring script is injected into the user's browser during execution), both of which have visibility to user actions. The capabilities supporting user management are aimed at answering questions such as these:

- Who are the application's users?
- Which applications are most critical to the business?
- Who is impacted if an application fails?
- What are the application's users doing and how are their devices responding?

UEM solutions provide insights garnered from a wide variety of monitoring methods. **Active monitoring** solutions incorporate robot scripts that quantify end-to-end performance, regardless of whether or not users are on a system. **Passive monitoring** solutions focus on real human interactions versus purely technical component behaviors. Both approaches lend themselves not only to IT-relevant metrics and **key performance indicators (KPI)**, but also to metrics supporting **service-level agreement (SLA)**[4] monitoring and insights into business-relevant information, such as online sales conversions. More detailed examinations of both APM and UEM product categories and features are provided later in this chapter.

ON-PREMISES AND SOFTWARE AS A SERVICE–BASED APPLICATION PERFORMANCE MANAGEMENT SOLUTION

In purchasing an APM solution, form factor is one of the first considerations that must be decided. The two most common form factors are shown in Figs. 12.1 and 12.2.

In either case, APM solutions are designed to gather, store, consolidate, and analyze a wide variety of operational data types. Data sources may include proprietary agents, logs, events, changes, and metrics [e.g., **Windows Management Instrumentation (WMI)**, simple network management protocol (SNMP), etc.]. They may also include messages from other systems that indicate changes in

---

[4]SLAs are discussed in Appendix A, which addresses Service-Level Management.

topologies or other relevant information. As an example, **release automation** solutions can provision and configure **virtual servers** as well as the applications and components that run on top of them. These solutions can then propagate topology and configuration changes to analytics systems for incorporation into automated topology maps.

Fig. 12.1 shows a simplified diagram of an on-premises APM solution. Operational data is gathered from agents supplied by the vendor, by third-party agents, and/or by operational protocols such as SNMP. All metrics are centralized, analyzed, and correlated on a central server that hosts the management software delivered by the vendor. All analytics functions, including topology modeling, analytics, and reporting, are done on the central server.

Operations staff are notified via emails, phone calls, pages, and such when the APM solution detects a problem. Operational users can also access real-time system status dashboards, supporting drill downs into underlying infrastructure and reporting software, typically via a web interface connection into the management system.

Security and fast processing are two of the key strengths of an on-premises APM solution. Management data sometimes includes sensitive data such as IP addresses, execution logs, and even network **passwords** ("community strings") that could compromise security if they fell into the wrong hands. Hosting the entire system on-premises eliminates this problem, at least to the extent that organizational borders are secured. Companies may also opt to host their own APM solution to minimize

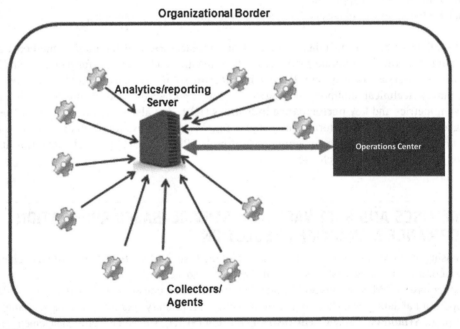

FIGURE 12.1

On-premises application performance management.

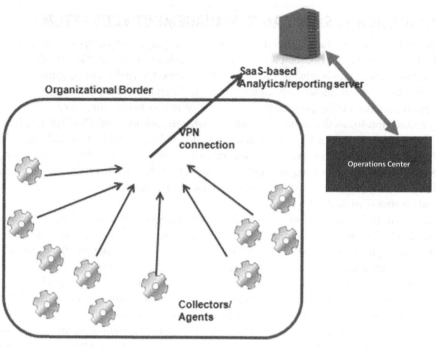

FIGURE 12.2

SaaS-based application performance management.

WAN utilization and latency. Due to the fact that the analytics server is within organizational borders, messaging to and from the server likely has minimal latency compared to the longer latency delays that may occur when the analytics are hosted in the cloud.

The primary drawbacks of an on-premise APM product are cost and time. Costs tend to be higher than software as a service (SaaS) options, and maintaining the analytics/reporting server—with updates, paging software, etc.—is a non-trivial affair. In actuality, most companies hosting management solutions on premises have tools teams in place to manage the management tools. In contrast, Fig. 12.2 shows a simplified diagram of a SaaS-based APM solution. The collection structure is virtually identical to that of an on-premises solution. However, instead of being routed to an on-premises management server, metrics are sent via a **virtual private network (VPN)** connection to a **cloud-hosted** system. Operations staff get the same notifications they would receive from an on-premises system and can access dashboards and reporting systems via a browser-based interface.

The choice of an on-premises or SaaS-based APM system is essentially a matter of customer preference. SaaS customers take advantage of world-class APM capabilities without needing to devote expensive personnel resources to system administration tasks and day-to-day maintenance, as well as ongoing updating of new software releases on the analytics server. However, some companies see operational risk in sending metrics to an external platform and prefer to use their own staff to maintain the APM software internally.

THE APPLICATION PERFORMANCE MANAGEMENT ECOSYSTEM

APM tools can be a unifying factor providing a common language and viewpoint for cross-functional teams with diverse training and skills. Particularly when such tools are capable of gathering data from multiple sources (data center hardware and software, network-focused metrics, application execution data, etc.), they create a centralized application perspective that is virtually impossible to duplicate via manual support processes or by pooling tribal knowledge across teams. Such tools can be critical for delivering application-focused insight to **development, operations, and DevOps** teams across the lifecycle. Preproduction application testing ensures that developers and testers find and fix problems early in the lifecycle—when they are easier and cheaper to remediate. Postdeployment testing detects production problems early, providing an opportunity to fix them before they impact users. Used in such a way, APM solutions provide a unifying bridge, enabling development, operations, and DevOps to communicate across silos more efficiently.

At the same time tools selection can be confusing, largely because of the wide range of technologies and solutions being bundled under the APM umbrella. Different types of APM tools deliver different perspectives on the same application. The APM story is similar to that of the elephant and the blindfolded man—touching a leg, a trunk, and a tail yield very different experiences. At the same time, viewed holistically, it's still an elephant. Tools choices are also complicated by the fact that they aim at an ever-changing target. As new types of technologies are incorporated into the data center, and as software ecosystems evolve, APM solutions must also evolve in a way that addresses the unique management challenges of each.

Fig. 12.3 shows the evolutions of development practices, application architectures, application deployments, and supporting infrastructure over time. As an example of APM evolution, the rise of **containers** and **microservices** shown in the Application Architecture column has driven the growth of

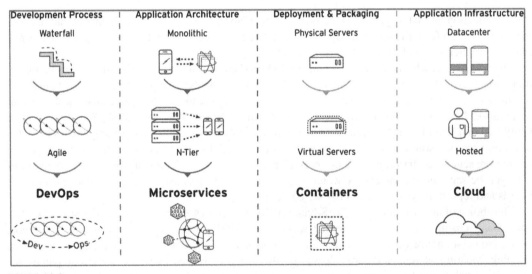

FIGURE 12.3

Evolution of development processes, application architectures, deployment platforms, and infrastructure.

©2016 courtesy of Red Hat, Inc.

API-connected applications as application components become increasingly granular. Microservices housed in containers are orchestrated into usable business services via APIs.

Public cloud services, owned and managed by external entities, are often part of the ecosystem as well. The reality for IT organizations consuming cloud services is that while they have a responsibility to their customers for performance and availability, they have little or no control over how—and at what levels—the service is delivered. To complicate matters further, the evolution of development practices (from waterfall to **agile**) created escalating rates of production change.

Each of these factors can adversely impact production. So as each evolution occurs, APM solutions must also evolve to support the massively connected, dynamically changing application environments that are becoming commonplace in modern clouds and data centers.

APM tools leverage analytics, encapsulated industry/technology expertise, and multiple monitoring protocols to develop visibility and control capabilities supporting applications and their underlying execution environments. They quantify application performance and automate the process of surfacing relationships among applications and infrastructure elements, making it easier to detect and diagnose issues and anomalies contributing to performance or availability problems. Without such a comprehensive, multidimensional approach, activities such as change management and root-cause analysis become increasingly expensive guessing games. It is also the case that many execution issues are never resolved, and therefore continue to recur.

While businesses are proficient at developing sophisticated applications, the statistics suggest that they are not as successful at maintaining and managing them. This is borne out with multiple research findings:

- More than 35% of IT professionals surveyed in 2015 indicated that they lacked the tools needed to support their application environments.
- More than 40% of application outages are reported by users versus management tools.
- Support costs consume 60–80% of the average IT budget. Although this statistic is so commonplace as to have become a cliché, there is a good reason for these high costs. In lieu of adequate management products, people are required to close the management gap—and people are expensive.

At the same time, while the industry coined the term end-to-end to describe the process of managing the application fabric, there is a notable lack of definition regarding what end-to-end actually means. For the purposes of this chapter, the term is used to describe the execution of an application, service, or transaction from start to finish.

Ideally, the process of managing a software service in a business context requires the ability to quantify and track performance and availability, to understand normal performance patterns (including time-based fluctuations), to auto discover dependencies and supporting infrastructure, and to monitor and notify on departures from the norm in real time. APM solutions are designed to address critical questions related to application performance. Examples include:

- **Dependency mapping**:
  - Which infrastructure elements support which applications?
  - What dependencies exist between applications and/or software components?
- **Capacity management**:
  - How are applications impacting the infrastructure that supports them?
  - Is overutilization of underlying resources adversely impacting performance?

- **Change management**:
  - What changed?
  - How will a proposed hardware or software change impact performance of existing applications?
  - Once a change to production is made, how is that change impacting production performance?
- **Proactive analysis**:
  - How can the business impacts of application and infrastructure problems be minimized?
- **Root-cause analysis**:
  - When performance slows or the application becomes unavailable, where is the problem and how can it be fixed?
- **Service-level management**:
  - How does the application normally behave, performancewise?
  - Are there performance variations based on time of day, day of month, and such?
  - How do the levels of performance and availability actually being delivered compare to contracted SLAs?[5]

As **containerization**, virtualization of every type, infrastructure abstraction, network centricity, and massively distributed applications become increasingly common, the answers to questions such as these are no longer straightforward or even forthcoming. To complicate matters, there is a wide variety of APM-related product flavors, most of which focus on specific subsets of the overall APM-related big picture.

INSTRUMENTATION AND DATA SOURCES SUPPORTING APPLICATION PERFORMANCE MANAGEMENT
ENTERPRISE MANAGEMENT ASSOCIATES APPLICATION MANAGEMENT SEMANTIC MODEL

To assist IT organizations in tools planning and acquisitions, EMA has developed an Application Management Semantic Model (see Fig. 12.4). This is a comprehensive approach to documenting the instrumentation points supporting delivery of the metrics required for the management of complex applications. The model also documents a tools framework supporting instrumentation of each major dimension of application execution as a basis and foundation for AIA tailored to APM practices.

The model assumes that gathering and analyzing execution information compiled from multiple vantage points (represented by the layers in the model) is ultimately necessary to build a management fabric. This fabric, in turn, will act as a foundation for the multiple functions performed by APM solutions, including analyzing, alerting, reporting, and ultimately fixing application-focused issues. Collectively, the layers of the model quantify the dimensions of visibility that are necessary to develop a holistic, 360 degree view of the execution ecosystem.

TOOLS, DATA, AND ANALYTICS, AND THE END-TO-END PERSPECTIVE

Table 12.1 is a functional breakdown that documents the function of each layer of the Application Management Semantic Model shown in Fig. 12.4. Each provides a unique execution perspective, gathered from direct instrumentation, protocols operating at that layer, or, in some cases (network, for example) by direct analysis of transactions or data flows occurring at that layer.

[5]See Appendix A.

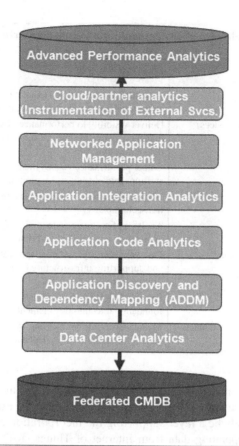

FIGURE 12.4

Enterprise Management Associates Application Management Semantic Model.

Needless to say, full automation requires that APM solutions include advanced analytics encompassing very high levels of built in industry expertise. It also requires near real-time monitoring and analysis based on insights into infrastructure performance, application topologies and dependencies, transaction execution, and system configurations. For this reason, in addition to instrumentation points, the model also includes layers supporting advanced performance analytics as well as a federated **configuration management database (CMDB),** also known as a **configuration management system (CMS).** Respectively, these layers support intelligent data analysis and real time topology modeling.

Today, the layers of the model support:

- Management of the predominantly custom versus packaged applications running in the majority of companies
- The emergence of massively componentized applications such as those deployed utilizing **service-oriented architecture (SOA)** and **web services**
- Widespread use of APIs and other **integration** technologies
- Use of public cloud
- Extensive use of virtualized systems hosted on premise and/or deployed into **infrastructure as a service** clouds

Table 12.1 Functional Breakdown of Instrumentation Points Supporting 360degree View of Application Execution

Layer	Function
Advanced performance analytics	Assimilate/analyze ecosystem data and metrics to deliver operational and business-relevant performance insight
Cloud/partner analytics (external services)	Deliver visibility to performance of systems hosted and/or managed by outside entities (i.e., public cloud or partner-delivered services)
Network	Gather performance-related metrics via real/synthetic transactions, sniffing, packet analysis, or other flow-centric analysis
Application integrations	Track and monitor transactions across middleware and variable transaction paths
Application code	Analysis of software code to identify, map, and monitor custom application execution in real time
Application discovery and dependency mapping	Discover, identify, and map applications, their interdependencies, and supporting infrastructure (via specialized application discovery tools)
Data center analytics	Discover, identify, monitor, and manage infrastructure and foundational technology elements (data/metrics from silo tools)
Federated configuration management database	Metadata repository modeling application and technology elements, configurations, dependencies

However, the intent of the model is to be flexible enough to support the data/metrics sources of the future that will evolve from the introduction of new technologies into the execution fabric. For example, one future addition will likely be a layer supporting the incorporation of big operational data into management systems. Incorporating data from Internet of Things (IoT) will become an important addition for many companies and we are already seeing IoT data integrated with back-end systems of record for a variety of business-focused analysis and reporting purposes—the addition of a data store and processing supporting big operational data will support these new use cases.

Each layer also addresses a specific viewpoint or perspective on the execution environments supporting today's distributed, virtualized, and tiered application architectures. In Fig. 12.5, instrumented data sources are shown in the left column, while supporting analytics and data/metadata repository functions are shown in the green and dark blue layers on the right-hand side of the diagram.

The ultimate goal of full instrumentation of each layer in the model is to provide the building blocks required to automate the process of creating and maintaining a dynamic model of the entire execution fabric that can be updated in real time. Doing so, of course, relies on APM solutions capable of analyzing the data rapidly enough to build and maintain such models. Finally, Fig. 12.6 documents the types of metrics generated and gathered at each instrumentation point. The vertical arrows show data flows to and from the analytics processing engine and, where relevant, the CMDB/CMS (to update topologies, dependencies, and configurations).

The analytics layer consumes data created and/or stored at the other layers to perform the analytics, correlation, and reporting functions. The CMDB/CMS provides an additional data source used by the analytics layer for information about dependencies, topologies, and configurations.

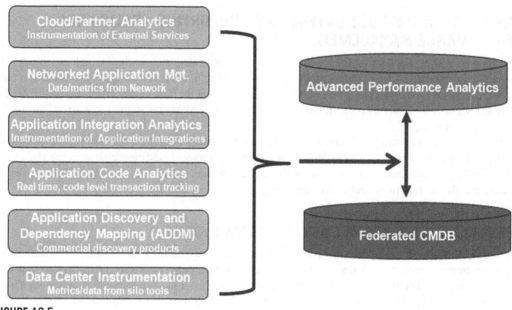

FIGURE 12.5

Instrumentation points providing visibility to application execution from multiple perspectives.

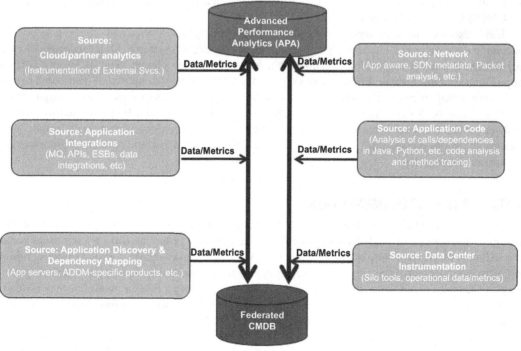

FIGURE 12.6

Runtime diagram showing data sources underlying each layer of the model.

TAXONOMY OF PRODUCT CATEGORIES SUPPORTING APPLICATION PERFORMANCE MANAGEMENT

To some extent, the model also defines a taxonomy of product categories, each of which contributes its own unique perspective to the management fabric. For example, element managers are still important for monitoring and gathering platform-specific health metrics at the data center layer. However, insight into these vertical components is of limited value to the overall APM task without context of the applications they support.

This context is provided by the five remaining vantage points: ADDM, application code analytics, application integration analytics, networked application management, and cloud/partner (external) analytics—and by the advanced performance analytics capabilities at the topmost layer. The following section details the functions and tools supporting each layer in additional detail.

THE CONFIGURATION MANAGEMENT DATABASE SYSTEM

Although the CMDB (or CMS) system is not explicitly responsible for gathering information about application execution, it does provide the context and data repository necessary to manage it. The federated CMDB/CMS system consists of data stores containing data and metadata about the end-to-end application fabric. In conjunction with modeling and management products, the CMDB/CMS ideally provides the key that describes how all the moving parts comprising the application interact with one another. EMA sees the CMDB/CMS as a prerequisite for end-to-end application management and a foundation for an efficient support process. EMA has written extensively about the CMDB/CMS in recent years and consulted with numerous companies worldwide on CMDB/CMS readiness and adoption.

EMA also sees metadata repositories, such as SOA registry/repositories and other repositories of execution data, becoming increasingly integrated with CMDB/CMS systems. Metadata provides critical information about application execution that helps build a big-picture view of loosely coupled application systems. Overall, EMA analysts believe the CMDB/CMS (composed of distributed repositories containing increasingly auto-discovered and self-maintained topologies and configurations) could become the Rosetta Stone, which, combined with analytics, would be positioned to translate isolated infrastructure elements into a holistic, application-focused context. Without such insight, managing applications is essentially a process of trial and error, heavily dependent on manual processes and organizational expertise.

DATA CENTER INSTRUMENTATION

The bottom layer of the model shown in Fig. 12.4, the data center layer, is one level of instrumentation that most organizations already have in place. Since the term data center has different meanings across the industry, for the purposes of the semantic model, the data center includes all the in-house hosted infrastructure elements necessary to deliver an application. From the tools perspective, tools at this level are the point products that manage servers, the network, and other foundational elements. Virtually all of these silo-focused tools include correlation capabilities designed to narrow down the potential sources of a given performance/availability issue for troubleshooting purposes.

There is nothing mysterious about these products as many have been in the marketplace for years. However, they are still foundational to managing the data center, and they also provide valuable data that is a fundamental element of application support.

This foundational layer provides insight into the health of the application's execution platform. It enables application issues to be correlated with infrastructure issues, when they exist, so they can be managed in context with one another. This is a prerequisite for efficient troubleshooting and root-cause analysis activities, among other functions.

Network management products are one example of a product that functions at this layer. The need to manage network devices drove the development of SNMP and its introduction to the industry in the 1980s. Not only is SNMP still widely used today, but multiple additional protocols and standards have been introduced over time as well. This market is very mature, with a host of quality products purpose-built to gather operational metrics from routers, servers, databases, storage, and almost every other platform in the data center. Even **uninterruptible power supplies (UPS)** have **SNMP MIBs**, allowing them to be monitored by SNMP-focused management stations.

APPLICATION DISCOVERY AND DEPENDENCY MAPPING

Application discovery and dependency mapping (ADDM) products are commercial solutions purpose-built to discover applications running in a production ecosystem and document them in context with supporting infrastructure and dependencies. Typically, such products utilize application signatures, or fingerprints, to discover applications, their downstream dependencies, and their supporting infrastructure, then assemble the resulting models into topology maps.

Commercial discovery and mapping products are shipped with prebuilt discovery signatures for an array of packaged applications. Since they lack signatures for custom applications, virtually all include tools designed to simplify the task of manually modeling custom applications so the automation under-stands how they are built.

ADDM vendors and products encompass varying levels of application awareness and functionality, along with varying levels of support for signatures and custom (usually homegrown) application support tools. However, most require a significant amount of manual scripting and grouping even after automated discoveries are complete, and these tasks are often performed as part of initial setup by vendor services organizations.

This product family is foundational to managing distributed applications for several reasons. These products document the links between applications and supporting infrastructure in an automated fashion. Further, they keep these links current, even within today's constantly changing IT systems. This information can then be used for multiple support tasks, including troubleshooting, root-cause analysis, and change management. In terms of change management, for example, they provide insight into upstream and downstream dependencies that may potentially be impacted by a given change.

However while ADDM technology continues to improve, it is also true that leading-edge APM solutions are starting to support a far greater level of topology modeling than they have in the past. Leading-edge APM solutions can automatically map component-based applications by watching intra-component interactions (see the auto-generated topology shown in Fig. 12.7, generated by IBM APM software). In many cases, these solutions mitigate or eliminate the need for ADDM solutions, since this function becomes part of the day-to-day, real-time topology modeling function.

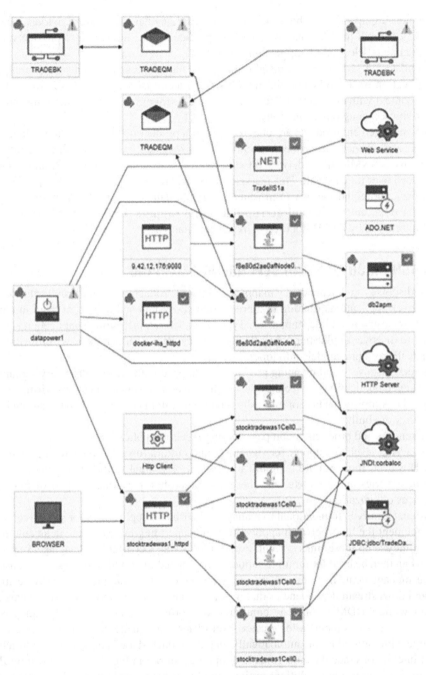

FIGURE 12.7

Automated topology map generated by IBM application performance management software.

APPLICATION CODE ANALYTICS

Code analytics products deliver deep insight into execution systems from the perspective of instrumented application servers. The value proposition of these solutions is that they are able to pinpoint execution-related problems down to a given piece of application code.

In some leading-edge APM solutions, code analysis also provides a basis for ADDM functionality by developing signatures or fingerprints for automatically discovering and mapping custom applications. Discovering custom applications is a problem for traditional application discovery products because no fingerprint exists to detect and identify the application. These products fill that gap by identifying executable code and, in doing so, generating a fingerprint by which custom applications can be tracked and identified.

There are a wide variety of products in this space, some of which have only recently come to market. The newest analyze application code predeployment and then use that analysis to discover and manage applications in production. Other products in this space monitor Java, node.js, and/or .NET executables during execution to identify availability and/or performance problems. They can break down execution into steps and quantify the time spent at each step. All of these capabilities facilitate root cause analysis of code-related issues for both custom and packaged applications and, in doing so, also helps identify opportunities for code redesign.

APPLICATION INTEGRATION ANALYTICS

This family of products tracks applications and transactions through the layers of integration that proliferate in **client/server**, web, and SOA-based applications. Many traditional application management products lack visibility to integration layers and technology touch points. Without this visibility, such products are unable to track a transaction across variable execution paths, multiple technologies, and complex middleware stacks. Integration technologies become, in essence, black boxes to the monitoring/management systems. This can be a source of significant risk, particularly if they support critical business applications.

Instrumentation supporting this layer covers the touch points between infrastructure elements, transactions, applications, components, and services. In addition to handoffs between infrastructure elements such as application server to database server, it can include interconnections among J2EE platforms, ESBs, registries and repositories, and related platforms that together route, execute, and manage underlying connections.

The most advanced products in this category can also track the variable routes that a transaction can take. Tracing these routes becomes particularly challenging when elements such as **XML** offloading, load balancing, WAN optimization, and similar technologies become part of the application execution chain. Products in this category are also essential for mapping real applications to real transactions and transaction paths, and for providing the insight into dependencies that is necessary for root-cause analysis. For example, **message queuing (MQ)** has been a standard method supporting data interchange for years, and many companies are still running hundreds of instances of MQ, allowing a wide variety of application types to interact. Still, many APM solutions as yet have minimal support for tracking MQ interactions as part of application execution. Other examples of integration technologies that could be addressed by this class of products include:

- ESB integrations: ESBs play a major role in SOAs by supporting rollouts of massively componentized software services. They enable businesses to link multiple discrete services together by normalizing across a wide variety of underlying data interchange methodologies.

- API integrations: Today, APIs are playing a central role in integrating companies with providers, suppliers, and customers. The so-called API Economy will likely continue to accelerate as APIs increasingly support the **container-based microservices** and **IoT** deployments of the future. API connections are now part of the execution chain as well, yet many companies have no way to track transactions (and consequently performance) across and through API connections.

NETWORKED APPLICATION MANAGEMENT

Networked application management solutions are playing an increasing role in providing user experience metrics quantifying Layer 8[6] performance for mobile, componentized, web, and cloud-based applications. These products differ from the standard network monitoring solutions that are part of the data center instrumentation layer by virtue of their visibility into the network traffic that carries application-related information. This visibility delivers higher-level functions such as user experience and performance/availability of external services.

Multiple solutions in this category have extremely varied capabilities and are rapidly evolving beyond their network management–centric roots. As applications are increasingly bound to the network, products that watch transaction flows and application exchanges become treasure troves of data relevant to managing applications.

As a product family, this new generation of networked application management solutions operates on transaction flows to gather application-relevant data related to network performance and transaction performance and, in some cases, the content included in the data flowing across the network. Some products in this category, for example, can perform such tasks as extracting business-relevant information from web traffic. This functionality would enable customers to track incoming sales transactions to maintain a running record of the day's online sales.

Packet analysis is another function performed by network facing solutions, and one that supports both performance management and business management capabilities. By utilizing "from-to" packet information, products in this category have the potential to automate the process of identifying and mapping transactions, regardless of the path the transaction takes as it traverses the execution environment. Automated **transaction tracing**, a technique utilized by a subset of products in the APM category, is one example of state of the art in this space.

Transactional reconstruction is done based on tagging transactions, then tracking them through the execution process. Solutions in this space utilize a combination of instrumentation and analytics to track transactions across diverse technology elements in real time, essentially automating the process of end-to-end transaction performance/availability management. Transaction tracing is useful for automating monitoring and management of complex transactions and mission-critical transactions such as those characteristic of equities trading and other financial systems.

Since these applications are network-centric, the challenge for vendors is to combine network-focused functionality with application-focused insights. The next few years will be pivotal for this market because its success relies on the ability of network vendors to make the paradigm shift to applications and to

---

[6]While the OSI model of networking has seven layers, Layer 8 refers to a hypothetical layer above Layer 7 (application) layer, often called the user layer. In reality, there is no Layer 8; however this is a sort of technical shorthand describing the applications that developers write and with which humans interact. One source for additional information on the OSI model is searchnetworking.techtarget.com/definition/OSI.

partner with application management vendors with similar vision. This will likely be a case where the most flexible and visionary vendors will be the most successful in the marketplace.

Theoretically, if all network connection points could be instrumented, this category of products could provide a way to automate 99% of the work involved in discovering, modeling, mapping, and monitoring virtually every transaction traversing a company's network. Observation of network traffic at wire-speed provides a basis for analysis of virtually all traffic interchanges for relevant content.

Today, a handful of network-focused solutions utilizes such analysis to support real-time application optimization, real-time reporting, troubleshooting, and **transaction management**. As analytics become increasingly sophisticated and as physical storage and processing power substantially escalate to support real time analytics, this product segment will likely be a primary data/metrics source for the fully automated data centers of the future. This type of real-time analysis will be essential for tracking and monitoring cloud bursts, dynamic deployments supported by **software-defined networking**, and similar automated functions.

ADVANCED IT ANALYTICS LAYER

AIA is EMA's term for analyzing operational big data for a variety of use cases. These include optimizing service performance, minimizing security issues, managing change, and optimizing capacity across internal IT and the extended enterprise (partners, service providers, suppliers, etc.). This data is also ultimately utilized for governing IT more effectively in support of the business it serves. This layer provides the "secret sauce" that distinguishes one vendor from another in virtually all the other layers. While it's not difficult to collect metrics and data from SNMP, WMI, logs, and similar technical sources, the difficulty lies in how that data is analyzed, once it is available. Analytics govern the way each vendor's solution correlates, combines, understands, and processes available data. And since analytics reflect the vendor's primary intellectual property supporting APM and UEM functions, many of the algorithms and heuristic capabilities utilized in these types of solutions are patented to prevent their use by competing vendors.

USER EXPERIENCE MANAGEMENT
INTRODUCTION

The expanding diversity of execution ecosystems has elevated **UEM** in prominence. As these ecosystems increasingly incorporate cloud, hybrid, virtual technologies, **SaaS**, and so on into transaction execution, UEM becomes one of the few constant and meaningful barometers for successful application delivery. EMA research bears this out. One study showed that UEM accelerated benefits from **cloud computing** across the board; benefits included accelerated service deployments, reductions in operational costs, and reductions in management complexity. It also found that service providers were nearly twice as likely to increase revenue from their cloud-related services by using UEM-related technologies for service monitoring.

There are diverse opinions regarding where UEM solutions fit on the enterprise management spectrum. Often the distinctions between APM and UEM definitions are very vendor-specific. Some view UEM as part of APM, while others view it as an adjunct, add-on function. The right answer is that UEM is both; indeed, multiple vendors have incorporated UEM functionality into APM solutions, providing customers with a consolidated view of application performance as experienced by the user in context to underlying hardware and software infrastructure elements.

From the perspective of the EMA Application Management Semantic Model shown in Fig. 12.4, UEM solutions are classified as part of the network layer because they focus on the performance of a single transaction or application as it traverses the network. Instead of simply doing silo monitoring focused on a single infrastructure element, UEM solutions track performance of a given transaction or user action across silos at the execution level. Depending on the type of product, UEM solutions may or may not link end-to-end execution with underlying execution elements. As a result, while some do provide information relevant to root-cause analysis, none provide the comprehensive visibility and analytics supporting root-cause analysis that APM solutions are built to deliver.

Because some UEM solutions—including those leveraging synthetic transactions—require no instrumentation on the platforms they monitor, they are the preferred monitoring platform for services delivered via the public cloud. More than 40% of today's IT organizations indicate that cloud application deployments are causing them to reevaluate management solution portfolios, and most of those without UEM solutions in place are considering purchases of these solutions. UEM solutions range from relatively inexpensive, compared to full-fledged APM solutions, to very expensive. Similarly, while some solutions require only minimal skills to manage and use, others require highly skilled coders and/or network engineers. Regardless of the specifics, these solutions (as a group) provide the number one way IT organizations plan to monitor and manage end-to-end transactions that access the cloud.

UEM solutions are specifically designed to monitor availability, as well as performance as experienced by the end user. They encompass a range of technology types. For example, active (synthetic transaction) and passive (**real user monitoring**) monitoring technologies, as well as client-side instrumentation and web server/browser instrumentation, all deliver visibility to specific aspects of overall performance and therefore provide insight on the user experience.

While each of these perspectives yields a partial view of application performance, most companies prefer to monitor mission-critical applications from multiple perspectives. The closer a company can get to end-to-end monitoring via automation, the less time is spent on triage and root-cause analysis. Suite solutions, encompassing both APM and UEM capabilities, do all of this by correlating and analyzing metrics from multiple locations into a single view of application performance. Often, these solutions pull in insights from infrastructure components, such as load balancers and middleware, to complete the end-to-end picture.

TYPES OF USER EXPERIENCE MANAGEMENT SOLUTIONS

Table 12.2 summarizes the key UEM product types and the primary functions of each type. The following section covers each product type in additional detail.

Active or synthetic transaction monitoring (synthetic transactions): Synthetic transactions, sometimes called robot transactions, are script-based tests that run at specified intervals against specified execution environments. They monitor transaction performance by automating the process of running tests against the application being monitored. These types of products are widely available, are capable of monitoring performance across the Internet, and provide an excellent entry point into UEM.

Synthetic transactions test performance and availability regardless of whether users are on a system or not. However, since they have little or no visibility of the underlying technology supporting the transaction, they are primarily used for high-level performance/availability analysis versus root-cause analysis. They yield two types of information. First, they test whether an actual transaction can be completed, in other words, whether the system is available or not. They also quantify the time spent for

Table 12.2 User Experience Management Products and Features

UEM Product/Capability Type	Function
Active or synthetic transaction monitoring	Synthetic transactions, sometimes called robot transactions, are script-based tests that run against an application at regular intervals
Passive or observed transaction monitoring	Also known as Real User Monitoring (or RUM), these tools leverage appliances placed at strategic points across the data center and/or end-user workstation to watch network or data flows, typically HTTP/HTTPS and similar
Browser injection	Monitor interactions between the web server and the browser by injecting code during execution
Client-side monitoring	Monitor performance and availability from the perspective of the user workstation

the transaction to complete, in other words, performance of the application. Unlike RUM, they do not require that anyone is actually working on the system. In other words, they monitor actual execution time, not the actual user experience. For this reason, they are often used for unattended testing. For example, many IT organizations run synthetic transactions around the clock regardless of whether or not users are on the system. This means that if something goes down overnight, the problem can be detected and fixed before users arrive and sign on in the morning.

Synthetic transactions start with scripting. Scripts are developed using programming languages or by point and click graphical interfaces, depending on the product. The scripts simulate a sequence of actions that a user might perform in the process of performing a task, such as entering a purchase order. The script is then run at given intervals against the system where purchase orders are entered—the company's enterprise resource planning system, for example.

These types of solutions are available as on-premises or cloud-based services. For example, cloud-based synthetic monitoring solutions have been available in the marketplace for quite some time from vendors such as Keynote and Gomez (now part of Dynatrace).

- Limitations: While these solutions advise IT support teams about basic performance and availability, the limitation is that most cannot pinpoint the source of a problem and why it is occurring. In addition, scripts often require maintenance if the underlying application changes, and some basic solutions even require script updates when a given web page changes. In addition, performance or availability issues vary significantly based on the origin of script execution. For example, if scripts are run within a company's **firewall**, they give little indication of what the user experience might look like from a remote office or on a mobile device.
- Use cases: These types of transactions are ideal for specific use cases. Since they are capable of monitoring performance whether or not users are on the system, they are often deployed as an early warning system to notify IT teams of execution issues occurring during off hours. Unlike real-user monitoring (RUM) solutions, they can test web-based applications running over the **WAN** or the Internet. Since they can also be run from or to multiple external locations, they are also useful for comparing performance across locations in corporate environments with multiple worldwide offices. IT executives often want to compare performance across geographies to ensure that contracted service levels are being maintained across the globe. Finally, synthetic transactions can be used to monitor internal or customer users, since no instrumentation is required to be installed on the endpoint.

Passive or observed transaction monitoring (RUM from the network): Products in this category are at the high end costwise and typically require network-focused skills to deploy and operate. RUM solutions monitor end-to-end transaction performance (for web and/or nonweb applications) from the perspective of the network, often collecting metrics from network taps[7] or span ports.[8] These types of solutions have visibility of the actual user actions, underlying network traffic, and interactions occurring during transaction execution; users must be on the system for these types of solutions to yield value.

RUM solutions see all network traffic traversing the monitored port. Virtually all are smart enough to analyze and report on specific types of Layer 7 traffic, including well-known protocols such as **FTP** and **HTTP**. However, an increasing number are also able to recognize and track Layer 8 traffic generated by commercial software packages developed by well-known business application vendors. They recognize these solutions using a combination of built-in analytics and the execution fingerprints of the commercial application. Some such solutions go deeper, utilizing packet analysis to actually break open the packets traversing the network to see the data contained in the packet, or even the payload. In other words, these solutions would be able to watch transactions to intelligently track sales information incoming from a website in real time, and so on.

RUM solutions give very deep insight into actual information flows, such as messaging and call sequences traversing the network. Since these message flows are the glue that binds transactions together, these network-oriented products can yield very useful application-related information. They can contribute valuable insight into the automated creation of topology models, for example, since they can see which nodes are talking to others and how they interact.

Because they have visibility to actual network traffic, these solutions can be very effective for general troubleshooting purposes. For example, one company experiencing application slowdowns every day at noon used a product of this type to trace the source to the fact that employees were turning on Internet radio while they ate lunch at their desks, leaving business-critical applications bandwidth-constrained in terms of network availability.

- Limitations: Network monitoring delivers visibility to network traffic and device-to-device interactions within a company's internal boundaries. Once the transaction exits organizational borders to the public Internet, for example, transaction visibility is lost. Some products in this class can track egress and reentry via transaction tagging; however, this capability varies by vendor. In contrast, server monitoring agents can passively observe transactions and interactions on any manageable endpoint. Cloud-based virtual servers, for example, can be included in the end-to-end monitoring ecosystem, as long as the cloud customer has the ability to provision an agent on the cloud-based system. In other words, once a transaction exits organizational boundaries, agents installed on the application server can take over end-to-end monitoring, if this feature is built into the monitoring solution provided by the vendor.

---

[7]A network tap is an external monitoring device that mirrors the traffic that passes between two network nodes. A tap (test access point) is a hardware device inserted at a specific point in the network to monitor data (from searchnetworking.techtarget.com/definition/Network-tap, accessed 2/15/2016).

[8]Port mirroring, also known as SPAN (switched port analyzer), is a method of monitoring network traffic. With port mirroring enabled, the switch sends a copy of all network packets seen on one port (or an entire VLAN) to another port, where the packet can be analyzed (from www.miarec.com/faq/what-is-port-mirroring, accessed 2/15/2016).

- Use cases: Since this class of solutions gathers data from network spans and taps, they are most useful for monitoring applications executing within the customer's own network. However, they can monitor performance of external clouds accessed by applications by watching egress (when a transaction leaves the data center) and ingress (when the transaction returns from the cloud). Comparing these two gives a quantification of time spent off premises. This is a useful metric when troubleshooting performance problems for **hybrid cloud** application configurations in which execution spans on premises and cloud. Finally, network-focused monitoring is best suited to monitoring internal or customer users, since, in most cases, these solutions have no visibility of external or public networks.

Passive or observed transaction monitoring (RUM from the application server): This set of solutions monitors network and user interactions from the perspective of the application server. Code-focused agent capabilities watch applications as they traverse Java or .NET platforms, while network interactions can be tracked by intercepting information from the network interfaces on each server. Although most such solutions are instrumented via agents installed on application servers, in some cases other types of servers and devices can also be instrumented depending on the types of agents provided by the RUM solution vendor.

- Limitations: While agent-based management systems are in wide use and such systems deliver very deep insight into applications, transactions, dependencies, and code, many companies find that the process of installing and maintaining hundreds or thousands of agents requires a significant amount of staff time. The resource overhead involved in managing the management system is also higher than that of network-focused RUM, for example, since installed agents talk to a centralized analytics and reporting server. So, in addition to installing agents, customers are also required to install and maintain the server. This has been alleviated by some vendors of agent-based solutions that moved analytics and reporting to the cloud. In this scenario, the link between agent and server is achieved via a virtual private network link, which adds security by shielding sensitive IP-address and topology data from unwanted intruders.
- Use cases: The network-focused RUM solutions described above monitor network and device traffic within a given company's operational boundaries. Once the transaction exits organizational borders to the public Internet, for example, transaction visibility is lost. In contrast, server monitoring agents can passively observe transactions and interactions on any manageable endpoint. Cloud-based virtual servers, for example, can be included in the end-to-end monitoring ecosystem, as long as the cloud customer has the ability to provision an agent on the cloud-based system.

Browser injection: This type of end user monitoring monitors interactions between the web server and the browser and, often, between the user and the application. In this scenario, the web server injects code into the browser, enabling monitoring of web traffic and performance as experienced by the user.

- Limitations: Products with injection capabilities are rarely available as standalone solutions. Instead, they add value to APM or UEM solutions by providing a depth of insight into actions on the endpoint that are not readily available via any other monitoring technique.
- Use cases: Since only the web server is instrumented, browser injection is one of the best ways to monitor web interactions as experienced by customers and other external users. Depending on the analytics capabilities delivered by the vendor as part of the analytics/reporting server, solutions of

this nature can yield detailed insights into web interactions impacting customer satisfaction or revenue. Browser injection provides accurate insights into user interactions with a web application, which can assist developers and marketing personnel in identifying user responses to the various steps of a sales transaction. Browser injection can, for example, track user actions to determine the points at which transactions are abandoned within a shopping cart application. This type of information can be used to make price adjustments and/or application redesigns, either of which may lead customers to complete future transactions.

Client-side monitoring: Client-side monitoring provides the best way to deliver comprehensive visibility to what has been called "the last two feet" of a transaction. This class of solutions delivers visibility to metrics and events on the desktop or mobile device, which other solutions lack. Like other products in the UEM/APM categories, these solutions also rely on a central server to aggregate, analyze, and correlate metrics and deliver real-time alerting and after-the-fact reports on the findings.

Client-side UEM solutions use actual client-side instrumentation to gather information about all things related to the internal customer and his or her workstation. They rely on agents installed on the endpoint to provide deep monitoring of the actions and experiences of internal users. This solution category is particularly useful for diagnosing application problems with sources originating on the endpoint. For example, old, underpowered PCs, software conflicts, and poorly configured devices can all impact perceived performance and are best diagnosed at the endpoint.

Due to their deep visibility to users and endpoints, as well as the fact that they are typically installed on every user's workstation, they provide unparalleled support for user management as well. They may, for example, reveal the need for user training in the use of an application, or for a device or network upgrade.

- Limitations: While these solutions provide deep visibility to the endpoint and some visibility back into the data center, they lack full visibility into end-to-end execution as the transaction traverses the data center. This means that while they are very good at quantifying the user experience, as solo solutions they lack the comprehensive breadth required to diagnose the root cause of the majority of problems not originating on the endpoint. In an effort to close this gap, endpoint monitoring vendors often partner with traditional APM vendors. Integrations between traditional APM and endpoint monitoring can provide the best of both worlds, yielding detailed correlations of endpoint behavior with application performance that cannot be equaled without endpoint instrumentation.
- Use cases: These solutions are ideal for supporting applications running on any physical or virtual Windows-based desktop. Depending on the vendor, they may also support mobile devices and native **mobile applications**. Granular insight into Citrix XenApp, **VDI**, Rich Client, Java and **Rich Internet Applications (RIAs)**, and asynchronous capabilities are available, depending on the specific product.

SUMMARY

Analytics, UEM, and APM are taking center stage as companies find that cloud, mobile, and container-supported software deployments are complicating the task of application support. With growing on-premises complexity and the march to the public cloud, APM and UEM solutions have become essential tools for development, DevOps, and operations personnel. These groups need faster, better, and cheaper ways to test, monitor, and manage application performance.

While APM and UEM solutions can help to ensure a high-quality user experience, the capabilities of a given tool or solution depend largely on the instrumentation and proprietary analytics delivered by the vendor. Products capable of observing and learning from their environments can minimize hands-on application support requirements, maximize staff and resource utilization, reduce business risk, and optimize application quality.

From a capability perspective, the combination of APM and UEM functions provides flexible, comprehensive coverage for transactions spanning cloud, mobile, and web. Analytics operating on combined metrics from real user interactions, infrastructure monitoring, and synthetic monitoring provide performance visibility and root-cause analysis regardless of whether users are on the system or not. This combination of capabilities enables an APM solution to preemptively monitor transactions, detect topology changes on an ongoing basis, and analyze real user metrics for UEM optimization. These are differentiating capabilities that are available primarily in high-end APM solutions.

In recent years, those APM solutions capable of supporting collectors and metrics from third-party solutions have become particularly attractive to medium-sized to enterprise-sized companies. Interoperability—the ability to share metrics with and consume metrics from third-party systems—maximizes the value proposition of existing management tools investments.

KEY TAKEAWAYS

- Traditionally, applications were supported with a combination of silo monitoring and tribal knowledge—knowledge built from the experience of the hands-on specialists supporting a company's enterprise applications. However, IT ecosystems have now become so massive and complex that it is no longer possible to manage them with silo knowledge alone.
- Analytics capable of transforming data and metrics into a human readable application or transaction perspective are what separates actual application monitoring from relatively simple silo monitoring.
- Analytics add the context necessary to understand the role of each moving part in end-to-end execution, a viewpoint that is absolutely critical for rapid—and eventually automated—problem determination and resolution. Without this context, these solutions would simply be operational data stores versus true tools capable of intelligent insight into application ecosystems.
- APM and UEM are not one-size-fits-all terms. There is a wide variety of permutations and tools options in each group.
- APM tools can be a unifying factor providing a common language and viewpoint for cross-functional teams with diverse training and skills. Particularly when such tools are capable of gathering data from multiple sources (data center hardware and software, network-focused metrics, application execution data, etc.), they create a centralized application perspective that is virtually impossible to duplicate manually or via tribal knowledge across teams.
- The expanding diversity of execution ecosystems has elevated UEM in prominence. As these ecosystems increasingly incorporate cloud, hybrid, virtual technologies, SaaS, and such into transaction execution, UEM becomes one of the few constant and meaningful barometers for successful application delivery.

Examples of vendors with products in this space:

Apica
AppDynamics
AppFirst
ASG
Appnomic
Aternity
BlazeMeter
BMC
Catchpoint
CA Technologies
Dyn (Acquired by Oracle)
Dynatrace
Dell Software
EMC
ExtraHop
HP
IBM
Idera
ManageEngine
Nastel
New Relic
NetScout
Netuitive
Push Technology
Riverbed
SmartBear
SOASTA
Splunk
Stackify
Sumo Logic

MANAGING CONTAINERIZED APPLICATIONS

In light of today's competitive realities, as outlined in our industry vision, enterprises must utilize leading-edge technologies like private PaaS and containerized apps to remain agile.
Bart Copeland

Virtualization will always have a segment, but generally people don't want to virtualize the whole operating system. They just want to run their app in a container.
Jevgeni Kabanov

INTRODUCTION

The introduction of containerized **applications** marks a pivotal moment in the trajectory of information technology (IT). The container concept was adapted from the freight industry, where the term "**containerization**" is used to describe a technique to simplify and speed up the transportation of freight in a secure and efficient manner. Different types of freight are placed in separate uniform size containers and transported using any number of different transportation methods, such as planes, trains, trucks, and ships to specified locations. Once packed, the freight is not unpacked until it reaches its final destination. In IT, the term "container" is applied to a technique whereby an application and data (freight) are securely and efficiently transported over local area and virtual networks to specific locations, such as desktop or laptop computers, servers, mobile devices, remote data centers, and public and private clouds, and are not unpacked until they reach their final destination (Fig. 13.1).

Containerization is sometimes referred to as lightweight virtualization or **container-based virtualization**. It is a Linux-based technology where a common operating system kernel runs multiple instances on a single operating system, eliminating the need for each instance to run on its own operating system (Fig. 13.2).

Although it has been heralded as the latest major technology shift in the IT industry, containers are not a new technology. Application containers have been used for more than a decade by virtual private server providers. However, as these companies switched to **virtual machines (VMs)** to get better performance, interest in container technology declined. Recently, IT organizations began to call for tools that provide more rapid deployment of applications. This led **platform as a service (PaaS)** vendors to adopt and standardize container technology to provide isolation and resource control, which consequently led to a renewed enthusiastic interest in containers. In fact, some analysts have speculated that containers are the next logical step in server consolidation.

FIGURE 13.1

Freight containers vis-a-vis application containers.

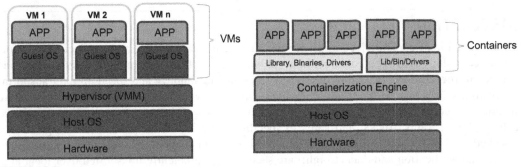

FIGURE 13.2

Hypervisor-based versus container-based virtualized architecture.

WHY CONTAINERIZE?

The most valuable benefit containers provide is a portable, reliable format that runs applications on a variety of hosts and reduces memory requirements, increases ease of migration and use of applications, enables faster deployment and backup, and frees up server capacity. In contrast to hypervisor-based virtualization, containers use the same host operating system repeatedly and the role of the hypervisor is handled by a **containerization engine** that is installed on top of the operating system. In this way, the container is notably smaller than a VM. The underlying concept of containerization is that virtual instances share a *single* host operating system and relevant libraries and drivers. As a consequence, significantly more containers can be hosted by a host server. It was estimated that 10–100 times the number of container instances can be hosted, compared with the number of VM instances on the same server. However, one of the reasons that containers lost some of their appeal was that applications all relied on a common OS kernel, so this approach could only work for applications that shared the same OS version.

THE REVITALIZATION OF CONTAINERS

One of the leaders driving the renewed interest in containers is **Docker**, an open-source project developed by dotCloud, a PaaS vendor. Docker was initially launched as an interactive tutorial in 2013 to address the issues of the lack of container portability caused by reliance on a common OS and the high level of Linux kernel experience required to develop containers. Docker offers a containerization engine that has an easy-to-use packaging format that envelops an application with its dependencies and container management tools, which empower a wider range of individual developers. The Docker containerization engine enables an application to run across a different Linux OS and is portable. In addition, developers can use any language to write an application and easily move the application across different devices. Software developers flocked to try this new approach, and within a year, Amazon and Red Hat had provided commercial support for Docker. Since then, a number of other vendors followed suit with products that rival or improve on the Docker concept of container-based systems. These include CoreOS Rocket, Cloud Foundry Garden, Google Omega, and Linux Containers (LXC).

To address the complex coordination issues associated with deploying multiple containers, that is, a **container cluster** or **container pool**, Google developed Kubernetes to manage a cluster of Linux containers as a single system. In the same way that containers empower individual developers by reducing much of the overhead associated with deploying a single container, the Kubernetes containerization cluster manager empowers teams of developers to create services involving multiple containers and directs these container clusters to follow a set of deployment rules to ensure correct operation. The ensuing **containers as a service (CaaS)** infrastructure is as reliable, fast, scalable, and flexible as any **infrastructure as a service (IaaS)** coupled with the ease of use of PaaS solutions (Fig. 13.3).

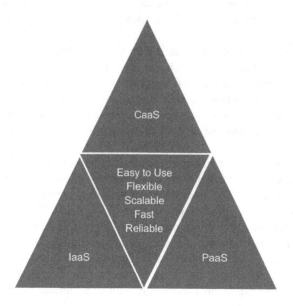

FIGURE 13.3

Evolution of the CaaS infrastructure.

At this point, it is important to note that the renewed and enthusiastic support for container-based virtualization does not mean that hypervisor-based virtualization is no longer a viable option. On the contrary, container-based virtualization and hypervisor-based virtualization should be viewed as complementary, not competing, technologies.

In different situations, they are both good choices for an IT organization, each providing a different solution to a different use case and even working together to provide the best solution. For example, if it is important that resources are distributed equally and performance is task independent, then hypervisor-based virtualization is the best choice.

Hypervisor-based virtualization is also the best fit for complex enterprise applications that depend on large data sets. On the other hand, container-based virtualization addresses scalability challenges, making it a good match for microservices-based architectures. For example, for an organization that executes many small isolated processes, container-based virtualization is the best option because it uses less overhead and performs better in those situations.

BENEFITS OF MANAGING CONTAINERIZED APPLICATIONS

From a management point of view, container-based virtualization offers new possibilities and flexibility for specific workloads because it enables applications to be available and quick to deploy. Unlike virtualization, which runs separate operating systems on each VM and thus can lead to high resource costs and more performance overhead, containerization generally simplifies application lifecycle management tasks by using a singular host OS and improving performance. In addition, the implementation of containers reduces memory requirements and consequently increases the ease of migrating applications. It also frees up server capacity for greater container storage for VMs to use, and the use of layers in containerized engines, such as Docker, improves security in application deployment.

In addition, while hypervisor-based virtualization uses resources more effectively than physical machines, container-based virtualization has shown a potential to further reduce overhead and improve the performance and utilization of data centers because everything runs on top of the same kernel. LXC is a kernel technology used in container-based virtualization that can run multiple processes in its own isolated environment. This isolation of processes can result in reduced overhead on major software deployments by decreasing deployment time, increasing application portability, and consuming fewer physical resources.

Another advantage of container-based virtualization that appeals to application development managers is increased developer productivity. Containers allow developers to write code in a standard way in any language. The number of applications inside a container can vary. Some organizations prefer the one application per container approach. This enables new stacks to be created without difficulty and applications can be built or rebuilt and managed easily but results in a large number of containers that must interact and more complex container management. Others favor multiple applications in one container, making them easier to manage but adding complexity to the building or rebuilding of applications. In either case, the increased level of efficiency introduced by containerization lends itself particularly well to a number of specific application management situations.

BALANCING MICROSERVICES IN THE CLOUD

Containerization really excels in the **microservices** architecture that are increasingly identified with cloud-native web applications. The introduction of containerization engines such as Docker, Cloud Foundry's Garden, and LXC motivated organizations to utilize the service as a means for cloud scalability. As a result, containerization is becoming increasingly popular among cloud providers. One of the largest users of containers in the cloud is Google. It is estimated that Google starts 3300 containers per second, 24 hours a day, 7 days a week. That is more than 2 billion containers per week. Google runs its container stack on Ubuntu (an open-source, Debian-based Linux operating system) with an emphasis on performance, rather than on ease of use.

To capitalize on this approach, Google developed Let Me Contain That For You (LMCTFY), its own LXC variation. LMCTFY isolates resources used by multiple applications running on a single machine and manages the workload by balancing needs of overcommitted machines with batch workloads. The fact that containers can be more densely packed on servers is a big advantage in the cloud where success or failure is measured by overall efficiency. As a result, Amazon Web Service and Microsoft are also enthusiastically embracing containers on their cloud hosts.

ENHANCING THE BRING YOUR OWN DEVICE EXPERIENCE

Containerizing applications is the predominant approach recommended by industry analysts for enhancing the bring your own device (BYOD) experience of organizations and employees. In the age of BYOD, **mobile device management (MDM)** is no longer simple. Gone are the days when corporate mobile devices were loaned to employees for business use. In the past, if a device was lost or an employee left the company, maintaining data and application security was as simple as remotely wiping all data and applications from the device. Now, when organizations set BYOD policies, administrators must consider the rights of its employees as device owners, as well as the security of organizational data and applications. In an environment where corporate and personal data coexist on personal devices, containerized enterprise mobile applications allow corporate applications and data to safely reside on personal devices under the control of the enterprise without infringing on the employee device owners' rights.

Application containerization provides each application and its data with its own secure runtime container that uses strong encryption, separate from native device encryption, and is controlled by a strong password policy. This enables IT managers to set and implement broader security policies confined to enterprise applications and implement features, such as sign-on authentication, data manipulation restrictions, and application-level encryption to protect sensitive corporate data and applications. The isolation provided by containerization reduces malware infection or privilege escalation from malicious applications on employee-owned devices. To assist in the adoption of these types of BYOD policies, it is important to preserve the look and feel of an employee's device to ensure a positive user experience. Containerization does this by securing enterprise applications without the need to cut over to a separate environment to use them. Caution still needs to be exercised, however, because containers are an effective layer in a security strategy, but the reality is that while creating a container raises the barrier of entry for data access, it will not necessarily prevent it.

INCREASING ADMINISTRATIVE CONTROL

To increase the level of administrative control, IT managers are using **app wrapping**, a useful containerization management technique. App wrapping also enhances the mobile application experience for the user. App wrapping essentially allows an administrator to take an application, implement extra security and management features on it, and redeploy it as a single containerized program. To achieve this, the mobile application management administrator must set management policies to create a set of dynamic libraries that are implemented on top of the application's native binary. For example, the policies might direct developers to add dynamic libraries to an application to make it behave differently when it is opened and determine whether authentication is required for a specific application when a certain type of communication occurs. Another management policy might be to establish whether data associated with an application can be stored on a device and/or whether file sharing is allowed. For example, app wrapping can be used to implement the BYOD security policies discussed in the previous section, thus saving time and reducing the complexity of developing mobile applications.

MANAGING THE ENTERPRISE APP STORE

Growing numbers of organizations are adopting **enterprise app stores**, which are driven by the increased use of enterprise mobile devices and the introduction of MDM. Applications that are downloaded from public app stores can disrupt IT security as well as application and procurement strategies. To overcome these issues, MDM providers are beginning to launch sophisticated app stores to enterprise and third-party applications for access by mobiles devices such as smartphones, tablets, and PCs.

Better management of the enterprise app store can be realized by effectively using containerized applications. To accomplish this, the IT organization must follow the maxim of "contain, control, and deliver." This is achieved by containerizing apps, data, and devices, controlling access based on identity and policies, and delivering a personalized app store to each user. In all cases, it is imperative that the IT organization views its enterprise app store as part of its application strategy and not its infrastructure strategy. Users must have a reason to use the enterprise app store. Therefore, the primary determinant of its success is supply and demand. To determine this, application managers must work collaboratively with **DevOps** teams to monitor downloads and usage to determine the value of its applications to users and regularly update enterprise app store offerings to reflect user needs.

TRANSFORMING THE DATA CENTER

The **containerized and modular data center facility (CMDF)** is an increasingly popular method for constructing and deploying data centers. With the introduction of this approach, the speed with which data can be handled has increased by orders of magnitude, allowing the data center to use the infrastructure more efficiently. With this new approach, IT developers can achieve faster deployments, reduced I/O latency, and lower operating and capital costs for IT managers through a set of replicable, preengineered, preassembled, and reliable components that produce the required capacity. An additional advantage is that, with a CMDF, organizations can increase or decrease their data centers' capacity in smaller, prescribed steps. As a result, for many organizations, containerized data centers were viewed as a quick fix to address an existing capacity shortfall. However, caution should be used when determining a CMDF's suitability as a strategic asset. It is important for CIOs and CTOs to assess not only facility needs but also the organization's overall IT architecture and its need for large-scale deployment of computing capacity before proceeding.

AUTOMATING DEVOPS

The introduction of containerized engine tools led to the automation of DevOps principles. By automating the software release pipeline, containers allow individual components and services to be viewed as discrete components that facilitate debugging or analyzing an application's architecture. Now integration-and-test means testing the relationship and interactions of the containerized modules, and management of the pipelines now becomes management of the containers. Instead of focusing on coding, IT operations personnel are freed up to work on business problems such as load balancing, capacity planning, disaster recovery, and distribution.

CHALLENGES OF MANAGING CONTAINERIZED APPLICATIONS

Despite the advantages that the container-based virtualization approach offers, it has its drawbacks. Some of these challenges and ways to manage them are discussed next:

Image Sprawl—The ease with which Docker-like images can be created can lead to image sprawl, which creates the same problems with managing security and compliance as VM sprawl, which was discussed in the previous chapter. Thus, the same management principles that apply to VM sprawl apply to image sprawl in a containerized environment.

Security and Data Confidentiality—When using containers in a mobile environment, data security can be compromised. Therefore, it is important to place applications in a secure container, that is, a third-party mobile application that acts as a storage area, authenticated and encrypted by software and governed by IT policies. This requires organizations to ask users to consent to full-device encryption and remote wipe before allowing them to use their own devices at work. Unfortunately, this can undermine the user experience.

Other considerations include cost and capability; security data containers must be purchased, deployed, and maintained. Organizations that lack established mobile application management practices may not have the necessary infrastructure to support large-scale implementation of secure containers. For these reasons, many organizations opt to use secure containers only for high-risk devices and for employees who need access to sensitive business data. Another approach, highlighted in recent research conducted by Enterprise Management Associates, is to deploy containers on top of VMs to leverage existing management tools and security practices related to VMs.

Network Management—Containers in distributed systems need advanced network support. However, the container platform was designed to assist developers in writing and testing code on a single host. This led to network management difficulties in production settings where interhost communication between containers is required. Because containers are not exposed directly to the layer-2 network, external systems that need to directly communicate with a container have to communicate with the IP of the container's host and a TCP socket. The larger the number of containers that are frequently accessed externally from the host, the greater is the complexity of network management. Fortunately, providers have acknowledged this management challenger and began to develop products to address this issue. For example, to extend network capabilities, Docker developed SocketPlane, a software-defined network technology that provides a plugin architecture for its product. SocketPlane puts control back into the hands of developers by creating an overlay network that allow containers to connect directly. Docker also created Libnetwork, an open-source project that offers an API for third-party solutions to provide network services. In contrast, Weaveworks takes an "under the hood" approach in Weave, their open-source network management offering. Weave simplifies application development and eliminates the need for developers to change their practices, code, and tools. This is accomplished through the use of Weave routers that automatically track the state of the network. These routers perform low-level networking tasks including tracking MAC addresses, encapsulating data, and routing packets.

Tooling—Containers do not share many of the same configuration attributes at the OS layer that physical and virtual servers do, nor do they have a well-developed set of tools for managing them. This means that application dependencies are no longer managed on a server or at the VM level; instead, they are managed *inside* the container. Consequently, IT personnel are required to manage the container software instead of the applications and their associated dependencies, and currently, container management tools are scarce.

One management tool that begins to address this challenge was developed by CA Technologies. Their Smart Containerization technology associates a policy describing security, performance, and support requirements with individual content, applications, or devices, thus protecting the target by enforcing policies that are appropriate to the type of content being managed. For example, a document may have a policy associated with it to prevent it from being stored locally on a device, or a mobile application may have a policy determining where it can execute. While other providers are also beginning to develop these much-needed management tools for container deployment, most of the tools are somewhat immature and open source with a resultant lack of a dedicated support structure present in proprietary software packages. In the meantime, until these emerging management tools become more mature, IT managers in large enterprises need to maintain a dedicated development staff to support containers. Unfortunately, this approach is not feasible in smaller companies that lack the necessary human resources.

Establishing Standards—Although some consider Docker as the de facto standard for container technology, at this point it is uncertain what the official standard for containers will be. However, a move is currently afoot to address this conundrum.

On June 22, 2015, the **Open Container Initiative (OCI)** was launched under the auspices of the Linux Foundation. OCI is an open-governance structure formed to expressly focus on open industry standards around container formats and runtime to ensure interoperability of different container technologies. The list of high-powered OCI sponsors is indicative of an increasingly high level of interest in and use of container-based technology. The sponsors include Apcera, AT&T, AWS, Cisco, ClusterHQ, COEOS, Datera, Docker, EMC, Fujitsu, Google, Goldman Sachs, HP, Huawei, IBM, Intel, Joyent, Kismatic, Kyup, Mesosphere, Microsoft, Midokura, Nutanix, Oracle, Pivotal, Polyverse, Rancher, Red Hat, Resin.io, SUSE, Sysdig, Twitter, Verizon, and VMware (the OCI will be addressed in greater detail in Chapter 16, "The Case for Standards").

SUMMARY

Containerization is a solution to allow software to run reliably when moved from one computing environment to another, such as a data center on a physical machine to a **virtual machine (VM)** in the cloud. Containers are much more lightweight and use far fewer resources than VMs, but are generally accepted to be somewhat less secure than VMs. As a result, it is likely that containers and virtualization will evolve into complementary, rather than competing, technologies. Although given that more and more microservices are being deployed in the cloud and containers enable faster deployment, more reliable services, and more efficient scalability and use fewer resources, it can been speculated that a greater number of next generation applications will be built using container-based virtualization rather than hypervisor-based virtualization.

Containers excel in the microservices architecture of the cloud and offer great potential for enhancing the BYOD user experience, increasing administrative control, managing the enterprise app store, transforming the data center, and automating DevOps.

However, it is important to note that containerization is not a panacea. Management challenges include network management, tooling, security issues, data confidentiality, and image sprawl. Added to these is the lack of robust management tools necessary to orchestrate a large number of containers or container clusters. This deficit is expected to be short-lived as more vendors step up to develop new tools or improve existing ones to create and manage containerized applications.

A move toward establishing common standards for containerization is under way, led by the Linux Foundation and a coalition of vendors, users, start-ups, and industry leaders. The project, known as the Open Container Initiative, expects to deliver final container standards by the end of 2017.

KEY TAKEAWAYS

- Containerization was initially understood by a select few and was unavailable to the vast majority of organizations because of the lack of Linux expertise and portability.
- The newly developed availability of containerization technologies has exponentially increased the economic advantage of microservices-based application architectures.
- Containerization and virtualization are both good choices but in different use cases.
- More management tools are needed to help manage containerized applications.
- Standards to oversee containerization are being developed by the Open Container Initiative.

APPLICATION MANAGEMENT IN A SOFTWARE-DEFINED DATA CENTER

Just as the world changed when isolated networks became the Internet, computing is about to make a quantum leap to 'data centers' abstracted from hardware that may reside in multiple physical locations. This pervasive abstraction will enable us to connect, aggregate, and configure computing resources in unprecedented ways.
Eric Knorr, Editor-in-Chief, *InfoWorld*

Enterprises will be able to use software-defined data centers to innovate with greater utilization, and cost savings on a unified platform for their applications.
Patrick Kerpan, CEO/CTO, CohesiveFT

INTRODUCTION TO THE SOFTWARE-DEFINED DATA CENTER

Enabled by the introduction of virtualization, **software-defined data centers (SDDCs)** are taking the information technology (IT) industry by storm. The goal of the SDDC is to decrease costs and increase agility, policy compliance and **security** by deploying, operating, managing, and maintaining applications. In addition, by providing organizations with their own private **cloud**, SDDCs provide greater flexibility by allowing organizations to have on-demand access to their data instead of having to request permission from their cloud provider.

It is estimated that the market share for SDDCs will grow from the current level of $22 billion to more than $77 billion in the next 5 years. As the use of SDDCs grows at this extraordinary rate, data center managers will be called up to scale their data centers exponentially at a moment's notice. Unfortunately, this is impossible to achieve using the traditional data center infrastructure.

A core belief of the SDDC concept is that the internal and external IT infrastructure must be controlled centrally and aligned with application and service requirements. The use of SDDCs is being driven by business units pressuring IT departments to accelerate their implementation. As a result, developers and application owners are quickly realizing that programming skills and cross-domain capabilities are critical requirements in their IT personnel.

The SDDC extends its focus beyond simply virtualizing servers, storage, and networking to a number of different software applications that contribute to performance improvement and more effective use of data center power use, networking, storage, and hardware. Consequently, in the SDDC, software placement and optimization decisions are based on business logic, not technical provisioning directives, requiring changes in culture, processes, structure, and technology.

Application Performance Management (APM) in the Digital Enterprise. http://dx.doi.org/10.1016/B978-0-12-804018-8.00014-0

The SDDC isolates the application layer from the physical infrastructure layer to facilitate faster and more effective deployment, **management**, and monitoring of diverse applications. This is achieved by finding each enterprise application an optimal home in a public or private cloud environment or draw from a diverse collection of resources.

FUNDAMENTAL RESOURCES OF THE SDDC

The fundamental resources of the SDDC are compute, storage, network, and security. Typically, the SDDC includes limited functionality of service portals, applications, **OS**, VM hardware, **hypervisors**, physical hardware, **software-defined networking (SDN)**, **software-defined storage (SDS)**, security layer, automation and management layers, catalogs, gateway interface module, and third-party plug-ins (Fig. 14.1).

COMPUTE (PHYSICAL AND VIRTUAL)

Traditionally, organizations maintained a combination of physical compute, legacy infrastructure, and virtualized compute nodes to support their core business applications. By stitching together these hardware and virtual components to systematically allocate resources to specific workloads, an overabundance of standalone systems emerged to monitor and manage server farms designed and sized based on projected workload. These infrastructure silos typically lead to resources that become underused, because most organizations using the traditional data center model cannot assess resource availability at a single, unified point because the tools were configured for incompatible legacy applications. As a result, an increasing number of organizations are moving toward developing enterprise-wide infrastructures to more efficiently resolve this issue.

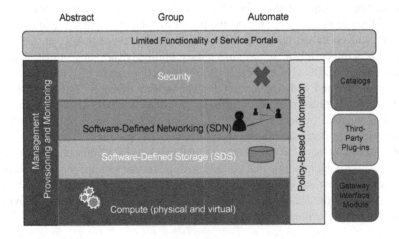

FIGURE 14.1

SDDC infrastructure architecture.

In response to changing workloads and accessibility requirements, the post–hypervisor programming environment and the cloud led to the emergence of **infrastructure as a service (IaaS)**, which offers shared infrastructure services and virtualized compute resources. Using IaaS, **virtualized data centers** can optimize the utilization of compute, storage, and networking through their hypervisors that are programmed to systematically allocate resources for specified applications. Essentially, hypervisors act as an **abstraction software layer** that virtualizes processing resources from physical hardware and integrates resources from a diversity of virtualized software-defined servers (IaaS is discussed at greater length in Chapter 5, "Application Management in the Cloud").

The resulting optimal utilization of resources decreases investment and effort associated with energy use, management overhead, software licenses, and general data center costs. In addition, it extends a data center manager's ability to monitor and create tools to support infrastructure and automation. The efficient and dynamic resource sharing enabled by software-defined server virtualization also results in balanced workloads that meet application requirements. This automatic load-balancing and increased availability is leading to a transition to even greater automation. As automation increases, so does the speed and reliability of compute-related operations and as more resources are abstracted and integrated into a software-defined model, the move to a full SDDC is possible.

SOFTWARE-DEFINED STORAGE

To realize the full benefits of the SDDC, it is necessary to include a **software-defined storage (SDS)** solution as a cost-effective way to gain real value from web-scale IT architectures. In light of unprecedented challenges in managing big data, SDS is quickly becoming an important aspect of a practical, proactive strategy for managing the rapidly increasing volume of enterprise data as organizations strive to gain greater flexibility in their IT architecture. SDS is hardware independent in that it can run on any standard server platform and has a distributed architecture that exceeds the limitations of **network attached storage (NAS)** or **storage area network (SAN)** storage. Ideally, the SDS should support standard data protocols including block, file, and object data services, run application workloads on storage nodes, and have a sophisticated management control plane to streamline and simplify access to the data. Second-generation SDS solutions, becoming available now, integrate **quality of service (QOS)** with storage services such as data protection and tiering. This approach automates QOS and provides the best opportunity for further capacity and performance optimization.

SOFTWARE-DEFINED NETWORKING

Network infrastructure must be abstracted for consumption by workloads in the SDDC. **Software-defined networking (SDN)** emerged as a critical enabler of network within the SDDC. The **Open Networking Foundation (ONF)**, a nonprofit consortium that maintains stewardship over the **OpenFlow** SDN protocol, defines SDN as the separation of the control and data planes in network devices, where the control plane is consolidated within a centralized controller that programs network flow rules into individual data plane devices.[1] In this way, SDN's ability to use a single, logically

---

[1] What is SDN? https://www.opennetworking.org/sdn-resources/sdn-definition.

isolated computing infrastructure within which discrete networks can easily be created allows organizations to move from production to development to test. Interestingly, decoupling the control plane and data plane was not the most important SDN characteristic identified by respondents to a 2016 Enterprise Management Associates End-User Research Report on the impacts of SDN and network virtualization on network management.[2] Table 14.1 shows the percentage of respondents who identified a variety of defining SDN characteristics that are important to the solutions they implement.

The OpenFlow protocol identified by respondents to the Enterprise Management Associates (EMA) survey was created by the **Open Networking Foundation (ONF)** to standardize critical elements of the SDN architecture and is the first standard interface designed specifically for SDN. The standard is designed to provide high-performance, granular traffic control across the network devices of multiple vendors. Table 14.2 shows the benefits that can be achieved by using the OpenFlow protocol.

OpenFlow began as a Stanford University research project in 2008. Vendors and large enterprises started productizing the technology and implementing SDN in 2011. Data center mega-user Google built its own SDN switches and was the first company to build a global software-driven network. Meanwhile, vendors including Microsoft, VMware, Cisco, and Brocade, released OpenFlow-friendly products, or other SDN technologies, such as software overlays or policy-based networking.

Table 14.1 SDN Defining Characteristics Important to Solution Implementation	
SDN Characteristic	**Percent (%)**
Centralized controller	35
Low-cost hardware	28
Fluid network architecture	25
Open source software	24
Software-only solutions with no hardware refresh	24
OpenFlow protocol	21
Decoupling the control plane and data plane	11

Table 14.2 Benefits of SDN OpenFlow Protocol
Centralized management and control of networking devices from multiple vendors
Improved automation and management
Rapid innovation through new network capabilities and services without the need to configure individual devices or wait for vendor releases
Programmability by operators, enterprises, independent software vendors and users
Increased network reliability and security
More granular network control with ability to apply comprehensive and wide-ranging policies at session, user, device, and application levels
Better end-user experience
Adapted from Software-Defined Networking: The New Norm for Networks, April 13, 2012. Accessible from: https://www.opennetworking.org/images/stories/downloads/sdn-resources/white-papers/wp-sdn-newnorm.pdf.

---

[2]McGillicuddy, S., 2016. Managing Tomorrow's Networks: The Impacts of SDN and Network Virtualization on Network Management. Enterprise Management Associates.

SECURITY

Overall, the SDDC is considered more secure than a virtualized data center that uses the cloud. The use of an SDN within the SDDC allows organizations to more easily and effectively secure their SDDC by microsegmenting the separate networks. Trying to achieve this with physical components and firewalls would be nearly impossible. A good example of this is a security improvement project undertaken by Starbucks. In the light of high-profile security breaches in companies such as Target, Neiman Marcus, and PF Changs, Starbucks sought tenders to improve the security of its data by segmenting it in an East vs. West fashion. In response, they received bids of at least $10 million and faced the onerous task of purchasing, implementing, and maintaining 90 physical firewalls. This appeared to be an almost impossible task to Starbucks' management, who simply could not justify the cost, time, or expertise it would take. As an alternative, they turned to an SDDC approach. By adopting VMware's NSX software-driven networking tool, they were able to use their existing network, and the total cost of the security improvement was $3 million. By choosing the SDDC approach to deliver automated, high-performance microsegmentation security inside their data center, Starbucks greatly improved their data center security for a fraction of the cost of the proposed $10 million traditional hardware-based approach.

WHY MOVE TO AN SDDC?

From a business perspective, the main reasons for transitioning to the SDDC are increased security, better business alignment of the IT infrastructure, and rapid application provisioning. Traditionally, data centers were characterized by dedicated and isolated hardware plagued by low resource utilization and very limited flexibility. Subsequently, second generation virtualized data centers used consolidated virtualized servers to improve resource utility. The SDDC can create a more flexible environment in which enterprise applications can be reconfigured and supported. The SDDC achieves this by reducing the steps needed to decrease the time it takes to deploy workloads into the production environment. In addition, the SDDC facilitates application definition and the specification of resource needs, including compute, storage, networking, and security by grouping the defined applications and needs to create a simplified application supported by the SDDC. Essentially, converting to the SDDC enables automation and provisions self-service for users by restructuring the data center software and the virtualization administrator's role to provide IaaS. The resulting simplistic application designs enable organizations to achieve greater agility and flexibility in their operations management. This supports and simplifies **application management**.

A software-defined infrastructure also accelerates the use of managed services that perform basic administration and configuration, as well as moving data center staff to performing value-added business services and managing the data created. Software-defined server virtualization enabled organizations to use SDDCs to more efficiently use resources, automate and balance workload, and minimize the need for physical hardware in the data center.

Transitioning to the SDDC enables organizations to achieve optimized utilization of resources, capacity on demand, greater business–IT alignment, improved agility, and flexibility of operations managements and cost savings (Fig. 14.2).

Typically, there are two approaches to implementing the SDDC project. Organizations can either make existing infrastructure more accessible to developers or adopt new infrastructure that offers comprehensive APIs for developer access. Large enterprises tend to add programmability to their existing

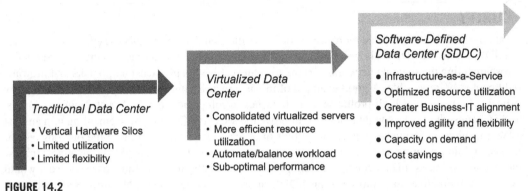

FIGURE 14.2

Data center evolution.

infrastructure while small and medium-sized organizations are more likely to adopt new programmable infrastructure. Very few organizations of any size follow a "rip and replace" approach to building the SDDC; instead, the vast majority gradually replace existing infrastructure and layer new programmable elements on top of legacy data center technologies.

Ultimately, the SDDC requires a change in culture, processes, organizational structure, and technology with a focus on deploying and constantly updating applications in the most efficient and effective manner. This is an ambitious vision that depends on a "logic layer" that is able to make policy-based application placement and management decisions by integrating with traditional IT disciplines, such as performance management, **capacity management**, and lifecycle management. Once the placement decision is made, orchestration and automation capabilities are needed to provision computer, network, and storage resources and the required software in a secure manner. In short, within the SDDC, software placement and optimization decisions are based on business logic instead of technical provisioning instructions.[3]

MANAGING SDDCs

Good management is critical to adopting and operating the SDDC and requires a very different approach from that used to manage a traditional data center. At first glance, the software architecture of the SDDC is easier to interchange than its hardware-based equivalent and might appear to be easier to manage, but that is not the case. There are numerous traps that organizations can fall into when transitioning from a hardware-based to software-defined data center. For example, it is important to verify existing configurations before exposing them to software-defined management because misconfigurations can cause major problems faster and be more difficult to identify in an automated environment.

---

[3]See part one of the EMA series of four blog posts on the baseline definition of the SDDC: http://blogs.enterprisemanagement.com/torstenvolk/2012/08/16/softwaredefined-datacenter-part-1-4-basics/.

It is also important to remember that traditional hardware-based data centers consist of tightly integrated vertical silos, each of which has a dedicated infrastructure tied to specific applications and has its own management tools, people, and processes. In the SDDC, these integrated vertical silos are transformed into loosely coupled horizontal layers consisting of abstracted infrastructure and applications with their own single set of tools that manage each horizontal layer regardless of the infrastructure or application.

In this type of environment, it is important to recognize that managing the SDDC is not just about managing virtual **CPU** and memory. First, each infrastructure topology layer must be addressed separately and the relationships between them must be understood so that problems across the different layers can be properly correlated and resolved. Next, data must be gathered to help make intelligent operations management decisions, including metric data from devices and element managers on a specific time cycle, logs to identify problems and issues, critical issues including faults, configurations settings to understand the current state, and configuration changes to determine root causes of problems. Finally, intelligent management operations include automating problem identification and resolution, monitoring performance, identifying abnormalities, conducting capacity and change management, managing logs, ensuring the SDDC conforms to best practices and more importantly to the organization's desired configuration and security stance, and, finally, being prepared to troubleshoot by searching the data collected by the software solution used in the SDDC.

The following sections discuss the different application management techniques needed to apply these principles and realize the full potential of the SDDC.

IMPLEMENT CENTRALIZED, POLICY-DRIVEN, AND APPLICATION-CENTRIC MANAGEMENT STYLE

Traditionally, data center managers had to focus on purchasing equipment, managing facilities, and equipment in their own data center and that of third parties. To reap the full benefit of the SDDC, managers have the added burden of carefully monitoring and controlling performance, compliance status, costs, and self-service provisioning for the SDDC users. Consequently, managing infrastructure in a centralized, policy-driven, and application-centric manner is generally regarded as the heart of SDDC management. This type of approach is a strategic shift that requires drastic changes in culture, organization, and processes, not just a change in technology. An application-centric and automated infrastructure is particularly important when addressing the networking component of the SDDC. To achieve this, it is critical to leverage software-defined networking and network virtualization that change the nature of the underlying network that supports SDDC, including the physical network devices and elements using control protocols such as OpenFlow.

CREATE BLENDED TEAMS WITH CROSS-DOMAIN EXPERTISE

As business units exert more and more pressure on their IT department to accelerate the SDDC adoption process, IT application and operations professionals have to obtain new skills such as programming and focusing on the development of **cross-domain expertise**. Consequently, IT managers have to provide their staff with a more well-rounded set of skills and a greater breadth of knowledge in their new roles.

To be successful, SDDC managers must coordinate diverse groups of people and infrastructure as part of their day-to-day duties. In large organizations, this might include architecture, engineering, integration, operations, and project management teams. A logical blending of teams might be architecture/engineering and integration/operations with a stand-alone project management team to oversee planning, execution, monitoring/controlling, and the ultimate closure of a project.

ORCHESTRATE A HANDS-ON APPROACH

As the blended SDDC teams emerge, it is essential that managers ensure teams are more hands-on than in a traditional data center and assume new responsibilities, such as evaluating partners, providing consistent management and security of all internal and external access points, and finding providers who include software developers on their teams. SDDC managers will also need to focus on ensuring that all teams are functioning and performing efficiently in managing the movement and security of on-site and off-site data, and motivating the newly formed teams to be more aggressive in automating discovery, provisioning, and location tasks with respect to space and power in the SDDC. Needless to say, the difficulty in orchestrating the hands-on approach will vary somewhat depending on the types of organization, and exponentially between organizations of different sizes. For example, upgrading a small number of **virtual machines** in a small–to–medium-sized enterprise can be relatively easy, while the level of complexity involved in upgrading 5000 virtual machines with intricate dependencies in a large Fortune 100 company would be far more difficult.

Temporarily switching staff between teams can be an effective way to achieve this. For instance, each month a small percentage of the architecture/engineering team would be moved to the integration/operations team for a week or two and vice versa, to allow them to appreciate the roles and challenges of the other team. This approach proved to be very effective by proponents of the **DevOps** concept in breaking down barriers between teams of analysts, developers, and operations personnel.

CULTIVATE POLICY-DRIVEN INFRASTRUCTURE PROVISIONING AND MANAGEMENT PROCESS

Although a number of strategically aligned vendors including EMC II, Pivotal, RSA, VCE, Virtustream, and VMware united to form the **EMC Federation** to provide customer solutions and choice for the software-defined enterprise and the cloud, there are currently no central management technologies to control and unify the entire data center and the public cloud. However, an IT operations mindset that focuses on reinventing the infrastructure provisioning and management process in a much more policy-driven manner can lead to successfully implementing the SDDC. Clearly, the SDDC cannot be implemented in the form of a technology project but rather constitutes a concept that describes guidelines that follow the multiyear vision of entirely closing the traditional gap between enterprise IT and the business.

INCREASE CAPACITY MANAGEMENT FOCUS

To preserve the CAPEX and OPEX savings realized by virtualization, the cloud, and the SDDC, the use of capacity management tools must be optimized. Too much guesswork results in overprovisioning, which often fails to deliver desired performance and reliability. As a result, a more intelligent approach needs to be taken in initial placement of applications and the ongoing optimization of application environments.

USE A MULTI-VIRTUALIZATION AND MULTI-CLOUD MANAGEMENT APPROACH

To enhance performance, costs, security, and SLA requirements, application and IT operations teams must assign the most effective selection of physical, virtual, and cloud platforms. Management software such as CSC ServiceMesh, Convirture, ASG Cloud Factor, or IBM SmartCloud Orchestrator provides this type of policy-driven central management capability.

CREATE AND PACKAGE REPEATABLE SOFTWARE AND INFRASTRUCTURE CONFIGURATION

To optimally run an application, configuration management is a critical component in enabling IT teams to consistently provision and manage the various SDDC resources. Configuration management also enables testing or simulating system updates and the consistent and continuous enforcement of policies and best practices across the SDDC, including the semiprivate and public cloud infrastructure. The ability to centrally create and package **repeatable software and infrastructure configuration** for application deployment is a core building block of the SDDC and can be delivered through configuration management software, such as Puppet, Chef, or CSC ServiceMesh. To achieve this, corporate policy must be in place to govern how developers or application administrators publish their applications to an environment of their choice. Only then can an organization take full advantage of all the components of the internal and public infrastructure.

TAKE ADVANTAGE OF IT VENDOR SUPPORT

IT vendors can provide assistance in the form of professional consulting and implementation services in the areas of "legacy infrastructure integration" and improved "IT alignment with business requirements."

CHALLENGES OF MANAGING AN SDDC

Moving to the SDDC is not a simple process. Enterprise architects perceive the SDDC as a strategic direction that consists of a complex web of technical, process, organizational, and cultural challenges. While virtualization facilitated hosting applications and server use, the SDDC further accelerates and expands this concept by eliminating more IT silos and more thoroughly decoupling IT infrastructure components. These additional changes can be met with resistance. In addition, many of the requisite technology components are still evolving and many organizations' existing IT infrastructures still use legacy products such as mainframes. Despite these challenges, demands for rapid change coupled with the need for organizations to be more agile, particularly in the application layer, are leading to a growth in the number of SDDCs.

In an EMA survey conducted with 235 visionary companies who had extensive experience, skill, and expertise regarding obstacles and priorities on their journey to the SDDC, IT silos and business pressure were identified as two major challenges faced on the SDDC journey.[4]

IT SILOS

Traditional data center silos (i.e., servers, network, storage, applications, and security) represent a key pain point within the context of the SDDC. This leads to security, OPEX, and integration issues. The issues associated with deploying software updates are magnified in large companies, while small companies experience more frequent issues with high OPEX and CAPEX related to the existence of IT silos. Security concerns and integration challenges of IT silos are most prevalent in medium-sized organizations. To satisfy business-driven IT initiatives, data center managers will have to be more project-centric across traditional silos. This will require establishing different priorities, oversight, and organizational and political control, because in most companies, the greater percentage of IT budgets is assigned to silos rather than to projects. Key pain points caused by the IT silos of storage, network, compute, middleware, security, and legacy groups in different-sized organizations are shown in Table 14.3.

Table 14.3 Pain Points Caused Between IT Silos	
Pain Point	**Percent (%)**
Security concerns	38
Increased operating cost	37
Integrating legacy with new technologies	35
Finding/hiring skilled staff	34
Lack of centralized control	34
Slow deployment of software updates	33
Slow provisioning of new application environments	32
Diagnostics and troubleshooting	32
Increased capital cost	30
Increased staff cost	29
Adapted from Volk, T., Frey, J., 2014. Obstacles and Priorities on the Journey to the Software-Defined Data Center: An Enterprise Management Associates (EMA) Research Report. EMA, Boulder, CO.	

[4]Volk, T., Frey, J., 2014. Obstacles and Priorities on the Journey to the Software-Defined Data Center: An Enterprise Management Associates (EMA) Research Report. EMA, Boulder, CO.

BUSINESS PRESSURE

The EMA survey reported that business units put tremendous pressure on traditional IT silos, leading to "added responsibilities and skill requirements," the "need for more cross domain knowledge," and IT groups asking for an "increase in staff." The latter applies more to small businesses, while mid-sized organizations are more focused on the cross-domain knowledge requirement to counter the breakdown of traditional IT processes under the load of business requests. Only 9% of study respondents did not see an impact of the SDDC on current infrastructure management, proving that the vast majority of companies (91%) are affected by this new set of challenges.

Table 14.4 shows the increasing number of resource requests from business units and their developers on the traditional roles of network, storage, database, application, and server administrators that were identified by the respondents.

Other challenges caused when transitioning to the SDDC relate to visibility and operations and software licensing.

PERFORMANCE VISIBILITY AND OPERATIONS

The transition to SDDCs and the associated utilization of software-defined networking (SDN), virtualized networks, and virtual firewalls requires new visibility, operations, and integration of networks, storage, servers, and security, all of which require highly integrated operations teams. Consequently, visibility and management across data center silos and across virtual and physical networks are critical.

Tools to address these visibility and operations challenges emerged, including Arkin's Visibility/Operations Platform, SDDC, and Cloud, and to provide end-to-end visibility across underlay and overlay. These tools also extend to **Amazon Web Services** to enable organizations to easily deploy and operate a microsegmentation-based network and security model.

Table 14.4 Impact of Business Requests on Traditional IT Roles	
Type of Business Requests	**Percent (%)**
Added responsibilities and skills required	44
More cross-domain knowledge needed	42
Increase in staff required	41
IT operations staff feels threatened by change	35
Traditional processes are breaking down under the load	34
Business units are bypassing IT and use public cloud services instead	31
Traditional IT roles stay unchanged	26
There is no increase in number of requests coming from business units	3
Adapted from Volk, T., Frey, J., 2014. Obstacles and Priorities on the Journey to the Software-Defined Data Center: An Enterprise Management Associates (EMA) Research Report. EMA, Boulder, CO.	

SOFTWARE LICENSING

Licensing can also be extremely challenging when moving to the heavily software-driven infrastructure of the SDDC. In today's highly virtualized world, the majority of software licensing models are still better suited to the traditional hardware/software infrastructure, and in some organizations that operate huge numbers of applications that change frequently, software licenses are too vast to inventory. In the heavily software-driven SDDC infrastructure, it is essential that managers seek efficient, effective, and user-friendly licensing models and monitor and control them in a systematic fashion.

SUMMARY

The SDDC directly addresses the shortcomings of many private and hybrid cloud implementation projects. However, implementing the SDDC should not be viewed as a simple technology challenge. Instead, it is important that it be approached as a comprehensive paradigm shift from a purely technology-centric approach to enterprise IT to one that truly focuses on delivering business solutions.

The SDDC virtualizes and delivers the IT infrastructure—computer, storage, network, and security—as a service. This means that provisioning and operating the IT infrastructure is entirely automated by software to increase its agility and flexibility. SDS and SDN are two critical components of the SDDC. The software-defined approach requires a different method for building networks, binding them with applications, and managing them. These new methods go beyond simply deploying a collection of technologies and processes. For instance, the requisite technology components are still evolving and the current state of many existing IT architectures are not conducive to automated deployment and management. To be successful, the transition needs to be approached as a strategic initiative that involves decision, planning, and execution phases for the provisioning of IT services. Management tools are emerging to assist with this process, including VMware's vCloud Suite and Red Hat's Cloud Infrastructure.

KEY TAKEAWAYS

- Key properties of the SDDC are centralized management, best-practice repeatable configurations of software and infrastructure for workload deployment, orchestration and automation to easily deploy applications across silos, and operational analytics.
- Implementing and operating the SDDC are not just technology challenges. They must be approached as a comprehensive paradigm shift from a purely technology-centric approach to enterprise IT to one that truly focuses on delivering business solutions.
- Management style in the SDDC must be policy driven and application centric.
- Cross-domain expertise and blended teams must be developed and nurtured.
- Implementing and operating the SDDC requires an increased focus on capacity management, **multi-virtualization** and **multi-cloud management**, and configuration management.
- Challenges of transitioning to the SDDC include IT silos, business pressure, performance visibility and operations, and software licensing.
- Vendors are collaborating to produce a fully integrated, engineered, tested, and validated solution to help accelerate organizations as they transition to the SDDC.

APPLICATION MANAGEMENT IN THE INTERNET OF THINGS

15

The Moving Finger writes: and, having writ,
Moves on: nor all thy piety nor wit
Shall lure it back to cancel half a line,
Nor all thy tears wash out a word of it.
Rubaiyat 51, Rubaiyat of Omar Khayyam

Before proceeding, it is first necessary to address the question of "What is meant by the **Internet of Things (IoT)**?" There are conflicting views about a concrete definition. The situation is reminiscent of the Indian fable of "The Blind Men and the Elephant." In that fable, a group of blind men are asked to describe an elephant. Each man felt only one part of the elephant. This resulted in each man having a very different perception of what an elephant was like (a pillar, a rope, a tree branch, a hand fan, a wall, a solid pipe, etc.) (Fig. 15.1).

There is still a great deal of confusion about IoT, much of it due to the phenomenon characterized by the fable of "The Blind Men and the Elephant." It is still a work in progress, with work going on in countless, semi-isolated groups around the world. An explosion taking place in slow motion would be another analogy. It will be at least a few years until IoT begins to stabilize, if that ever happens. However, for the sake of this chapter, it is important to provide some definition of the space even if those definitions are superseded in coming years. For this book, we will rely on a definition developed by Enterprise Management Associates. "The Internet of Things (IoT) is an interconnected web of sensor-enabled devices that communicate between each other and a series of intermediary collection points. This web of devices provides sensor information on device operation, status, and location" (Fig. 15.2).[1]

IoT is a concept that has been around since at least the 1990s. However, it was not until the 21st century that the necessary technologies emerged and began to coalesce. The developments that were needed to take IoT from an academic pipe dream to reality include:

- Miniaturization of components
- Commoditization of components leading to substantially lower costs
- Concise, compact software (microcode)
- Ubiquitous connectivity

---

[1]"The Rise of the Internet of Things: Connecting Our World One Device at a Time." Myers and Wise, EMA, 2016.

FIGURE 15.1

Blind men and the elephant.

"The Internet of Things (IoT) is an interconnected web of sensor-enabled devices that communicate between each other and a series of intermediary collection points. This web of devices provides sensor information on device operation, status, and location."[2]

Commercial Devices operating within room temperature environments with access to connectivity bandwidth and electrical power to enable device processing and analysis

Industrial devices hardened to operate in harsh environments with limited access to connectivity, power, and processing

Edge data collection to bridge between industrial devices and streaming data platforms, as well as providing edge processing and analysis

Streaming data platforms to provide real-time connectivity between devices and geographic data stores

Geographic data stores to provide mid-stage operational visibility analytics and cross-device operational process information

Traditional data integration moves data from geographic data stores for historical and organization-wise analysis

Historical environments based on the EMA Hybrid Data Ecosystem to augment IoT data with operational, customer, and product information as well as historical analysis

FIGURE 15.2

IoT Ecosystem Reference Architecture.[3]

[2]Ibid.
[3]Ibid.

- Low overhead communications protocols
- Technology for processing vast amounts of data (i.e., Big Data and analytics)
- Methods for uniquely identifying devices

Every time a new technical innovation emerges, there is a period in which the market struggles to sort out the nature of the innovation, how it will be applied, and what terminology will be used to describe it. Concurrent with this is something like a cattle stampede, as vendors rush to try to capture a share of the new market, or at least leverage the excitement around it to stimulate sales of their existing product(s). Each company has its own marketing messages, each with a unique interpretation of what the new technology is or how it can be used, and/or how it impacts other current markets. While generally well intentioned, this multitude of perspectives does make it difficult to sort out the true nature of that innovation.

It is not possible to know how many objects are currently deployed with instrumentation for IoT purposes. Even the best attempts to estimate that number are little more than educated guesses. It is enough to know that there is a very large number (currently in the billions) of objects deployed and that number is likely to increase by orders of magnitude in the next few decades.

The market for IoT products can be divided between consumer and commercial and government applications. For consumers, IoT applications range from frivolous to life-saving. The following are some categories with a few examples. It is important to realize that these categories are only examples and that there are many others (Fig. 15.3).

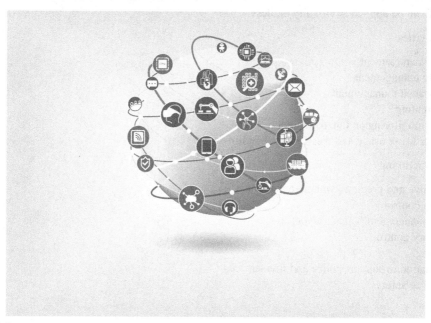

FIGURE 15.3

IoT connecting everything to everything.

Health

Monitor vital signs (applications for all ages)
Ensure that medication is taken
Implanted devices
Track activity levels
Track location

Home

Security (smart access)
Home automation (smart appliances)
Energy efficiency (lighting, heating, and cooling)
Irrigation

Lifestyle

Toys
Drones
Wearables (smart watches, FitBit, etc.)
Smart cars (autopilot, preventative maintenance, etc.)

Below is a similar list for IoT applications in business and government sectors. Again, it is important to realize that this is just a list of examples and is not intended to be exhaustive. There are many other areas where IoT will be applied (e.g., mining, military, hospitality industry, etc.). The list of areas where IoT can be applied is virtually endless.

Smart cities

Traffic management
Parking management
Mass transit management
Area lighting
Crowd monitoring and management
Monitor water usage and waste water handling

Manufacturing

Preventive and predictive maintenance
Quality control
Flow management (smart valves)
Inventory control
Tracking
Information to support police and fire services
Employee safety

Retail

Inventory control
Loss prevention
Targeted marketing

Smart lighting
Track customer behavior
Adaptive pricing

Agriculture

Livestock monitoring (health and location)
Discrete application of fertilizer
On-demand irrigation
Monitor plant health
Inventory control (seed stocks, harvested crops, etc.)

Health

Ambulance telemetry
Hospital asset tracking
Access control
Implanted devices
Patient monitoring
Asset management

Energy

Smart grid (electrical distribution)
Flow management (pipelines)
Smart valves
Smart meters
Smart air conditioning controls (utility can turn off during peak demand periods)

Natural resources

Wildlife monitoring and tracking
Forest management (health and prevent illegal logging)
Wildfire crew tracking
Monitor human impacts

INSTRUMENTATION

The first point that must be understood about IoT is that it is not a "thing." It is not a tangible object that can be touched, weighed, or measured. It is not an intangible article such as software, nor is it a service to which one can subscribe. It is more accurate to think of IoT as a phenomenon. It consists of billions of objects around the world that are instrumented, and the instrumentation is generating unimaginable amounts of data. It is that instrumentation that is the enabling force behind IoT and it is the instrumentation that is central to IoT.

For IoT to work, there must be instrumentation with the following attributes:

- Power source(s)
- Memory
- Operating system and application software

- Data collection by the associated object
- Ability to communicate with a higher level system
- Control over the associated object (optional)

Those are the attributes of the instrumentation, but what is the instrumentation? That is, what form does the instrumentation take? In the simplest terms, the instrumentation required for an object to be part of IoT is a computer system. Most commonly, that computer system consists of some microcode running on a single chip or a board. However, in principle, code running on a **PC** or even a server could perform the same functions and in the case of large complex systems (e.g., manufacturing, traffic control, etc.), a larger system may be better suited.

Generally, the IoT remote system will reside within the object with which it is associated. However, it is possible for the IoT system to be external to its object. In either case, the IoT system must be attached to data sources. Those data sources may be sensors that were embedded to collect data for the IoT system. Alternatively, the IoT system may utilize data that is collected by the object for operational purposes. In the case of the latter, the IoT system must have a way to extract that operational data.

IMPLEMENTATION

Because of the magnitude of the IoT space, the diversity of uses, and the absence of widely accepted standards, a significant disparity in implementations is inevitable; therefore, it is inescapable that there will be many exceptions to the following description. Nonetheless, the definition presents the most common approach to implement IoT.

The software for an IoT component is written on **non-volatile memory (NVM)**. That is necessary so the code will be secure and remain intact if there is a loss of power. Being secure means that it is not possible for the code to be altered or reverse engineered. Likewise, any **encryption** keys that are used must be fully protected from discovery or alteration. It is important to remember that objects with IoT instrumentation will often be found in remote locations where there is little or no physical security. Also, the environmental conditions may be extreme. Any solution must be able to perform satisfactorily in such environments.

The use of **one-time programmable memory (OTP)** memory, including PROM and ROM, will typically achieve these objectives. The software is printed on a **complementary metal–oxide semiconductor (CMOS)**[4] chip, using standard manufacturing processes. Once printed, the information on the chip is relatively secure.

MANAGEMENT

Management of IoT applications poses some unique challenges, and in other ways is much simpler than traditional applications. There are two parts to IoT applications: the portion that runs on and monitors a remote object and the software that resides upstream from the remote software.

The upstream applications are the ones that collect data from the remote applications. They reside on a much more robust system (whether it is a PC, server, or mainframe of something else is irrelevant). At a minimum, the upstream applications collect data from the remote applications and store that data

---

[4]CMOS is a technology for constructing integrated circuits (chips). It offers the advantages of low power consumption and low waste heat. Both traits are important in IoT components. CMOS is the dominant form of integrated circuit manufacturing.

in some kind of repository. That repository may be proximate to the application or situated remotely. That is, the remote repository for data at rest may be on the same chip as the remote application, or it may be stored elsewhere on the remote device.

Each of the upstream applications is in every sense an application and the management of them is the same as it is for any other application, regardless of the environment where they run (e.g., local server, PC, mainframe, cloud-based systems, etc.). The same management functions (fault, performance, accounting, and security) are required and the same tools can be used as would be used for any other applications running in the same operating environment (i.e., with the same operating system).

CONFIGURATION

The situation is very different with the remote applications. In simplest terms, the application can be viewed as installed and configured at the time of the manufacture of the chip set on which it resides and runs. If the designer elected to use NVM OTP CMOS technologies for the implementation, then like the quote at the beginning of this chapter, it is finished. It would seem that there is no practical way to change what was written. However, there does need to be a way to capture user preferences, local access codes, etc. Also, in order to avoid having to replace an entire IoT remote system, the designer may elect to allow patches or new copies of the code to be written to the chip. Currently, there are multiple techniques available for accomplishing this and new ones are likely to emerge in the future. While a thorough discussion of the technical details of how this can be done is beyond the scope of this book, it is important to note that if changes are allowed, the security of that application is weakened.

A designer can select a variety of chip options, including **programmable read-only memory (PROM), field programmable read-only memory (FPROM), erasable programmable read-only memory (EPROM),** and others. Any of these may be chosen for special IoT applications to meet the individual architectural and use requirements of the intended IoT applications, but each also has limitations and/or special requirements (power and/or UV light) that limit their usefulness in certain environments or use cases, thus affecting it for widespread use for IoT. Also, use of one of these alternatives can compromise the integrity of the software due to environmental factors or external threats.

SECURITY

One may be tempted to question the importance of the need for security for IoT applications – especially when thinking about consumer-focused applications such as the smart home (e.g., lighting, smart thermostats, smart appliances, etc.) or some wearables. However, there are many more important uses for IoT applications such as traffic control, mass transit (i.e., trains and subways), oil refineries, utilities, factories, hospitals, etc. with the potential for catastrophic consequences from an error caused by a cyber attack. We live in a world where acts of terror are commonplace, where some people find enjoyment in simply proving that they are able to hack into a system regardless of the consequences, and where state-sponsored cyber attacks are rampant. Thus far, the latter have been relatively benign, possibly intended only to ensure that the capabilities exist if there is ever a need to call on them. However, state-sponsored attacks have potential to wreak havoc throughout a country. Even if IoT is more passive (i.e., just collecting data and forwarding it to an upstream system), it is important to ensure that the application and its data are secure. That is because that data can form the basis for future actions and some with potentially serious or even deadly consequences if the wrong action is taken.

The use of NVM OTP CMOS technologies enables relatively tight security for the application. Together, these technologies can make it difficult or (depending on the design) even impossible to alter the software on the chip(s). The data that is captured by the remote application and stored remotely must also be protected. It is vulnerable unless it is encrypted. Therefore, encryption for both the data stored on the IoT remote system (data at rest) and data in transit is necessary. Even when stored data is encrypted, it may be possible to delete data and thus cause harm. In all honesty, for most cases, this is a relatively esoteric discussion. Destruction of data requires an attacker to have physical access to remote IoT systems, or to have compromised the encryption used for communication with the upstream application(s) and any additional security measures that were implemented. Certainly, it is possible to do that. However, to do so requires the dedication of a tremendous amount of resources (or the assistance of an insider). Attacks involving the assistance of an insider are much more difficult to prevent. Some would say, depending on the role of the insider, it is nearly impossible to prevent successful insider attacks (Fig. 15.4).

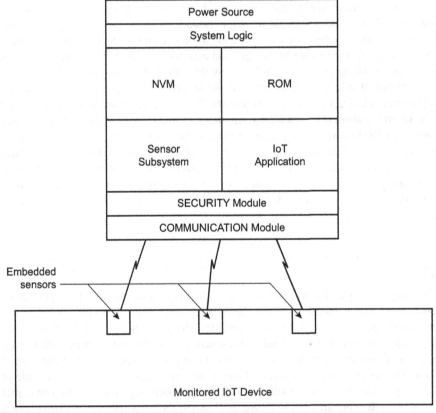

FIGURE 15.4

Simplified view of remote IoT device.

As mentioned earlier, data in transit encryption is a crucial consideration for the security of the collected data to be maintained. This form of encryption prevents "man in the middle" attacks. However, data in transit encryption is only part of the strategy. Next, the network itself must be secured with latest techniques available. However, at a minimum, the network needs to utilize IPsec, SSL, SSH, WPA, etc. or an equivalent technology to encrypt each packet and to authenticate each node in the communication stream. The use of other **virtual private network (VPN)** capabilities may also be warranted along with security these measures.

FAULT

Limited monitoring is possible with an IoT remote application, but only if the application was designed to support management queries. While it is possible to incorporate a management agent, the design objective of minimum use of memory conflicts with this. Instead, awareness of the health of the remote application and system (i.e., chip set) on which it runs is largely a function of interpreting the data supplied by the remote application, recognizing when it is no longer communicating, and understanding that the data it is communicating outside of the expected range. In that event, it may be possible to remotely interact with the system to run some form of testing or power cycle the system on which the IoT remote application resides. If that fails to resolve the problem or if the system does not support remote power cycling, then it is necessary to dispatch someone to replace the failed system. At this point, it is important to remember that most IoT systems (units) are inexpensive to the point of being disposable.

PERFORMANCE

The overall performance of the remote application is equivalent to end-to-end response time in real-time systems. It is a composite of the performance of sensors, the remote application, and the network over which the data from the remote application is transported. Obviously, network performance is something that can be managed and fine-tuned, and that is routinely done. The performance of the remote application is determined at the design and testing stage. In general, once the application is burned on the chip, its performance is permanently defined. The exception to this is if there are user-defined parameters that can impact the performance of the application. If there are, then those can be adjusted with their overall performance increased or decreased accordingly. Hopefully those adjustments to user parameters can be changed remotely, otherwise someone will have to travel to the location of the remote application to make the change. Unless the remote application was specifically designed to capture and report certain metrics about its performance, it will not be possible to capture that information.

ACCOUNTING

As explained in Chapter 3, the accounting component of **application management** of applications consists of two basic functions: asset management and tracking of resource utilization. In fact, such information would most likely be of limited value given the relatively static nature of the remote application. The system on which the remote application runs is a closed environment. The remote application can only use resources that are part of that system (with the possible exception of power).

The other aspect of accounting is asset management, which is definitely relevant to the management of IoT remote applications. Each system should have a unique identifier. It may be a MAC address, a serial number assigned to the chip on which the remote application runs, or a custom identifier developed by the designer (or the designer's employer). Through this unique identifier, it is possible to individually account for each IoT system. That identifier can also be tied to the IP address for each system to more granularly identify the system and has an additional benefit of enabling additional security features in some designs.

> In 2015, researchers discovered that makers of a wide assortment of embedded devices were reusing HTTPS certificates and SSH keys. In doing so, they were potentially defeating the very security that was supposed to be enabled by those certificates and keys.

Passive Identifiers

Passive, permanent identifiers such as barcodes, **quick response codes (QR codes)**, and **radio frequency identification (RFID)** tags are *not* part of the Internet of Things. It is true that they represent data that can be collected, but that data is static. It is fixed at the time of manufacture of that object or when the label or tag is attached. They are actually quite similar to a brand (or ear tag) on a cow or a retina pattern in a person's eye. Each is unique and can be read. They certainly contribute to the exponential increase in the volume of data being captured and stored. However, they lack the data collection and communication attributes required for them to be part of IoT.

The devices that read the passive identifiers are sensors in the IoT hierarchy. Those devices are likely to also include the remote applications necessary to communicate the data collected with an upstream application. The passive identifiers represent data points that are detected by a sensor, just as a sensor might detect engine temperature or atmospheric pressure.

SUMMARY

The Internet of Things (IoT) is a technology experiencing explosive growth. It holds the promise to revolutionize how we live and work. Successful realization of the potential of IoT requires the effective management of the applications that make it possible. Management of applications that are physically attached to the objects that they collect data from (i.e., remote applications) requires special attention at the design/test stage and once they are deployed and operational.

Upstream applications (i.e., the ones that receive data from remote applications) do not require any special management consideration. They can be managed like any other application running in the same environment (mainframe, server, PC, etc.).

KEY TAKEAWAYS

- There are billions of IoT objects currently deployed and the number will continue to grow dramatically.
- IoT devices will have a dramatic impact on how people live and work. Because of that, it is imperative that the IoT applications be well designed and manageable.

- Management of host-based (mainframe, server, PC, etc.) applications is comparable to the management of any other application in the same environment.
- Remote applications will usually reside on a single CMOS chip.
- Applications that are printed to a chip using OTP NVM CMOS are difficult to modify. Thus, management is more difficult.
- Greater care must be taken when designing and testing applications that will be installed on remote objects.
- Since IoT devices are often remote and unattended, greater attention must be given to designing the system to be secure.

THE CASE FOR STANDARDS

16

As cloud computing models emerge and evolve in a significant way to deliver reliable, automated services across private, hosted and public environments, standards provide a base of consistent, interoperable management across different cloud service implementations.
Brad Anderson, Microsoft General Manager, Management and Services Division

As every market matures, so evolves the need for standards. HP sees that the right balance between industry standards and proprietary technologies propels the industry forward, fostering collaboration and innovation.
James Mouton, Hewlett–Packard, Chief Technology Officer, Technology Solutions Group

It is not only about open standards, but it is about how these standards all play together for the benefit of the customer.
Angel Diaz, VP IBM Standards, Open Source and Cloud Labs

INTRODUCTION

One of the priorities of **application management** is monitoring and controlling application performance, security, and **total cost of ownership (TCO)**. To address the rising costs associated with these tasks and to further facilitate the management of applications, a number of industry, vendor, and neutral organizations have focused their efforts on creating standards and **management information bases (MIBs)**. Some of the most prolific groups to lead these efforts include the **Institute of Electrical and Electronics Engineers (IEEE)**, the **Internet Engineering Task Force (IETF)**, the **Desktop Management Task Force (DMTF)**, and the **International Organization of Standardization and International Electro-Technical Commission (ISO/IEC)**.

Standards establish consistent protocols that can be widely understood and adopted to facilitate performance, security, compatibility, and interoperability. Standards also simplify application development by speeding time-to-market and expediting the comparison of competing products. Standards are essential to ensure interconnectivity and interoperability requirements and verify new products and new markets. Without standards, application development, implementation, and management would be far less consistent and much more complex.

Over the years, numerous standards relevant to application management were developed. As changes occur in the nature of the applications themselves, the types of infrastructure on which they exist and the way in which they are managed (automated vs. manual) formed committees and task forces to address the ongoing need for new or updated standards. The following sections introduce the composition and purpose of each of the standards' organizations, and discusses the management standards they developed and their relevance to various aspects of application management.

Application Performance Management (APM) in the Digital Enterprise. http://dx.doi.org/10.1016/B978-0-12-804018-8.00016-4

MANAGING WITH INTERNET ENGINEERING TASK FORCE STANDARDS

The IETF is a large, open community of network designers, operators, vendors, users, and researchers that produce high-quality, relevant technical documents that influence the way people design, use, and manage the Internet. The IETF's standards development efforts are organized into several areas, which include applications and real-time, general, Internet, operations and management, routing, security, and transport. These working groups develop and review specifications for Internet standards in their area of expertise. The IETF standards process includes developing a specification that undergoes several iterations of review by the Internet community, making appropriate revisions, adopting the specification as a standard, and publishing the standard. According to the IEFT,[1] the goals of the IETF Internet standards process are:

- Technical excellence
- Prior implementation and testing
- Clear, concise, and easily understood documentation
- Openness and fairness
- Timeliness

More information on IETF membership requirements, processes, structure, and procedures can be found on their website at ietf.org.

Each IETF standard consists of a document that contains the standard's specifications. All documents published by IETF are designated as requests for comments (RFC) and allocated a unique identifier. The most popular and widely used IETF application management standards are **simple network management protocol (SNMP), system application MIB (sysApplMIB), and application management MIB (ApplMIB)**.

SNMP NETWORK MANAGEMENT PROTOCOL (SNMP V1, V2, V2C, V3)

SNMP was first conceived as an application-layer protocol for exchanging management information between network devices. Since its inception in 1988, the various iterations of SNMP have gained widespread acceptance and proved to be a highly successful standard. SNMP v1 was initially created to provide network device monitoring for TCP/IP networks and defined in RFC 1155 and 1157. Subsequently, users became aware of functional deficiencies in SNMP v1, such as the inability to easily specify the transfer of bulk data and security deficiencies that included the lack of authentication and privacy mechanisms.

In 1993 SNMP v2, defined in RFCs 1441–1452, was released to address both the functional and security deficiencies in SNMP v1. Unfortunately, the security facility in SNMP v2 was criticized for deficiencies in the definition. Consequently, SNMP v2 was revised and released as SNMP v2c in 1996, defined in RFCs 1901, 1905, 1906, and 2578. The new version retained the functional enhancements of SNMP2 but eliminated the security facility. Instead, SNMP v2c contained a simple and unsecure password-based authentication feature, referred to as the community feature. Security was afforded a much greater emphasis in SNMP v3, defined in RFCs 2271–2275 and published in 1998. SNMP v3 defines a framework for integrating security features into the overarching capabilities of SNMP v1 or SNMP v3 and specifies a set of capabilities for network security and access control.

---

[1]The IETF Standards Process. Available from: ietf.org/about/standards-process-html.

The primary goal of the SNMP is to reduce the amount and complexity of management functions. SNMP achieves this by decreasing development costs for the management agent software required to support the protocol, which increases the degree of management functions remotely to allow best use of internet resources and impose the fewest possible restrictions on the form and sophistication of the management tools. It also simplifies the set of management functions to make it easier for developers to understanding and use. Another goal of SNMP is that the functional paradigm for monitoring and control be sufficiently extensible to accommodate additional, possibly unanticipated, aspects of network operation and management. Finally, it seeks to be independent of the architecture and mechanisms of particular hosts or particular gateways.[2]

Two key components of SNMP are the **object identifier (OID)** and **MIB**. The OID is structured and follows a hierarchical tree format, and the MIB describes the managed device parameters. Typically, the MIB contains a standard set of statistical and control values defined for hardware nodes on a network that forms the basis for various management queries. As the management community developed additional MIBs evolved, in 1998 the first application management MIB was published as part of the SNMP v2 Network Management Framework under the direction of the Application MIB Working Group.

The new working group bifurcated its efforts to first develop the sysApplMIB, defined in RFC 2287 and published in September 1998, followed by the development of the ApplMIB, defined as RFC 2564 and published in May 1999.

SYSTEMS APPLICATION MIB

The primary purpose of the sysApplMIB was to define the nature of the applications to be managed. In the sysApplMIB, an application is defined as, "One or more units of executable code and other resources, installed on a single host system."[3] Thus, by definition, the Application MIB Working Group did *not* limit the term "application" to a particular category of applications but instead made it generic to *any* type of application installed or running on a single system. The group also specified that an application be modeled both as a whole and as its individual elements, such as files and executables. In this way, the sysApplMIB models information regarding installed applications and their elements that are running or have previously run on the host and provides the necessary link for associating applications with their executing processes.

The purpose of the sysApplMIB is to provide a basic systems-level view of the applications and their components on a single-host system. The sysApplMIB also models activity information on applications and their components that are running or have previously run on the host system to link associating executing processes with the corresponding part of the application. The objects in the sysApplMIB are arranged into three groups (Systems Application Installed Group, Systems Application Group, and Systems Application Map Group). Each group has one or more information tables and/or scalars (see Table 16.1).

The sysApplMIB restricts the managed objects to information that can be determined from the system itself and does not require instrumentation within the applications to make the information available.

---

[2]A Simple Network Management Protocol, 1990. Available from: https://tools.ietf.org/html/rfc1157.
[3]MIB for Applications. Accessed from: http://www.ietf.org/rfc/rfc2287.txt.

Table 16.1 SysApplMIB Group Tables

Group	Table	Purpose
System application installed group	1. sysApplInstallPkgTable	List application installed on a particular host.
	2. sysApplInstallElmtTable	Provide information about executables and nonexecutable files or elements that collectively compose an application.
System application run group	1. sysApplRunTable	Contain application instances currently running on the host. Each time application is invoked, a new entry is created to provide information about that particular invocation of the application. Entries remain until the application instance terminates, then entry will be deleted from sysApplRunTable and placed in the sysApplPastRunTable.
	2. sysApplPastRunTable	Maintain history of instances of applications previously executed on the host. Entries are made when an invoked application from sysApplRunTable terminates. Size of this table is controlled by two scalars—sysApplPastRunMaxRows specifies maximum number of entries in the table, sysApplPastRunTblTimeLimit specifies the maximum age of table entries. Oldest entries are removed first.
	3. sysApplElmtRunTable	Contain an entry for EVERY process currently running on the host, not just those processes that are running as part of an identified application. Entry is created for each process at the time it is started and remains in the table until the process terminates. When processes terminate, only information from entries corresponding to elements of an identified application are moved to the sysApplElmtPastRunTable. If the process cannot be associated with any "parent" application, it is simply removed from the sysApplElemtRunTable.
	4. sysApplElmtPastRunTable	Maintain a history of processes previously executed on the host as part of an application. To control the size of this table, two scalars are defined—sysApplElmtPastRunMaxRows specifies maximum number of entries and sysApplElmtPastRunTblLimit specifies maximum age of entry of the table. Oldest entries are removed first.
	Scalars	Control size of each of the past run tables by number of entries and age of entries.
System application map group	1. sysApplMapTable	Provide a backward mapping to determine the invoked application, installed element, and installed application package given a known process ID number.

APPLICATION MANAGEMENT MIB

In May 1999, the Application MIB Working Group published the Application Management MIB (applMIB), defined in RFC 2564, to provide a more granular level of detail about the management objects and expand the sysApplMIB to include attributes that typically require instrumentation within the managed resource. Its purpose is to describe a basic set of management objects for fault, configuration, and performance management of applications from a systems perspective.

To ensure ease and speed of implementation while allowing room for growth, the applMIB defines a model for application information resident on a host computer that can be determined from the system itself and not from the individual applications. This system-level view of applications is designed to provide information about software applications installed and running on the host system without requiring modifications and code additions to the applications themselves. To support configuration, fault, and performance management, the information described by the objects in the applMIB represent some of the basic attributes of application software from a nonapplication specific perspective. In this way, the applications are described as collections of executables and files installed and executing on a host computer.[4] The applMIB was last updated in March 2013.

To use SNMP to enhance application management, it is necessary to create an MIB to map the application attributes for monitoring and corrective action. With an MIB in place, SNMP can be used to query and set the attribute variables. When the state of a variable changes during normal operations, SNMP will trigger automated or manual management actions. In this way, the MIB becomes a base that is accessible to the entire management system and customized to support a specific application.

Numerous software products evolved using SNMP to troubleshoot network problems and distributed applications and ensure that critical systems, applications, and services are always available. These include Microsoft Network Monitor, Nagios, OpenNMS, Capsa Free, and Fiddler.

MANAGING WITH THE INSTITUTE OF ELECTRONIC AND ELECTRICAL ENGINEERS STANDARDS

The IEEE is the world's largest technical professional society with approximately 400,000 members worldwide. The IEEE is designed to serve professionals involved in all aspects of the electrical, electronic, and computing fields and related areas of science and technology. The main objective of the IEEE is to foster technological innovation and excellence through the educational and technical advancement of electrical and electronic engineering, telecommunications, computing, and associated disciplines. To achieve this aim, the IEEE has established itself as one of the leading standards-making organizations in the world and has developed more than 900 active standards with another 500 under development in a wide range of industries, including healthcare, power and energy, robotics, telecommunications, transportation, information assurance, and information technology.

Two of the most important IEEE standards that apply to application management are the **IEEE 1220 Standard for Application and Management of the Systems Engineering Process** and the **Portable Operating System Interface (POSIX) 1387.2**.

IEEE 1220—APPLICATION AND MANAGEMENT OF THE SYSTEMS ENGINEERING PROCESS

The stated purpose of the IEEE 1220 is to provide a standard for managing a system from initialization through development, operations, and disposal. The IEEE 1220 defines the systems engineering course as a generic problem-solving process that provides mechanisms for identifying and evolving the product and process definitions of a system.

The IEEE 1220 was first released for trial use in 1995. The first fully fledged **IEEE 1220** was originally developed in 1998, superseded by IEEE 1220:2005 in 2005, and reaffirmed in 2011.

IEEE 1220 defines the interdisciplinary tasks required through a system's lifecycle to change customer needs, requirements, and constraints into a system solution. In addition, the IEEE 1220 specifies the

---

[4]Application Management MIB. Accessible from: tools.ietf.org/html/rfc2564.

requirements for the systems engineering process and its applications throughout the product lifecycle. The six processes of the Systems Engineering Process model outlined in IEEE 1220 are:

1. Requirements analysis
2. Requirements validation
3. Functional analysis
4. Functional verification
5. Synthesis
6. Physical verification

These six systems engineering processes are connected by five control processes: data management, configuration management, interface management, risk management, and performance-based progress measurements. The focus of IEEE 1220 is on engineering activities required to guide product development while ensuring proper design to make it affordable to produce, own, operate, maintain, and dispose of without undue risk to health and environment. IEEE is widely used in the public and private sectors and has not changed significantly since its trial issue.

POSIX 1387.2 SOFTWARE ADMINISTRATION STANDARD

POSIX 1387.2 provides the basis for standardized software administration. Developed in 1995, POSIX 1387.2 is part of the IEEE POSIX series of standards for applications and user interfaces to open systems. POSIX 1387.2 consists of three main components:

1. **Standard application structures and application packaging layout**
   a. Defines a hierarchical set of structures that enable application developers to organize software files into management components
   b. Defines layout of distribution media containing packaged applications to provide portability of installation media including serial and directory access formats
2. **Standard utilities and application catalog information**
   a. Provides a standard interface for administering applications to avoid retraining of system administrators and simplify installation documentation
   b. Provides utilities to package application files into distributions using software packaging layouts, including utilities to install applications from distribution onto target systems, manage applications on the system, and manage distributions and intersystem distributed applications
   c. Creates an application catalog to drive the management utilities including listing, verifying, or removing an application throughout its lifecycle
3. **Distributed application administration**
   a. Defines concepts and utility syntax for application management in a distributed environment

Once an application is created, it must be logically organized and packaged for distribution. Packing, distributing, and controlling applications is a critical and time-consuming task for application developers and administrators. POSIX 1387.2 is a set of processes that guides an application from one state into another, for example, from development to distribution or distribution to postimplementation. To achieve this, POSIX 1387.2 addresses distributed software administration, standard software structures and software packaging layout, standard utilities and software catalog information and defines the roles relevant to application development, operation, and use. This structured set of definitions of processes and roles helps managers to consistently assign tasks and package and distribute any application, with a minimum of effort and expense.

Initially, the IEEE working group that created POSIX 1387.2 focused their efforts on Unix systems, but over the years they have widened its scope to apply to other operating systems, including those that support personal computers. Interestingly, while POSIX 1387.2 does not address the issue of interoperability, it does define the distributed environment by defining six distributed roles. To fully understand the distributed aspect of POSIX 1387.2, it helps to present these distributed roles[5] as provided in the POSIX 1387.2 rationale (see Fig. 16.1). In the distributed environment, each of these roles can be on the same system for local operations and a separate system for distributed operations.

A complete description of POSIX 1387.2 software structures, configuration scripts, software packaging layout, standard utilities, software catalog information, and distributed software administration can be found in "Foundations of Application Management"[6] or "Go Solo 2."[7]

MANAGING WITH THE TIVOLI SYSTEMS APPLICATION MANAGEMENT SPECIFICATION

The **Tivoli Application Management Specification (AMS)** is a roadmap for application developers to make applications management-ready. It does so by capturing information about an application in a central repository to enable an AMS-compliant management tool to manage the application. The AMS describes the following application management tasks:

- Structure and topology
- Deployment and distribution
- Installation
- Dependency checking
- Monitoring and events
- Verification
- Operational control

The core of the AMS is a definition of a set of **application description files (ADFs)** that contains all the information needed to effectively carry out the management tasks listed above and include the following information:

- **Topology**—description of each component of the distributed application and the relationships between the components
- **Distribution**—list of source files and directories
- **Installation**—custom scripts that run before or after application distribution
- **Dependency checking**—custom scripts that check hardware and software configurations of target systems to ensure application requirements are met
- **Monitoring**—specification of metrics and events accessible from the application and how to access them
- **Operational control**—custom scripts to perform an arbitrary set of operational control tasks

[5]POSIX Software Administration. Available from http://www.unix.org/version2/whatsnew/softadmin.html.
[6]Sturm, R., Bumpus, W., 1999. Foundations of Application Management. John Wiley and Sons, Ltd., New York, NY.
[7]Open Group, 1997. Go Solo 2: The Authorized Guide to Version two of the Single UNIX Specification. Josey, A. (Ed.).

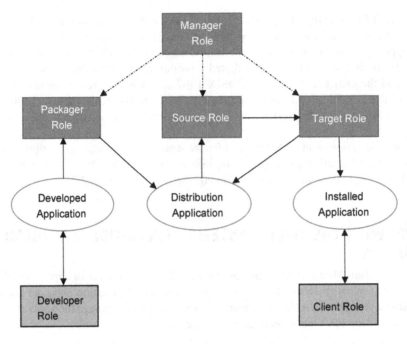

FIGURE 16.1

POSIX 1387.2 distributed roles.

- **Developer Role**—specifically outside the scope of the standard, in the developer role the application is constructed (developed software) into the form that can be accepted by the packager role. Activities performed by the developer role include compilation, source control, etc.
- **Manager Role**—provides for distributed control of the application administration process and tasks are initiated. The manager role is the one in which the administrator directly interacts through the command line interface provided in the standard or through a management application. The manager role directs the other roles to actually package, install, or manage the application.
- **Packager Role**—transforms application from locations where it exists after being developed into the standard packaging layout suitable for distribution. The packager role can package directly to media or to file system-based distributions that can later be copied to media, or from where installation can be performed directly.
- **Source Role**—serves the files in the application distribution source to the target role for actual installation onto a target system or for copying to a second distribution. The source role also makes logical software structures available to the manager role for user selection of software to be operated on.
- **Target Role**—actually installs the application and places it into a form in which it will eventually be used. Normally the application is installed on the system where the application is run, in which case the application is also configured. However, while this is usually the case, the target role is not necessarily on the system that will run the application but instead may be on a file server that serves the installed application to other client systems.
- **Client Role**—actually configures the application so that it is in a state where it can be executed. Configuration typically takes place on the system and architecture on which the application will be run. In this case, the standard supports configuration independent of installation. Installed applications may be subject to being configured several times. How the installed application is made available to the client role is also outside the scope of POXIS 1387.2. In addition to making the installed application files available to the client, an implementation must also make the installed application catalog information available so that clients can be configured by running configure scripts.

The ADF format is based on the Distributed Management Task Force's **Management Information Format (MIF)**, which is described in the next section. While the format of each ADF is common for all applications, the content of each set of ADFs is different since each set describes a different application with a unique set of characteristics. A typical ADF would include a single **global description file (GDF)** and multiple **component description files (CDFs).**

Information in the GDF includes:

- Application make
- Version identifier
- Manufacturer/author
- A free-form description of the application
- A reference to each application component
- Other miscellaneous fields of information that are global to the application.

Information included in each CDF includes:

- Component name
- Textual description
- Version identifier

Each CDF includes a reference back to the GDF to allow a management application to treat a distributed application as a cohesive whole. A stand-alone, single-system application supported by AMS has a single component (Fig. 16.2).

Administrators managing a distributed application need to understand both the type of application components and the relationship(s) among various components. AMS enables the application provider to define relationship specifications that include name, type, and related component type. With this relationship information, a management tool can provide an interface through which the administrator can view and modify existing application topology.

Distribution and installation are simplified by AMS support for automated software distribution, which breaks a distributed application into platform-specific components. In this way, the administrator can easily choose which parts of the application should be distributed and where the application should be installed. Component definitions include executables, data, scripts, etc. organized according to the target directory in which they reside on the target system.

In instrumented (i.e., management-ready) applications, in the component definition the administrator can include the types of programs required during the distribution or removal process, depending on

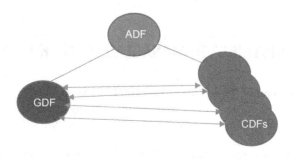

FIGURE 16.2

ADF structure for a distributed system.

whether additional programs need to run before, after, and during the process. Application types include:

- Before
- After
- Before removal
- After removal
- Commit
- On error

Other features of AMS allow the administrator to define application dependencies (both component-dependency instances and predefined dependency types), monitoring, and events and operational control tasks.

The AMS defines the following monitor types:

- Synchronous monitor (general)
- Asynchronous monitor (general)
- Log file monitor
- SNMP monitor
- Custom monitor definitions

Operational tasks include start, stop, backup or restore, and sending a message to a particular application user. Application provides can specify application-specific tasks, such as supporting a control task, by providing a program or script that, when executed, performs the desired function. The following information must be included in the CDF for each task:

- Name of task
- Description of task
- Command that, when executed on the system where the component resides, performs the control function
- Description of arguments required by the command

The AMS encourages creation of software element management information when the software is created and several vendors integrated AMS plug-ins into their products to automatically generate management data as part of software development. Tivoli submitted their work on AMS to DMTF to be used as input in the development of the Common Information Model. A full description of AMS can be found in *Foundations of Application Management.*[8]

MANAGING WITH DISTRIBUTED MANAGEMENT TASK FORCE, INC. STANDARDS

The **Distributed Management Task Force, Inc. (DMTF)** is an industry standards organization that works to simplify the manageability of mobile and cloud systems through open and collaborative efforts of leading technology companies that include Broadcom, CA, Dell, Emerson Network

---

[8]Sturm, R., Bumpus, W., 1999. Foundations of Application Management. John Wiley and Sons, Ltd., New York, NY.

Power, Hitachi, Hewlett Packard, Intel, Lenovo, Microsoft, NetApp, Software AG, TIM, and VmWare. The group has 160 member companies and more than 4000 active participants in 43 countries. DMTF develops and guides worldwide adoption of its interoperable management standards to enable the management of diverse traditional and emerging technologies. An interesting animation that shows the relationship between the various management technologies and DMTF standards can be found at: http://www.dmtf.org/managementtechnologiesdiagram. The three DMTF standards most relevant to application management are the **Common Information Model (CIM), Cloud Auditing Data Federation (CADF)**, and the **Web-Services Management (WS-MAN)** specification.

COMMON INFORMATION MODEL (CIM, CIM V2)

The Common Information Model (CIM) is a DMTF computer industry standard that methodically defines device and application characteristics to enable systems administrators and managers to control devices and applications across different vendors. In this way, products can be controlled based on the same kind of information (e.g., device name, model, serial number, network location, capacity, etc.). The CIM infrastructure approaches systems and network management by applying basic object-oriented structuring and conceptualization techniques. Using several defined Extensible Markup Language (XML) schemas, hardware and software vendors can supply CIM information about their product. CIM builds on the SNMP to provide relationship information to help track the source and status of application concerns. Originally released in 2005, CIM was most recently updated as CIM v2.45 in January 2016. The complete and most current CIM specification can be found at http://www.dmtf.org/standards/cim.

To use CIM to enhance application management, it is necessary to choose the CIM schema that reflects organizational needs, including the core schema. This CIM would reflect organizational ways of thinking that are applicable to all management areas, plus any common schemas that reflect on particular management areas of interest (e.g., applications, databases, security). If desired, extension schemas can be developed to represent organizational extensions of the common schema. Next, tools need to be selected to use this application management information. Finally, logical management systems that are understood and used by IT personnel operating the system on which the application resides would be constructed.

CLOUD AUDITING DATA FEDERATION

The Cloud Auditing Data Federation (CADF) is an open standard published by DMTF that was primarily designed to assure organizations, with cloud deployments, that their required security policies are as consistently managed and enforced in the cloud as they would be in the enterprise. Additionally, the CADF can provide accurate measurement data that can be used for SLA monitoring, real-time analytics, and problem diagnosis in cloud infrastructures.

CADF defines an event model for use in filling the essential data needed to certify, self-manage, and self-audit application security in the cloud and enables cross-vendor information sharing via its data format and information definitions. In this way, CADF delivers increased levels of insight into a provider's hardware, software, and network infrastructure used to run specific consumer applications in a multivendor environment in a private, public, or hybrid cloud.

CADF has a robust query interface that can be modified to reflect the unique resources of each provider. This standard also defines:

- Attachment of domain-specific identifiers
- Event classification values
- Tags to dynamically generate customized logs and report for cloud subscribers and customers

To enhance application management, CADF can be used to perform log-based periodic audits and meter, and monitor real-time performance to ensure quality of customer service. In doing so, it is important to demonstrate the value of CADF to the user. Show them that what they get is practical and that using a standard such as CADF is not merely an academic exercise using another new technology.

WEB-SERVICES MANAGEMENT SPECIFICATION

The Web Services Management (WS-Man) specification is a simple object access protocol for management-specific domains such as PCs, servers, smart devices, Web services, and other applications. It helps systems and network-based services collaborate seamlessly, provides interoperability between management applications and managed resources, and identifies a core set of web service specifications and usage requirements.

WS-Man addresses the cost and complexity of information technology (IT) management by providing a common way for systems to access and exchange management information across the entire IT infrastructure. It is used as a network access protocol by CIM-based management solutions, including **Desktop and Mobile Architecture for System Hardware (DASH)** and **System Management Architecture for Server Management (SMASH)**. WS-Man has the following capabilities:

- Get, put (update), create, and delete individual resource instances, such as settings and dynamic values
- Enumerate the contents of containers and collections, such as large tables and logs
- Subscribe to events emitted by managed resources
- Execute specific management methods with strongly typed input and output parameters

The WS-Man specification provides a standard for constructing XML messages using different web service standards such as WS-Addressing and WS-Transfer. These standards define XML schemas for web service messages. The messages refer to a resource using a resource URL. WS-Man adds a set of definitions for management operations and values. For example, WS-Transfer defines the Get, Put, Create, and Delete operations for a resource. WS-Man adds Rename, Partial Get, and Partial Put.

Version one of WS-Man was released in 2008, and WS-Man v1.2 was published in 2014. The objectives of WS-Man v1.2 include:

- Constrain web services protocols and formats to enable web services to be implemented with a small footprint in hardware and software management services
- Define minimum requirements for compliance with containing richer implementations
- Ensure backward compatibility and interoperability with MS-Man version 1.0 and 1.1
- Ensure composability with other web services specifications

In 2013, WS-Man was confirmed and published as an international standard by the ISO, designated as **ISO/IEC 17963:2013**. WS-MAN assists in application management by promoting interoperability between managed applications and managed resources. It also enables you to:

- Discover the presence of management resources, as well as provide navigation among them
- View and write to individual management resources, such as settings and dynamic values
- Obtain a list for contents of containers and collections, such as system components and log entries
- Run management methods

More information on implementing and deploying a WS-Man environment to remotely manage IT infrastructure can be found at http://www.dmtf.org/standards/wsman.

OPEN VIRTUALIZATION FORMAT

The OVF 2.0.0 standard published in August 2014[9] was formally known as DSP0243 **Open Virtualization Format (OVF)** V1.0.0. OVF 2.0.0 describes an open, secure, and portable format for the packaging and distribution of software run in virtual machines. Originally developed by DMTF, the OVF has been formalized as ISO/IEC as **ISO/IEC 17203:2011**. OVF provides a platform independent, efficient, open, and extensible packaging and distribution format that facilitates portability and deployment of virtual appliances and provides customers with platform independence. Once installed, an OVF package adds to the user's infrastructure a self-contained, self-consistent software application that provides a particular service or services. For example, an OVF package might contain a fully functional and tested web-server, database, and OS combination, such as a LAMP stack (Linux + Apache + MySQL + PHP), or it may contain a virus checker, including its update software, spyware detector, etc.

The OVF specification describes a hypervisor-neutral, efficient, extensible, and open format for the packaging and distribution of virtual appliances composed of one or more virtual systems. It aims to facilitate the automated and secure management not only of individual virtual systems but also of the virtual appliance as a functional unit. To be successful, OVF was developed and endorsed by a wide range of vendors. The OVF specification promotes customer confidence through the collaborative development of common standards for portability and interchange of virtual systems between different vendors' virtualization platforms. OVF is intended to be immediately useful, to solve an immediate business need, and to facilitate the rapid adoption of a common, backward compatible, yet rich format for packaging virtual appliances.

Within the OVF remit is the concept of the certification and integrity of a packaged virtual appliance. This concept allows the platform to determine the provenance of the appliance and permits the end-user to make the appropriate trust decisions. The OVF specification was constructed so that the appliance is responsible for its own configuration and modification. In particular, this means that the virtualization platform does not need to be able to read from the appliance's file systems. This decoupling of platform from the appliance means that OVF packages may be implemented by using any operating system and installed on any virtualization platform that supports the OVF format. A specific mechanism is provided for appliances to detect and react to the platform on which they are installed. This mechanism allows platforms to extend this specification in unique ways without breaking compatibility of appliances across the industry.

---

[9]DSP2017 – Open Virtualization Format White Paper. Available from: http://www.dmtf.org/standards/ovf.

The OVF format has several specific features that are designed for complex, multitier services and their associated distribution, installation, configuration, and execution:

- Provides direct support for the configuration of multitier applications and the composition of virtual systems to deliver composed services
- Permits the specification of both virtual system and application-level configuration
- Has robust mechanisms for validation of the contents of the OVF and full support for unattended installation to ease the burden of deployment for users and thereby enhance the user's experience
- Uses commercially accepted procedures for integrity checking of the OVF contents through the use of signatures and trusted third parties. This serves to reassure the consumer that an appliance was not modified because it is signed by the creator of the appliance. This assurance is seen as critical to the success of the virtual appliance market and to the viability of independent creation and online download of appliances
- Allows commercial interests of the appliance vendor and user to be respected, by providing a basic method for presentation and acknowledgment of licensing terms associated with the appliance

A detailed description of OVF 2.0.0 is available from http://www.dmtf.org/standards/ovf.

OVF can be used in many situations, for example, by software vendors to produce an application, data center operators to transport an application from one data center to another, and customers to archive an application.

MANAGING WITH ASL-BISL FOUNDATION STANDARDS

The **ASL-BiSL Foundation** is a meeting place (http://aslbislfoundation.org) for professionals with a common interest to encourage improvement in working methods and promote the exchange of best practices. The ASL-BiSL Foundation contributes to international standards for application management and information management organizations, in collaboration with ISO/IEC and NEN, the Dutch Standardization Institute.

Sound guidance for application management and development can be found in the Application Services Library (ASL) that is currently managed by the ASL-BiSL Foundation.

APPLICATION SERVICES LIBRARY

The ASL consists of a framework of processes and a library of best practices in the area of application management. Closely related to the Information Technology Infrastructure Library (ITIL) that supports service management, the ASL is a framework whose main objective is to professionalize the field of application management by supporting application management best practices.

The vendor-independent library consists of a set of books that describe best practices in the IT industry. ASL includes all processes and activities required to keep current the functionality of an application for the lifetime of the business process it supports. Originally developed in the Netherlands in

2002, the current version, ASL2, was published in 2009 in the Netherlands and released in English in 2012. ASL2 consists of:

- Standard terminology
- Generic descriptions of all ASL processes including process inputs and outputs, activities within the processes, relationships between process, and the roles of those involved in executing the processes
- Templates for important documents, such as, annual plans, management plans, SLAs, agreements and procedures, etc.

The structure of the ASL framework has not changed significantly since its first release. The main differences between the two versions relate to the positioning of internal and external IT vendors that affect how application management processes are implemented currently and in the future due to fluctuations in supply and demand. ASL2 consists of 26 processes, contained in six clusters across three levels of application management (Fig. 16.3).

The operational level consists of eleven processes that fall into three clusters to provide guidance in the operation processes for services and applications:

1. Application Support—four processes (use support, continuity management, configuration management, and IT operations management) support the day-to-day use of IT to ensure that applications perform as expected
2. Connecting Processes, Operational Level—two processes (change management and software control/ distribution) focus on synchronizing service organization/operations and development and maintenance with an emphasis on transferring from day-to-day operations to maintenance and vice versa
3. Application Maintenance and Renewal—five processes (impact analysis, design, realization, testing, and implementation) guide application design, programming, and testing to ensure optimal availability of applications currently being used to support business processes with a minimum of resources and disruption and defines and discusses changing an application in response to disruptions and new requirements from defining consequences of a change request to supporting the customer in acceptance testing

The managing level has a total of five processes that fall into one cluster: management processes. The five processes of the management processes cluster (contract management, planning and control, quality management, financial management, and supplier management) are used to manage the activities that occur within the three operational level clusters. In ASL2's management processes, all areas of application management are controlled and managed and agreements with customers and suppliers are defined.

The strategic level consists of 10 processes that fall into two clusters:

1. Applications Strategy—five processes (IT development strategy, customer organizations strategy, customer environment strategy, application lifecycle management, and application portfolio management) focus on future application demands of the application portfolio of customers
2. Application Management Organization Strategy—five processes (account and market definition, capabilities definition, technology definition, supplier definition, and service delivery definition) deal with the creation of their own organization's management strategies for maintaining and enhancing necessary skills, capabilities, markets, and customers

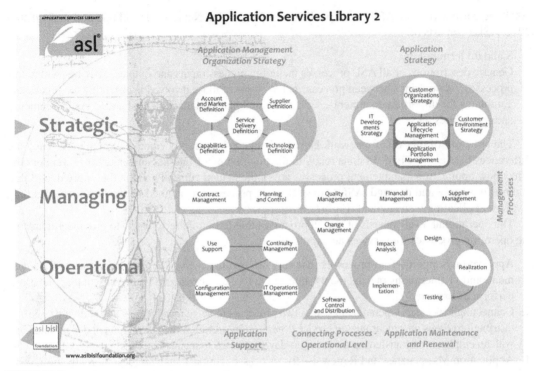

FIGURE 16.3

ASL 2.

www.aslbislfoundation.org.

For use in conjunction with ASL2, the ASL Foundation has developed an ASL2 Maturity Model (Fig. 16.4) to enable organizations to measure their progress in adopting and using the 26 processes defined in the ASL2 framework.

Similar in purpose and scope to the capability maturity model (CMMI) used to evaluate the current state of business processes, the ASL2 maturity model is a useful tool for application managers charged with making process improvements across a project or division or an entire organization.

The ASL framework helps IT professionals work and gain greater credibility for their profession. It can be used for all forms of application management such as outsourced and internal IT services. Based on best practices, the framework serves as a guide for the division of tasks and defines processes to direct the execution of those tasks. ASL can also be used to provide guidance to help structure and visualize activities that take place within application management and identify gaps between what should be done and what is done. In addition, ASL is a useful communication tool. For example, by providing a common set of terms and a clear definition of concepts and activities, ASL can facilitate communication between hardware and application management staff.

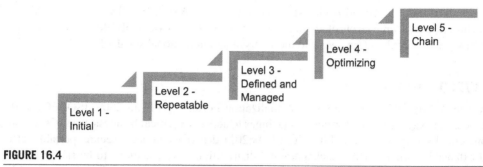

FIGURE 16.4

ASL2 maturity model.

MANAGING WITH ISO/IEC STANDARDS

The ISO and IEC are two international organizations that form a specialized system for worldwide standardization (ISO/IEC). National bodies that are members of the ISO or IEC develop international standards for particular fields of technical activity through technical committees established by the respective organization. These technical committees work together in fields of mutual interest and collaborate with other international government and nongovernment organizations to develop ISO/IEC standards. In the field of information technology, ISO and IEC have established a joint technical committee, ISO/IEC JTC 1. The ISO/IEC standards that are of greatest interest for application management are **ISO/IEC 16350** for Application Management, ISO/IEC 17203:2011 (formerly known as the Open Virtualization Format (OVF) developed by DMTF), and ISO/IEC 17963:2013 that was described earlier as DMTF's WS-MAN.

ISO/IEC 16350 FOR APPLICATION MANAGEMENT

A closer look at the standards discussed so far reveals an emphasis on the initial stages of application development. Few of these frameworks and standards address the operation, maintenance, and use of applications where the majority of TCO is spent. ISO/IEC 16350 was developed to address this shortfall in application management standards. In 2007, the Dutch Standardization Institute, NEN, introduced NEN 3434. This Dutch Standard for Application Management was developed in cooperation with the ASL BiSL Foundation and is heavily based on ASL. With the help of an international study group, the Dutch standard NEN3434 evolved into ISO/IEC 16350 for Application for Management, the international standard for application management published in August 2015.

ISO 16350:2015 establishes a common framework for application management processes using well-defined terminology referenceable by the software industry. ISO/IEC 16350:2015 contains processes, activities, and tasks that apply during the stage of operation and use. It is written from the point of view of the supplier organization that enhances, maintains, and renews the application software and the software-related products such as data-structures, architecture, designs, and other documentation. It applies to supply, maintenance, and renewal of applications, whether performed internally or externally with respect to the organization that uses the applications.

The structure of ISO/IEC 16350 is almost identical to that of ASL2. ISO/IEC 16350 has 26 processes, six clusters across three levels of application management, and essentially elevates the concepts of ASL from those of a guiding framework to the status of an international standard.

ISO/IEC 17203: 2011

Originally released by DMTF as the Open Virtualization Format (OVF) in 2009, ISO/IEC 17203 offers a standard packaging format for virtual machines to address a critical business need of software vendors and cloud service providers. ISO/IEC 17203:2011 describes an open, secure, portable, efficient, and extensible format for the packaging and distribution of applications to be run in virtual machines. The focus of this standard is on the software engineering activities that are involved in software development. It also ensures proper design to make the application affordable to produce, own, operate, maintain, and retire.

OPEN STANDARDS

In addition to the standards organizations discussed, a number of other groups have developed some interesting open standards that are important to enhancing application management. Described next are Open Group's Applications Response Measurement (ARM) and the **Cloud Application Management for Platforms (CAMP)** initially developed by an industry consortium and confirmed by the **Organization for Advancing Open Standards for the Information Society (OASIS)**.

APPLICATIONS RESPONSE MEASUREMENT

Application Response Measurement (ARM) is an open standard initially developed by Tivoli and Hewlett–Packard in 1996 and published by The Open Group later that same year as a specification entitled, "Systems Management: Application Response Measurement (ARM) API" v1.0 (API = application programming interface). The Open Group is an international vendor-neutral consortium upon which buyers and suppliers of technology can rely to lead the development of IT standards and certifications. The objective of The Open Group is to ensure interoperability and vendor neutrality, provide guidance in an open environment, and provide organizations with access to key industry peers, suppliers, and best practices. Founded in 1996 by X/Open Company Ltd., and the Open Software Foundation, The Open Group is supported by most of the world's largest user organizations, information systems vendors, and software suppliers. The Open Group operates in all phases of open systems technology lifecycle including innovation, market adoption, product development, and proliferation. The Open Group published a diverse assortment of technical documentation focused on technical standards and product documentation.

Subsequently, the ARM v2 (API) specification was issued in 1997 and finally approved for publication as an Open Group Technical Standard in March 1998. ARM v4 was released in 2003 and revised in 2004, followed by ARM v4.1. The current version of the ARM standard is ARM 4v2. An ARM 4v2 Software Development Kit (SDK) using Java and C bindings and a library of convenience function API calls used to manipulate ARM four structures are available for download from opengroup.org.

The purpose of ARM is to monitor and diagnose performance bottlenecks of loosely coupled or service-oriented enterprise applications in a single system or distributed environment. The ARM standard describes a universal method for integrating applications as manageable entities by allowing users to engage in end-to-end transaction and application response time monitoring and performance management. ARM monitors user-visible business transactions and those visible only within the IT infrastructure by embedding simple calls into an application that are captured by an agent supporting the ARM API in either C or Java. Timing information from each step in a processing transaction is logged to a remote server for later analysis. This captured data allows the application to be monitored and analyzed for availability, service levels, and capacity.

To help organizations comply with the ARM standard, many applications have already instrumented some of their offerings with ARM calls, including:

- Apache HTTP Server
- Baan 5
- IBM WebSphere Application Server
- IBM HTTP Server
- IBM DB2 Database Server
- IBM Tivoli Access Manager
- Mozilla Firefox
- SAS

ARM is easy to use. It uses a small number of calls and parameters and can be called from many different programming languages. To use ARM, the sequence of steps shown in Fig. 16.5 and described next should be followed.

Identify and Select Transactions—before an application in a production environment can be monitored and analyzed, the units of work must be identified and selected. In ARM, a unit of work is referred to as an ARM transaction. Typical examples are transactions initiated by a user and transactions with servers. Transactions selected should be ones that need to be measured and monitored and for which corrective action can be initiated if performance is subpar. Next, the application must be instrumented with calls to the ARM interface.

Instrument the Application—when the application is initialized, define transaction names and register definitions with the ARM implementation using the appropriate API to instrument the client and server applications. Once registered, the names can be used to measure transactions by judiciously inserting Start and Stop calls that define the start and end of important business transactions to the ARM

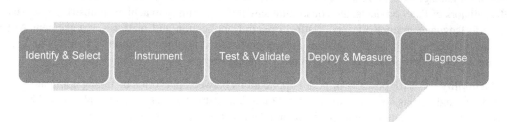

FIGURE 16.5

Application Response Measurement (ARM) v4.1

API. To build the correlation between the client and server measurements, the ARM start call creates an ARM correlator token to pass to the server within the SOAP-request measurement.

Test and Validate Measurements—provide a meaningful transaction name to test. Confirm that measured responses times are within an expected range of values. Provide the status of the transaction (i.e., success or fail). Pass the appropriate parent correlator to the child(ren) correlator(s).

Deploy and Measure Transactions—deploy instrumented applications with an ARM interface. Measure selected business or technical ARM transactions. Measurements are processed and forwarded to a configured database.

Diagnose Measurement Data—analyze specific transaction measurements and review summary of all measured transactions. Identify users on a per-transaction basis. Implement appropriate corrective action.

Many of the standards discussed so far were created by developers as an engineering exercise. The ARM API provides unique capabilities that other solutions cannot provide because it focuses heavily on the business. As a result, customers have shown a strong interest in ARM, which translates into the need for vendors to integrate an ARM API into their products to remain competitive.

CLOUD APPLICATION MANAGEMENT FOR PLATFORMS

CAMP is a platform-as-a-service management API specification designed to facilitate the management of applications in public and private clouds throughout their lifecycle. It is the first attempt to standardize the PaaS management interface by providing a common basis for developing multicloud management tools together with a representational state transfer-based approach to application management for vendors and consumers.

CAMP specification v1.0 was developed in 2012 by a consortium of vendors consisting of CloudBees, Cloudsoft, Huawei, Oracle, Rackspace, Red Hat, and Software AG.

One of the major pain points for PaaS consumers is portability, that is, the need to use a different plug-in for applications produced by different vendors due to the diverse proprietary APIs that individual providers use. Existing PaaS offerings use different languages (Java, Python, Ruby, etc.), frameworks (Springs, Rails, etc.), and APIs.

CAMP provides common development terminology and an API that can operate across multiple cloud environments without excessive adaptation. Using CAMP organizations can redeploy applications across cloud platforms from different vendors, thus reducing the effort required to move applications and provide service assurance through interoperability.

It was widely recognized that in order to enable the PaaS space to evolve, the problem of divergent application management APIs needed to be addressed. Since the features of APIs are not viewed as differentiators of PaaS products, the consortium saw the opportunity to achieve industry consensus on a generic language, framework, and platform neutral application and platform management API to effectively address the growing concerns around portability and interoperability in mobile and cloud systems. CAMP address these concerns in the following ways:

- **Portability**—CAMP portably migrates applications between platforms by taking application artifacts and putting some metadata around them to construct a package and deploy it. CAMP can also export a package from one platform and deploy it on another platform.
- **Interoperability**—CAMP supports management of applications and their use of the platform by defining basic application lifecycle operations (upload, deploy, configure/customize, start/stop, suspend, restart, and delete an application) and enables monitoring of the applications.

In August 2012, the consortium submitted the CAMP v1.0 specification to the Organization for Advancing Open Standards for the Information Society (OASIS), a nonprofit consortium that drives the development, convergence, and adoption of open standards for the global information society. OASIS develops international standards focused on security, Internet of Things, cloud computing, energy, content technologies, emergency management, and other IT areas.

OASIS established the OASIS CAMP Technical Committee to refine CAMP v1.0 and produce an OASIS Standard specification. The OASIS CAMP Technical Committee consisting of Cloudsoft, Fujitsu, NetApp, Oracle, Rackspace, Red Hat, and Vnomic came together to refine the CAMP v1.0 specification by further leveraging the similarities in current PaaS APIs. The OASIS CAMP TC also solicited input from the public at large through two public reviews in August 2013 and February 2014. Feedback received from the reviews led to a simplified resource model as shown in Fig. 16.6, a single-step deployment process and resource type inheritance. Subsequently, CAMP v1.1 was published in November 2014, and nCAMP, a proof-of-concept implementation of CAMP v1.1, was developed by the OASIS CAMP Technical committee to test the concepts and constructs of CAMP v1.1.

The CAMP specification consists of three components:

1. **Domain Specific Language**—defines application artifacts, services needed to execute them, and relationships between artifacts and services
2. **Resource Model**—represents the applications and their components, supports interoperability between diverse PaaS offerings, HTTP-based, REST-based protocol using JSON, highly extensible for future evolution
3. **Packaging Format**—moves applications between clouds, supports ZIP, TAR, or TGZ, YAM metadata, and is highly extensible

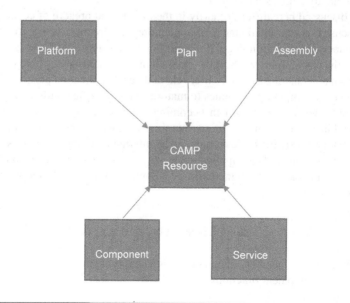

FIGURE 16.6

CAMP v1.1 resource model.

Although CAMP is not yet an official OASIS standard, it shows great potential for enhancing application management by addressing interoperability and portability issues in the cloud and as such is worthy of inclusion in this chapter. When addressing these two issues, creating a complex specification/standard is time consuming and labor intensive. Interoperability in particular has a large number of issues that need to be addressed. The OASIS CAMP TC is attacking the small problems first to gain "quick wins" by currently limiting CAMP v1.1's scope to a minimal set of known problems such as extensibility and versioning in the hope that those providers who adopt CAMP will extend it to fit their own applications. In this way, the OASIS CAMP TC will be able to integrate those extensions into upcoming versions of CAMP to improve the specification even further.

SUMMARY

The importance of standards in application management is reflected by the large number of standards that are evolving and the commercial and open-source applications that already use them. These applications benefit from the interoperability and portability the standards provide, along with shared functionality provided by numerous vendors that are developing tools to capitalize on the power of these application management standards.

Increasingly, software applications are the result of the integration of a diverse collection of executable and nonexecutable components dispersed over a network. Different components are often provided by different vendors that simultaneously compose different systems. These components can change rapidly and independently, making it difficult to deploy and manage a system in a consistent manner. Two key factors for the applicability and interoperability of the system are the completeness and standardization of the information structures that support the system. Standards are one way to effectively and efficiently address these issues.

The standards discussed here differ primarily in their depth and breadth of coverage. For example, early standards focused on the initial stages of application development where they proved useful in establishing a common set of terminology, processes, and roles associated with application management. Viewed over the past 25-plus years, it can be seen that standards as a whole provide a consistent and holistic approach to managing the entire lifecycle of diverse application portfolios (see Table 16.2).

As mobile and cloud computing continues to mature, even more standards will emerge. For example, VMWare recently voiced an interest in becoming a new entrant into Application Management Standards in the mobile environment. As greater numbers of standards created by industry task groups such as IETF, DMFT, and ASL-BiSL are recognized by international organizations such as ISO/IEC, it is expected that the use of standards for application management will gain even greater favor among the following groups who are charged with increasingly complex application development, operation, and management responsibilities:

- Business application owners
- Individuals responsible for application-dependent business processes
- Systems integrators
- Technical staff, including members of an application support team
- Heads of systems development functions
- System developers
- IT auditors

Table 16.2 Application Management Standards at a Glance

Year	Name of Standard	Developer	Objectives
2015	ISO/IEC 16350	ISO/IEC	Establish common framework for application management processes using well-defined referenceable terminology
	CIM v2	DMTF	Update CIM v1
2014	CAMP v1.1	OASIS	Refine resource model, create a single-step deployment process, provide resource-type inheritance
	CADF	DMTF	Address need to certify, self-manage, and self-audit application security in the cloud and enables cross-vendor information sharing via its data format and information definitions
	WS-Man v1.2	DMTF	Constrain web services protocols and formats to enable implementation of web services with a small hardware and software management services footprint
2013	ISO/IEC 17963:2013	ISO/IEC	Confirm WS-Man as an international standard
2012	ASL2 (English version)	ASL-BiSL	English version of ASL2
	CAMP v1	CAMP TC	
2011	ISO/IEC 17203	ISO/IEC	Formalize OVF
	IEEE1220-2011	IEEE	Reaffirm IEEE 1220–2005
2009	ASL2 (Dutch version)	ASL-BiSL	Extend ASL to address positioning of internal and external IT vendors and how they impact implementation application management processes now and in the future due to fluctuations in supply and demand
	OVF	DMTF	Offer standard packaging format for virtual machines to address critical business needs of vendors and providers
2008	WS-Man	DMTF	Provide interoperability between management applications and managed resources and identify a core set of web service specifications and usage requirements
2007	ARM v4.1	Open group	Add new capabilities (e.g., instrumentation control interface to query an implementation) to determine amount of useful transaction information, interfaces to improve ARM's usefulness in messaging and workflow
2005	CIM v1	DMTF	Methodologically define device and application characteristics to enable systems administrations and managers to control devices and applications across different vendors
	IEEE 1220–2005	IEEE	Reaffirm IEEE 1220–1998
2004	ARM v4	Open group	Richer and more flexible than ARM v3 (e.g., specify identity of application and transaction), reports changes in transaction attributes on a per-instance basis, bind a transaction to a thread
2002	ASL (Dutch version)	ASL-BiSL	Professionalize field of application management and provide a vendor-independent library of a set of books that describes application management best practices

Continued

Table 16.2 Application Management Standards at a Glance—cont'd

Year	Name of Standard	Developer	Objectives
2001	ARM v3	Open group	Increase flexibility of ARM v2, e.g., add ability to identify a user on a per-transaction basis, add Java bindings
1998	SNMP v3	IETF	Define a framework for integrating security features into overarching capabilities of SNMP v1 and SNMP v2 and define specific set of capabilities for network security and access control
	IEEE 1220–1998	IEEE	Describe systems engineering activities and process required throughout a system's lifecycle to develop systems meeting customer needs, requirements, and constraints
1997	ARM v2	Open group	Add ability to correlate parent and child transactions and collect other transaction measurements using C bindings
1996	SNMP v2c	IETF	Added a simple and unsecured password-based authentication "community" feature to SNMP v2
	ARM v1	Tivoli/HP	Measured response time and status of business transactions using C bindings
1995	Tivoli AMS	Tivoli	Provide central repository of information about an application to enable a management tool to manage the application
	POSIX 1387.2	IEEE	Define application layout, information about application and set of utility programs to manipulate the application and its information in stand-alone and distributed computing environments
1995	IEEE 1220 trial use	IEEE	Provide a standard for managing a system from initial concept through development, operations, and disposal
1993	SNMP v2	IETF	Improve SNMP v1 by addressing functional and security deficiencies of SNMP v1
1988	SNMP v1	IETF	Provide network device monitoring for TCP/IP networks

- Vendors
- Policy administrators
- Chief information officer (CIO)
- Chief finance officer (CFO)
- Chief compliance officer (CCO)
- Chief information security officer (CISO)

It is important to remember that when managing with standards, it is not necessarily a question of choosing just one standard. Depending on the specific needs of a given organization, several standards may be used together to gain most improvement in consistency and quality of management across the application lifecycle. According to the ISO, standards "facilitate trade, spread knowledge, disseminate innovative advances in technology, and share good management and conformity assessment practices."[10]

---

[10]ISO Standards – What's the Bottom Line? Accessible from: http://www.iso.org/iso/home/standards/benefitsofstandards.htm.

In application management, standards enable IT professionals to benefit from the expert opinion without having to call on those experts directly. Standardization also begins to simplify the increasingly complex application management environment, particularly the issues of interoperability, security, and portability. As the number of mobile and cloud applications increases, compliance with standards in product development will provide application managers and other IT professionals with insights for making better decisions about product choice and the management of their diverse application portfolios.

KEY TAKEAWAYS

- Key focus of cloud standards is on interoperability, portability, and security.
- Standards represent the knowledge and skills of a large number of industry leaders resulting in best practices.
- Standards facilitate application instrumentation. An application that is instrumented for management reduces its TCO.
- Early standards focused on the initial stages of the application lifecycle, but the existing suite of standards now covers the entire lifecycle.
- As mobile and cloud computing evolve further and the proliferation of available applications to support this complex environment increases, standards-based management solutions become even more critical to facilitate a seamless user experience.
- Since standards are very much an engineering exercise, it is important to keep the user perspective and requirements in mind.

LOOKING AHEAD

17

The future is software deploying software delivering software.
Lori MacVittie, Principal Technical Evangelist, F5 Networks

To help manage, monitor, and secure the next-generation of enterprise mobile apps, IT will need to incorporate dynamic policy rules that change instantly based on the behaviors of the applications.
Alan Murray, Sr. VP of Products, Apperian

INTRODUCTION

Ten years ago, there were no smartphones or other individual mobile devices that allowed employees to check email, access work systems, or share information with colleagues. In the past 10 years, technologies matured to produce cloud computing, mobile, big data, and social media, and over the next 10 years, we expect to see these new technologies fueling the digital transformation of work and changing the face of application management.

Gone are the days when the responsibilities of an application manager focused on what applications they had, where they were, when they were used, and keeping everything running. The focus today is on managing and automating integration and security in the cloud, **software-defined data centers (SDDCs)**, as well as mobile devices and optimizing application performance. The key changes in **application lifecycle management** that evolved as the computing environment moved from a stable to an agile environment are captured in Table 17.1.[1]

Although application management has matured greatly in the past 10 years, the next 10 years will see many ways in which the running of mobile and cloud applications will change significantly. **Hyperavailability** will become an absolute requirement and an executive-led, enterprise-wide **digital transformation strategy** to leverage technology to improve business processes will be necessary for organizations to stay competitive. Just as IT professionals 10 years ago would never have imagined they could set up and provide access to multiple servers, storage, and various new applications to employees around the globe within 24 hours, we anticipate that many more changes than we can imagine will occur.

The next sections present and discuss expected changes in application management that will occur within the next 10 years. Based on current indicators, and in the absence of the IT equivalent of *Gray's Sports Almanac* that Biff found in "Back to the Future," these are our best predictions of how application management will change as we move forward into the next decade.

---

[1]Craig, J., 2011. Modernizing application lifecycle management through software as a service. EMA Research Report.

Application Performance Management (APM) in the Digital Enterprise. http://dx.doi.org/10.1016/B978-0-12-804018-8.00017-6

Table 17.1 Evolution of ALM Practices

Stable	Agile
Structured ALM practices siloed by discipline (development, quality assurance, etc.)	Team collaboration and changing requirements necessitate improved traceability among project artifacts, adherence to established process and workflow Dynamic and real-time access to project state through KPIs Ongoing stakeholder input, evolving requirements across the lifecycle
Point development and testing solutions	Solutions integrated to one central repository
Teams co-located, working in isolation issues handled through whiteboards	Ability to accommodate and facilitate geographically distributed teams with external contributors (e.g., suppliers)
Rigid, sequential ALM methodologies	Flexible, iterative ALM methodologies
Monolithic applications	Composite applications

CLOUD COMPUTING INNOVATIONS

It is most likely that future breakthroughs in application management will occur through innovations in cloud computing. For example, some cloud vendors are already offering built-in management functions to shift the burden from the development organization to the cloud vendor. While this approach does not entirely relieve developers of the management burden, it does shift the nature of the work from primary responsibility to that of an assistant. Examples include data center-wide patch management (the cloud patching service) or abstracting **middleware as a service (MaaS).** MaaS delivers built-in monitoring, problem and change management services, pooled support resources, policies for scaling up and down, and metering and optional chargeback on consumed resources.

THE CHANGING FACE OF APPLICATIONS

Applications will continue to proliferate, particularly as the concept and reality of the **Internet of Things (IoT)** matures. The numbers of apps will be staggering. We will see discrete pieces of code that are smaller, but nanotechnology will have all these codes doing their own thing.

Applications are also going to be less visible as more human-like interfaces become available, such as IpSoft Amelia chat sessions. User perspective apps will be thought of in a different way. Applications will just be there, always on, always available, and the functions they perform will be more complex. Increasing dependencies between applications will prevent one application from functioning. As processors get bigger and faster, the speed of management and line of business applications will increase. As a result, the requirement will be for faster time to resolve problems, enabling faster problem resolution time. Thus, the complexity of applications themselves will grow along with the complexities of managing them.

This increased demand for the deployment of huge numbers of hyperavailable cloud and mobile applications will require organizations to be proactive in adequately funding, staffing, and training their infrastructure and operations teams to handle increasing demands in terms of quantity, accessibility, and reliability. It is also important to realize that not all applications will be running in public or private clouds. It is probable that we will see greater use of virtualized technologies over the next several years.

SOFTWARE-DEFINED EVERYTHING

Recent data collected on the use of **software-defined networking (SDN)** and SDDCs shows they are already adopted fairly widely. However, companies do not yet have a good handle on how these factors will affect their enterprise management initiatives going forward. From our perspective, the move toward software-defined versus hard-wired configurations will increase rates of change in a similar way as vMotions changed the virtualization story. As companies become more adept at rolling out these technologies, network and data center configurations can change based on time of day, time of month, etc., or, ultimately, in real-time based on applications in use and their bandwidth requirements. Just as network **QoS** specifications changed the game in the past, via SDN entire network segments will ultimately be provisioned, de-provisioned, or configured in real-time based on a given set of rules. In a similar way, network definitions may well become part of application deployment, such that network configurations are built at the same time the application is deployed to production.

All of these things lead up to one key point, and this was the crux of application management for many years. IT is still struggling with topologies, that is, the ability to relate underlying hardware and software to the applications they support (ideally in an automated fashion). Recent research shows that this is still a major problem, both with applications hosted on-site and hybrid apps executing across on-site and third party systems. As infrastructure becomes increasingly defined and provisioned as software, changing topologies will create an even bigger support challenge, as support personnel may well have no idea when, where, and how configurations are being changed. The bottom line relative to software-defined everything is that troubleshooting and root cause analysis will become increasingly difficult, and **application performance management (APM)** and **app discovery/dependency mapping (ADDM)** vendors will have to develop increasingly innovative ways of discovering and mapping application execution paths.

ADVANCED PREDICTIVE ANALYTICS FOR PERFORMANCE MANAGEMENT

As distributed applications in virtual environments and cloud computing increase in complexity, application performance management will become overwhelming. **Advanced predictive analytics** may hold the answer to easing the burden on application managers of the future by sifting through mounds of log and performance data to learn how systems work together and predict problems related to workload slowdowns and outages. Properly configured and used predictive analytics not only report on application, database, network, and storage performance, but also can detect issues from the end user's perspective.

Choosing the best, advanced predictive analytics software will require diligence. Steps to follow in making this choice should include:

1. Determining if the software can deal with the newest generation of BYODs.
2. Ensuring the software can detect everything in use in the IT infrastructure and suggest needed changes.
3. Determining if the software can manage workloads and not just provide alerts and reporting.
4. Requesting a demo or proof-of-concept to experience how complex and time-consuming installation, configuration, testing, and use will be.

5. Talking to references who already implemented the software.
6. Considering the cost-effectiveness of the software in the environment in which you will use it.

DYNAMIC POLICY RULES

The command-and-control approach to mobile device management is rapidly becoming outdated. As the behavior of enterprise applications changes based on how employees use them, rules and security measures will be created and integrated into mobile applications based on employee roles, location, and manner in which the application is being used. Application provisioning and security settings will also mature to accommodate heightened employee mobility, changing work styles, and increased collaboration with colleagues across multiple time zones.

To help manage, monitor, and secure future enterprise mobile applications, **dynamic policy rules** that change instantly will be essential to send updates and alerts and alleviate the need for the continual monitoring of employee application usage. Foreseeing this turn of events, Apperian recently released its patented Dynamic Policy Engine. The Dynamic Policy Engine provides customers with a diverse set of app wrapping policies that administrators can directly apply to applications to enhance behavior and functionality, depending on the policy. Moving forward, other vendors are expected to follow Apperian's lead in developing products that apply business and security logic to individual applications that already compiled.

AUTONOMICS AND COGNITIVE COMPUTING

In the future, **autonomics and cognitive systems** will become the norm. As result, we will see a dramatic improvement in application availability, a significant reduction in the lower-skilled IT services industry workforce, and the aggressive adoption of intelligent automation by service providers.

On June 29, 2016, Chetan Dube, CEO of IPsoft, opened the IPsoft Autonomic Center and previewed Apollo, IPsoft's next-generation cognitive IT management platform. Apollo layers cognitive competence on an autonomic backbone to disintermediate large components of IT overhead and leads the way for running unmanned network operations. As this type of innovative technology matures, IT applications of the future will be able to understand the business directly, eliminate the need for large service centers, and drive the market toward a digital labor model. Other vendors who are developing products in this space include IBM Watson, Ikarus, Ayehu, Ignio, and Syntbots.

HEIGHTENED SECURITY NEEDS

As organizations continue to enjoy the opportunities afforded them by cloud and mobile applications, companies will have to relax traditional boundaries and connect greater amounts of valuable and sensitive data to external sources to meet customer needs. These needs will drive businesses to work hard to meet the demand for online shopping, banking, and leisure (such as reading online, sharing social media links, gaming, and watching movies). At the same time, organizations will need to stay abreast of the extreme security threats posed by these cloud and mobile initiatives. As hackers become more and more sophisticated, including those in China, the importance of developing and deploying complex security measures will increase. Unfortunately, all indications are that organizations will continue to ignore the need for security. If application management is an afterthought, then the need for security in particular will be overlooked as companies continue to fail to acknowledge the importance of putting in place effective security initiatives unless and until they find themselves in a Target or Home Depot situation.

NORMALIZING DEVOPS

The best practice of integrating engineers, developers, operations managers, application managers, and business leaders, that is, **DevOps**, will come of age over the next 5 years and obliterate the distinction between development and operations. To fully realize the full benefits of mobile and cloud computing, virtualization, SDE, and cognitive computing, DevOps must become the norm in application management. Without it, the barriers between siloes of IT workers will adversely affect the benefits that each of these IT innovations has to offer. One of the harsh realities is that creating technology solutions is the easiest part. Processes that must change to accommodate the new technologies, along with new marketplace demands, are more difficult to achieve. Most difficult of all can be the cultural change needed to achieve best results. DevOps requires a major culture change, so achieving the normalization of DevOps will not be easy, but those companies that persevere and make it a priority will reap the benefits.

CLOUD MANAGEMENT STANDARDS

It has been a long struggle with application management standards overall, and **cloud standards** in particular are just emerging. In the future, standards will become more important as they establish a norm for vendors to follow and facilitate application choice. As the ISO/IEC and **IEEE** formally acknowledge cloud standards, more vendors will develop standards-based products and continue to do so to stay competitive.

An interesting twist would be the standardizing of the actual enterprise application management strategy to enable comparable reporting across programs and projects. However, organizations considering this move would need to build in some flexibility in their standard to accommodate the different needs of individual programs and projects within an organization's portfolio and the different methodologies used.

CHANGING OF THE GUARD

Many high-revenue companies already traded in MS Servers for Linux servers and all indications are that this trend will continue. Linux is open-source based and runs on everything. Microsoft runs only on X86 and, like Apple, has a long history of being a closed system. Although Microsoft is trying hard to reverse this trend, it is likely that they will have difficulty matching their more agile competitors. On the desktop, Google is merging its chrome OS (which runs on devices) with the chrome browser. In addition, there are rumors to the effect that Google is in the process of merging chrome OS with Android. As a result, thousands of android apps running on mobile devices will be able to run on a Linux-based Android desktop/laptop. If and when this happens, Microsoft's effectiveness will be limited to its Azure assets. The transition will take a while due to the millions of desktops running .NET front ends, even after

Google makes its move. However, it is anticipated that Google will ultimately assume leadership in the desktop market, starting primarily with the non-US market followed by domination in the US market. This will cause APM vendors to ramp up support for Linux, Chrome OS, and Android since Android, in particular, becomes the front end for a new breed of complex, component-based applications.

Increasingly, component-based applications will reintroduce issues relating to latency (with many more network interactions, the potential for performance impact increases). APIs will supplant traditional methods of integration, particularly for those integrations that are not performance critical (in other words, most of the financial world will still run on proprietary platforms and/or high-scale integration pipes). From the app perspective, "big operational data" coming from IoT can go into a similar (separate but equal) bucket as the "big operational data" coming from execution systems. This makes analytics the key differentiator between management solutions—this is the case today, and the transition from pure analytics to actionable analytics is already under way.

OTHER POSSIBLE INNOVATIONS

In the next 10 years, we are likely to see other innovations such as **customizable patterns** in the form of **multiple-use templates** to speed application development and deployment. There are also indicators that **in-context collaboration**, **real-time planning**, **lifecycle traceability**, and **development intelligence** will be available in the cloud as part of a full application lifecycle approach rooted in current practices but extending the model in new ways.

BACK TO THE FUTURE WITH ACME

As we come to the end of this book, it seems appropriate to revisit Acme Manufacturing sometime in the not-too-distant future. Things have changed a lot from the situation portrayed in the earlier chapters. The people we introduced earlier moved on to other jobs, some within Acme and some elsewhere. Acme, unlike some of its competitors, has not outsourced any of its IT functions. Acme management believes that IT is too important and too strategic to put it in the hands of another company. Let's take a look.

Meet Jake. He is a client service manager (CSM) in Acme's IT Department. He graduated 2 years ago with a BS in computer science from nearby NIWOT State College. His is an entry-level position

that Acme uses to onboard most of its new hires in IT Operations. Acme's IT management feels that this is a good spot to give new employees a broad perspective of the role of IT and its importance to the company. It is intended for this to be the beginning of a career path within Acme's IT organization.

Jake's manager, Fiona, stops. She knows from checking an app on her tablet that everything is on track.

Fiona: How's it going, Dave?

Dave: Fine. It's pretty quiet today. (Thinking to himself "Isn't it always?") A couple of hours ago EARL (the autonomic, cognitive management system) detected a voltage fluctuation on the storage system used for the inventory control database. Once he noticed it, he pointed the inventory control system to the backup database and took that storage system off-line for preventive maintenance. He also created a new backup copy on an alternate storage system. That's been about it.

Fiona: That's good. Good, but not unusual.

Dave: I have to say that this job is pretty low-key. Mainly, we need to follow up on things. You know, like making sure that EARL hasn't lost his mind—ensure that the actions that he takes make sense. Also, we need to make sure that changes requested by our clients actually get implemented by LISA (the automated change control and processing system used by both clients and IT staff).

Fiona: (chuckling) Yes, that is true, but you need to keep a couple of things in mind. First, it's very important that someone is looking over the virtual shoulders of systems like EARL and LISA. They're very good and extremely accurate in what they do—far more accurate and reliable than the people who used to do their jobs. However, as you've seen, they aren't perfect. Maybe someday we'll get to the point that we can "fire and forget" with systems like EARL and LISA. The other thing to remember is that this is as much about getting you broad exposure to our systems, our clients, the people in IT, and our overall business. This is a steppingstone for you to more interesting jobs in the future. No matter how good the automation, we always need people for higher-level tasks that can't be automated like planning and strategy, application development, etc.

SUMMARY

Moving forward, many organizations will be creating a malleable hybrid cloud environment that combines public and private cloud computing. This approach will require new strategies for application management that enable software components to create an appropriate image for any target environment. The mix of public and private cloud computing will also require linking resource, configuration, and cloud management. With budget a big concern, organizations will need to update their applications portfolios; review a cost-benefit analysis of cloud, social media, and mobile; and take meaningful action to choose the right providers and negotiating the best terms and conditions from them.

Security will be an ongoing critical part of application management. Organizations that acknowledge and embrace the need for more and stricter security initiatives will benefit from the investment. As new application management techniques and methodologies evolve, tools must evolve to accommodate them to enable organizations to focus on business innovation versus retooling and retraining.

In the future, organizations must embrace and absorb cloud, mobile, social, and big data technologies and recognize digital transformation as an important business strategy, not just as a technology fad. To achieve and maintain a competitive advantage, organizations will need to integrate digital technologies into their business processes to help them solve infrastructure problems, particularly those related to the network, that often cause enterprise-wide application performance issues.

Appendix A

Service-Level Management

Say what you mean, mean what you say, and do what you said you would.
Barbara Colorosso

Service-level management (SLM)—it is a topic that is really simple and straightforward, but one that many people seem to have difficulty understanding or feel a need to make it more complex than it really is. The essence of SLM is embodied in the quote, although the associated processes are definitely more formal than that. Serviceable management is about ensuring that customers (internal or external) get what they are paying for and that what they receive matches their expectations. While the subjects of SLM and service-level agreements (SLAs) are most commonly associated with information technology (IT) and telecommunications, they are equally applicable to any kind of service. There are SLAs for every imaginable kind of service, ranging from baggage handling at large airports to weed control in Australian parks.

Much has been written about SLM (including the top-selling book on the topic by one of the authors, titled *Foundations of Service Level Management*). The objective of this chapter is not to address the subject in depth, but rather to provide the reader with a brief overview.

TERMINOLOGY

One of the big problems with SLM is that it is riddled with acronyms that are tossed about, without a proper definition of underlying terms. This ambiguity works to the disadvantage of the IT manager or service provider hoping to address it. Ambiguity fosters confusion. That confusion may lead to inaction or, worse, it may lead to inappropriate action (as in the case of purchasing the wrong tool to help with SLM). Before we can really begin our discussion of SLM, it is necessary to establish some common ground.

To begin, we must look at the term "**service**." Contrary to common supposition, SLM is not limited to IT and telecom organizations. It applies anywhere a "service" is delivered. However, this statement just further begs the question, "What is a service?" In the simplest terms, a service is any task performed by a person or group for another person or group.

SLM is often mistakenly equated with SLAs, but the two are very different. SLM is a process for delivering services that consistently meet client requirements. It entails defining, managing, and improving the levels of those services. This is true regardless of the type of service that is being delivered. It is just as applicable for an airline as it is for an MSP or the IT department in a large company.

An SLA is a component of an effective SLM program. Interestingly, it is possible to have an SLA without a program for managing service levels and conversely, an SLM program may be established without creating SLAs. While both approaches are possible, neither is advisable. *The most fundamental aspect of an SLA is that it represents an agreement (or contract) between the service provider and the client, which defines the service to be provided and the level (or quality) of service that will be delivered.*

There are many facets to an SLA. It is a communication vehicle between the client and the service provider. Central to the SLA is the definition of terms in a way that will be meaningful to both parties. For example, the agreement must define the service that is covered, the level of service that will be provided, etc. It is this latter point that leads to one of the key benefits of an SLA: managing expectations.

Operational-level agreements (OLAs) are a specialized form of an SLA. OLAs are used within the service provider's organization to address subsets of the overall service. For example, an OLA related to an online billing system might address the network used by the client to communicate with the application. OLAs are more technical than an SLA with a client organization. Using the example of an online billing system, the SLA would focus on the end-to-end availability of the application and the overall response time or time to process a transaction. However, in an OLA, the network portion of that same service may include metrics for such things as: buffer miss ratio, buffer utilization, CPU utilization, line utilization, faults, discards, latency, error rate, packet loss, etc. These metrics are not normally meaningful to a client but are important to IT management, particularly those directly responsible for that network.

Next are two closely related terms: **service-level objective (SLO)** and **service-level guarantee (SLG)**. The main difference between these is contractual in nature. The SLO represents the level of service that the service provider and customer have agreed will be delivered during the term of the SLA. This means that the service provider agreed to meet that commitment. In order to agree to it, the service provider (including IT organizations) must be reasonably certain that it is possible to meet the commitment within the existing constraints (e.g., budget, staff, technology, etc.). In turn, the client's agreement means that they determined that they can function properly at this level of service.

The step from SLO to SLG is very small. It is often a legal difference. The term service-level guarantee (SLG) is far more common in formal, legally binding contracts between companies than in internal SLAs. An SLG is simply a guarantee by the service provider that the SLO will be met. It is common for the contract to include some form of penalty that will be imposed if the service provider fails to meet the guarantee.

SLM PROCESS

The minimal functions of SLM are to:

Define
Measure
Assess
Set objectives
Monitor
Refine and improve (Fig. A.1)

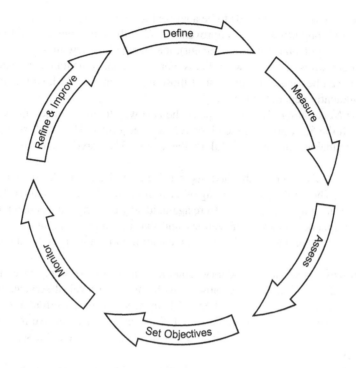

FIGURE A.1

SLM functions.

These six functions assume that there are other associated activities taking place in parallel (e.g., reporting, client dialogue, negotiating SLOs, negotiating SLAs, etc.). Also, this is an iterative process with feedback loops incorporated.

Define: Before any work can be done on SLM, you need to first determine which service you wish to manage. You also need to decide what metrics are available, or may be captured, that will give an indication of the level of service that is being provided.

Measure: The starting point for the process of SLM is to establish a set of baseline data. Of course, this should include the data that was identified in the definition phase as being representative of the level of service. However, that is probably not going to be sufficient. Data should also be captured that will allow system and network experts in your organization determine what would need to be done to improve the service. Some organizations find that the management tools they already have are sufficient for this part of the process, at least initially. Others find that they simply do not have the ability to acquire adequate information. They are then faced with the choice of abandoning the project or purchasing the additional tools. However, it is rare that an organization does not have access to any of the data necessary to assess the level of service provided. If none of the necessary information is available, then that service provider probably has much more serious problems than implementing a formal SLM process. They are probably facing the problem of sheer survival.

Assess: Once captured, the data needs to be analyzed to understand the current state. It also needs to be studied to identify opportunities for improvement. With these two pieces of information (current level of service and the potential for improvement), management is now in a position to engage in a serious dialogue about levels of service with clients. For now, management knows what it is delivering, what improvements can be made, and the cost of those improvements. Without this information, it is not possible to confidently negotiate SLAs.

Set Objectives: Negotiating SLAs is normally the best way to go about setting objectives for service levels. Through the SLA process, the objectives are set jointly. The result should be something that is realistic, attainable, and meaningful to the client. The targets that are set also must be affordable.

Monitor: Once the SLOs are established, the service provider must take steps to ensure that the SLOs are at least met. There follows an ongoing process of monitoring the actual level of service being delivered and measuring it against the SLO. Here again, ideally existing management tools will be sufficient. However, in practice, many organizations find that the monitoring and reporting part of the SLM process is improved (or made possible) with the addition of some specialized tools aimed at that function.

Refine and Improve: A service provider (whether it is an IT organization, carrier, ISP, or any other type of service provider) should never be satisfied with any given level of service, even if that level completely satisfies its obligations to its clients. There needs to be an effort aimed at continuous improvement of the level of service being delivered. This can be for defensive reasons (e.g., staying ahead of the competition). It may also be seen as a way to add more value to the service and ultimately derive more revenue.

Finally, the unstated seventh step of the SLM process is **repeat**. The process must be regularly scrutinized for relevance, accuracy, etc. The manager or executive responsible for providing the service covered by the SLM process must always be scrutinizing both the process and the service, looking for ways to improve both.

SERVICE-LEVEL AGREEMENTS

An SLA is a contract between the service provider and the client. If the service provider is part of the client's enterprise, the agreement can be less formal. Certainly, it will not normally be a formal, legally binding contract.

As shown in Table A.1, an SLA has several key components.

Table A.1 SLA Components

Parties	Reporting
Term	Reviews
Scope	Revisions
Service-level objectives (metrics)	Responsibilities
Nonperformance	Approvals
Exclusions	

Parties: This part of the SLA simply identifies the client and the service provider(s).

Term: An SLA does not run indefinitely. That is because the changes that occur over time will eventually make any SLA obsolete. Therefore, the SLA needs to have a duration specified. Having an expiration date forces periodic reviews of requirements, capabilities, and costs.

Scope: The scope section is where the services covered by the SLA are defined.

Service-Level Objectives: The SLOs represent the level of service that the parties to the SLA have agreed will be delivered. The level of service is expressed and measured by metrics. It is those metrics that are used in the SLOs. In the context of IT, metrics are generally about either availability of an application or its performance. Availability is usually represented by such details as total hours of availability, hours or minutes of outage, mean time to repair, etc. However, whatever metrics are chosen must indicative of the clients' actual experience.

Performance is significantly more difficult to measure than availability. The challenge is determining which aspect of performance is appropriate for the SLA being written. As with availability, strive for simplicity in performance metrics and try to make them as indicative of the client experience as possible. Usually, performance has a speed dimension to it. Speed may be represented by such things as response time, data transfer rate, etc. For online systems, the SLA should always include a metric for response time. Another common performance characteristic is volume. Volume may be reflected in such statistics as the amount of data transferred, the number of transactions processed, etc. There is no place in an SLA for such details as error rate, packet loss, percent of frames delivered, network latency, etc. Also, like availability, keep performance metrics as simple as possible. There is something seductive about performance metrics. They make us want to drill down into more and more detail. However, when writing an SLA, resist that temptation and go only as deep as necessary to accurately reflect the user **experience**.

Metrics for SLAs must be:
- Attainable
- Measurable
- Meaningful/understandable
- Controllable
- Mutually acceptable
- Cost-effective

METRICS

Metrics should always be defined from the perspective of the user rather than from that of the service provider. That is because SLAs are always about the users' experiences. Therefore, availability and performance of individual components together comprise the service but are not relevant to the user. The user sees and cares about their ability to access the functionality afforded by an application. That is what the SLA should reflect.

Attainable—The target service levels that are defined in the SLA have to reflect reality and not just wishful thinking. The service provider must know, or reasonably expect, that the objectives defined in the agreement can be achieved. To do otherwise is simply foolish.

Measurable—There is absolutely no point of including a metric for something that cannot be measured. In that case, how will you be able to assess whether or not you met the commitment?

For example, it might seem like a good idea to include end-to-end response time as a metric. However, if you do not have the ability to measure the actual response time that is delivered, then it is useless.

Meaningful/Understandable—There is a tendency by IT organizations to proposed metrics for an SLA that are not meaningful to the client. The metrics need to be defined in terms that reflect the clients' experience and that the clients can relate to.

Controllable—The service provider must be able to control any of the factors reflected in the SLA. If the service provider is not able to control a factor, then that factor should not be reflected in the SLA.

Mutually Acceptable—SLAs are supposed to be created with a sense of equality and partnership. Therefore, any metrics need to be acceptable to both parties. While it may be possible for the client to dictate terms to the service provider, or vice versa, it is a mistake to do so. Dictating terms defeats the purpose of the SLA.

Cost-effective—Restraint must be exercised when defining a set of metrics for an SLA. It can be tempting to define a wonderful set of metrics that would be prohibitively expensive to actually measure. Thus, when defining metrics, there is often a tradeoff between cost and precision of the data.

NONPERFORMANCE

A nagging question regarding SLAs is what to do about situations in which the service provider does not deliver the level of service promised in the agreement. This is an important question and it must be addressed in the SLA, but the question remains: what is the appropriate action in such a situation?

Thinking about this question usually flows along a path of reasoning that assumes that there should be penalties for failing to meet service-level commitments (nonperformance). It is also assumed that the penalties should be financial. However, at this point, popular thinking starts to bog down. If there is to be a penalty, how large should it be? Also, there is the problem of in-house service providers. If they are penalized financially, will that simply result in making it harder, or impossible, for them to meet the service commitments? Won't they still need to have adequate funding to operate?

If there is a penalty for nonperformance, should it be financial? For external groups, a financial penalty is appropriate, though not the only option. Service providers often like to offer free service as compensation for poor service. That can be compared to the experience of being served a bad meal at a restaurant and then being offered a free meal in the future as compensation. Does that actually mean that I will have a better meal or just another bad meal for free? Sometimes it may make sense to accept that offer, but more often it is not.

The key point of any penalty for nonperformance, whether for an in-house or an external group, is that the penalty must be significant. One must be pragmatic and realize that the purpose of a penalty is not to compensate to offset the impact of the substandard level of service. It is a virtual certainty that it will never be possible to negotiate such a penalty. Instead, the penalty must cause enough discomfort or pain to the service provider that avoiding it acts as an incentive to meet the service commitment.

There have been cases in which a service provider made service-level guarantees. Subsequently, the service provider decides that it is cheaper to pay the penalty than to provision to meet the service. This is obviously an unethical approach to business and one that is ultimately self-limiting, as customers desert when their contracts expire. However, setting aside the ethical aspect, the key point to notice is that in such a case, the penalty does not cause enough pain for the service provider to want to avoid it.

How can penalties be made more painful? One obvious answer is to make the dollar amount of the penalty very large. Naturally, service providers are usually unwilling to accept agreements with very large financial penalties. The secret is to be creative. Pain can be caused by many things, not just the size of a penalty check. Things such as escalation or creating obligations for their executives, etc., should be explored to find possible alternatives.

Applying a financial penalty may be a viable alternative with an external service provider, however, with an in-house provider (such as IT), it is a dubious proposition. If money is taken away from an IT group, that may very well guarantee that they won't have enough money to meet the guarantees in the future. Just as with the external service provider, the secret lies in being creative. Remember, the goal is to cause pain, not to hinder the group's ability to provide services in the future.

Behavioral psychologists have long known that positive reinforcement is far more effective in modifying behavior than negative reinforcement. That is worth considering when negotiating service-level agreements. Consider rewards for meeting or exceeding guarantees rather than penalties for nonperformance. Bonuses for in-house staff can be an option. More radical are incentive payments to external service providers that deliver a high level of service.

Remember that when contemplating the creation of consequences for nonperformance, it is essential to be creative and remain flexible. Think outside the box. Consider both positive and negative alternatives and always remember that financial penalties may not be the best answer for your situation. Penalties for nonperformance cannot ensure that SLOss will always be met; however, they can significantly increase the likelihood of those objectives being met.

EXCLUSIONS

While the client and service writer can come to an agreement on the SLOs in other major aspects of an SLA, there are times or circumstances that should be excluded from consideration when calculating whether the SLA commitments were met. Those exclusions need to be defined and incorporated into the SLA. For example, holidays may not warrant the same level of service, or it may not be possible to deliver the same level of service on some holidays. Likewise, it may be necessary to make a provision for maintenance windows for the network, the systems, or even the applications. Acts of God, excess volume, third-party errors, problems caused by the client, etc. are other examples of things that may warrant exclusion from the agreement.

REPORTING

An SLA requires reports so that both the service provider and the client can see whether or not the SLOs are being met. The SLA should define the reports that will be produced in support of the agreement and who will be responsible for producing those reports. Normally, the reports will be the responsibility of the service provider. At a minimum, there should be periodic reports that identified the service covered by the SLA, the date the report was created, the period of time covered by the report, and for each metric included, the actual result versus the objective.

REVIEWS

Periodically, the SLA should be reviewed by both parties. Reviews should take place once or twice per year. That frequency should be spelled out in the SLA.

REVISIONS

The SLA should include a description of the process for making revisions to the agreement. The environments through which the services are delivered are never static. They are constantly changing. Likewise, the needs of the client will change and evolve over time. Therefore, the SLA needs to be adjusted to reflect those changes.

RESPONSIBLE PARTIES

Although really just a formality, as with any other contract, the parties to the agreement need to be identified in the agreement. This actually defines who must approve the SLA.

APPROVALS

Finally, the agreement needs to be signed (approved) by a client representative and a representative of the service provider, each with the necessary authority to do so.

SUMMARY

Within the context of IT and its clients, SLM is not just about applications, but applications are almost always part of SLM. Having an SLM program in place does not guarantee that clients will experience higher levels of service, but it does provide a mechanism for setting realistic expectations. It also defines what will happen if the level of service falls below what is promised in the SLA. In short, it provides the basis for an objective and dispassionate relationship between the service provider and the client(s).

Appendix B

The Configuration Management Database and Configuration Management System

There is no question that **application performance** and the performance of the business services they support, as well as initiatives such as **DevOps** and **agile**, all depend on managing change effectively across the broader application infrastructure. The requirements to do this have only accelerated, given the more dynamic and heterogeneous environments of public and **private cloud**, the move to virtualization, and even the need to provide more effective approaches for managing **containers** and **microservices**.

Ongoing research and dialogue with information technology (IT) organizations reaffirm that despite current industry controversy (including a fair amount of "bad press"), solutions related to **configuration management databases (CMDBs)**, **configuration management systems (CMS)**, and **application discovery and dependency mapping (ADDM)** are actually on the rise in terms of innovation and relevance. This is because the need to discover, capture, and optimize application-to-application and application-to-infrastructure interdependencies could not be more critical given dynamic, heterogeneous infrastructures. The use cases relevant to understanding service interdependencies range from **performance management**, to **change management**, to **asset management**, to data center consolidation, to security concerns.

This appendix, taken from *CMDB Systems: Making Change Work in the Age of Cloud and Agile*,[1] explores the processes and the technologies relevant to CMDB systems as they evolve to become more automated, more analytics-aware, and more supportive of transforming IT efficiencies and effectiveness.

Given the manifold debates about issues and values in CMDB systems, it comes as no surprise that few topics in IT today are as confusing and misunderstood as the CMDB. Some people define the CMDB and the CMS by their strict **IT Infrastructure Library (ITIL)** definitions, while others use one of the many descriptions given by the CMDB vendors in the market. Still others see the CMDB as a homegrown collection of data that never found its way to being useful. One common misconception is that a CMDB contains only configuration information on servers and devices in the infrastructure. Depending on the particular deployment, a CMDB may also contain information on applications, middleware, documentation, people, processes, providers, and other relevant information in addition to infrastructure components.

This appendix will examine the two foundations for the CMDB system: ITIL processes and associated CMDB-related technologies, as shown in Fig. B.1. These two foundations are not always understood from a common set of balanced perspectives. Processes are often favored by one set of

---

[1]Drogseth, D.N., Sturm, R., Twing, D., 2015. CMDB Systems: Making Change Work in the Age of Cloud and Agile. Morgan Kaufmann.

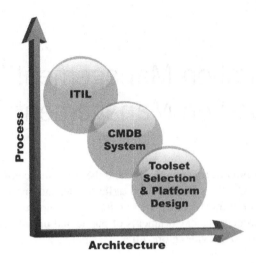

FIGURE B.1

The CMDB system's two foundations.

stakeholders, while other stakeholders may be fully consumed by technologies, integration issues, and architecture. If there is one central idea behind optimizing CMDB system deployments, it is the need to promote balanced attention and facilitate dialogue to both process and technology.

CMDB FOUNDATIONS PART 1: PROCESS

ITIL may not be perfect, and it is categorically best if viewed as a "departure point" rather than an ideology (as some might claim). However, ITIL offers well-thought-out guidelines that also pose questions with the potential to spark valuable analysis as IT managers and practitioners seek to adopt ITIL recommendations within their own unique environments.

ITIL is:

- A common lexicon for disparate disciplines
- Holistic—a place where the full IT process mosaic can come together
- A high-level set of recommendations for what processes should be in place
- A valuable catalyst

ITIL is not:

- A standard
- Completely prescriptive
- A perfect answer for a perfect world
- A panacea for all of IT's ailments

The ITIL framework is based on a service lifecycle and consists of five lifecycle stages: *Service Strategy, Service Design, Service Transition, Service Operation,* and *Continual Service Improvement.* There is a supporting publication for each of these stages as well as a set of complementary ITIL publications that provide guidance specific to industry sectors, organization types, operating models, and technology architectures.

ITIL'S CONFIGURATION MANAGEMENT DATABASE

CMDB is defined as a database used to store configuration items throughout their lifecycle. The CMS maintains one or more CMDBs, each of which stores attributes of configuration items and relationships with other configuration items.

ITIL defines **configuration item** (CI) as "any component or other service asset that needs to be managed in order to deliver an IT service." Additionally, "service transition" clarifies that CIs "typically include IT services, hardware, software, buildings, people, and formal documentation such as process documentation and service-level agreements." Defining, managing, and optimizing CIs and their interdependencies are at the heart of CMDB system deployments.

The dimensionality and range of configuration items open up a whole world of interdependencies and insights for which ITIL should be given a great deal of credit. We are no longer talking about just managing things—we are talking about managing IT services in their fully human and technical dimensions.

THE CONFIGURATION MANAGEMENT SYSTEM

In understanding the real impact of the CMS, it is best to stay focused on the term "system," as ITIL's CMS includes both a sense of federation and potentially more dynamism than a single, standalone CMDB.

According to ITIL, a CMS is:

> ...a system that supports configuration management through effective data assimilation and toolsets that track, aggregate, analyze, and showcase critical information regarding configuration items and CI relationships. The CMS may also include information about incidents, problems, known errors, changes and releases. The CMS is...used by all *IT service management* processes.

This definition of CMS (in ITIL V2, largely used to define the CMDB itself) allows for more flexibility with "incidents, problems, known errors, changes and releases." As such, the CMS can become a foundation for empowering virtually any IT process or requirement, which increasingly includes operations and even **development**—well beyond ITIL's traditional service desk roots. Note the concluding sentence in the ITIL definition: "The CMS is...used by all IT service management processes." In the real world, this is a statement of potential that needs to be addressed in phases. Remember, despite its potential to bring about huge benefits, the CMDB system is not a single magic bullet. In its entirety, and in real deployments, the CMS represents a much more streamlined, systemic, and dynamic approach than the market stereotype for the traditional CMDB, in which service modeling and discovery are beginning to take center stage, supplanting data storage as the true "spine" of the system.

THE SERVICE KNOWLEDGE MANAGEMENT SYSTEM

ITIL's definition of CMS brings up yet another term: the **service knowledge management system (SKMS)**, which may be ITIL V3's single most visionary idea. If the CMS can house multiple CMDBs optimized for different levels of detail and relevance, the CMS is itself an enabler for this even larger vision—the SKMS.

ITIL defines the SKMS as:

> ...a resource that encompasses the Configuration Management System along with other databases and information repositories. It is a true service management system that can acquire, analyze, update, store, and display all the information that an IT service provider needs access to in order to offer the most complete and precise IT services for their customers.

The SKMS is far from just being about collecting data and storing it in a single physical database; it is a system that facilitates the analysis and presentation of knowledge to support the "full lifecycle of IT services." If you want to achieve value through your CMDB system and you completely ignore the need for analyzing and presenting knowledge (not to mention automation), you will never optimize your efforts (Fig. B.2).

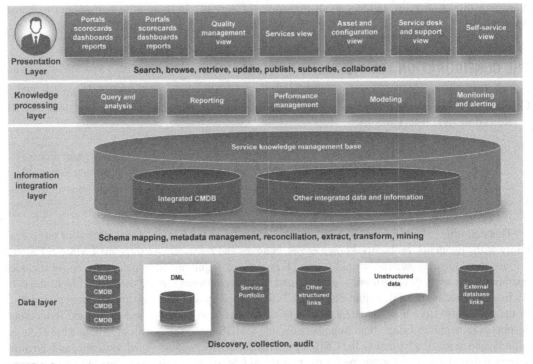

FIGURE B.2

The primary goal of ITIL V3's SKMS.

Figure B.2 shows an advanced logical architecture in which a core or "integrated" CMDB is federated with multiple CMDBs optimized in content and granularity for separate stakeholder groups (EMA's term for this is "citizen CMDB"). Core CMDBs enable the full IT organizations to enjoy a cohesive and reconciled view of services and their interdependencies.

CMDB DATA AND CONFIGURATION ITEMS: A SECOND LOOK

Understanding CMDB-related data and CIs is central to CMDB system success. ITIL V2 grouped CMDB-relevant data into the following logical categories:

Technology data—Includes asset data such as costs, locations, hardware and software configurations, related contracts, software licenses, and maintenance and support histories, physical and logical topology data, and operational data, such as availability, performance, and capacity.

Process data—Includes service models that map assets to services, business process models that map services to business processes, and IT service management process workflows.

People data—Includes asset-to-user mapping and user information, such as roles and responsibilities. It also includes IT staff member data, such as asset-to-support mapping useful for incident escalation (indicating which IT staff members support which assets).

Provider data—Includes which service providers engage, when, and under what conditions.

ITIL 2011 also refines how to better understand CIs and CI categories beyond broad groupings of hardware, software, buildings, people, documentation, etc. For example, ITIL 2011 also includes the following:

Service lifecycle CIs—Including business cases, release documentation, test plans, etc.

Internal CIs—Comprising those required for individual projects internal to the IT organization.

External CIs—Such as external customer requirements and agreements, releases from suppliers or subcontractors, and external services.

Interface CIs—Those required to deliver the end-to-end service across an ecosystem of multiple service providers, for example, an escalation document that specifies how incidents will be transferred between two service providers.

This last category is especially intriguing as it shows how ITIL is setting the stage for the very real and growing challenges of managing services across many separate political entities, which may nonetheless constitute a true business ecosystem of partners, suppliers, and service providers of all varieties (Fig. B.3).

Another key foundational concept from ITIL is the CI attribute, defined as, "A piece of information about a configuration item. Examples are name, location, version number, and cost. Attributes of CIs are recorded in a configuration management database (CMDB) and maintained as part of a configuration management system (CMS)." In real CMDB system deployments, CI attributes can extend to multiple sources through a consistent service modeling system (as described in the following section on technology) to support unique use case requirements, from capacity to performance, or state to financial data.

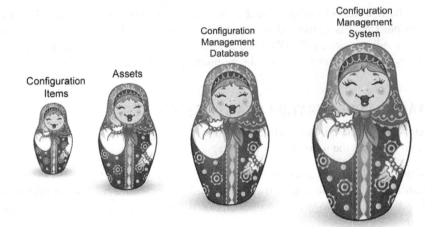

FIGURE B.3

Russian nesting dolls as an analogy for the relationship between CIs, assets, the CMDB, and the CMS.

CMDB FOUNDATIONS PART 2: CMDB SYSTEM TECHNOLOGIES AT A GLANCE

The fact is that the CMDB system is not a single technology, which in itself has become a major source of confusion. Sadly, the CMDB, and to a lesser degree the CMS, were largely defined by various constituencies according to what is most convenient for them. These include vendors that develop (or attack) CMDB/CMS-related solutions and technologies, consultants and systems integrators with processes and game plans associated with CMDB-related deployments, analysts seeking to cram the CMDB into a two-dimensional technology market, and even IT executives and professionals who have narrowly construed wishes for a magic bullet tailor-made for them.

EMA often refers to the challenge of CMDB-related deployments as an issue of the blind men and the elephant, in which a group of blind men touch an elephant to learn what it is. Each man feels only one part of the elephant, such as the tusk or the leg, and they compare notes. The men learn that they are in complete disagreement about the elephant. The same is true regarding the challenge of CMDB-related deployments. While the siloed perspectives usually include debates between those wedded to process (sometimes too firmly) and those who see the CMDB system primarily in terms of technology, the analogy can just as well be applied to the confusion and prejudice arising from the relevant technologies alone.

CMDB SYSTEM TECHNOLOGIES: A CLOSER LOOK

Critical CMDB system foundational technologies include the CMDB itself, application discovery and dependency mapping, other discovery and inventory tools, automation, analytics, dashboard and visualization, and other investments.

Configuration Management Database

The CMDB's core functions are to assimilate and reconcile critical data sources through manual population, bulk updates, or automation, informed by policies, dialogues, and increasingly by analytics. In turn, CMDB-supported modeling can help to articulate, access, and promote the critical service interdependencies that will ultimately make the CMDB investment worthwhile. How the CMDB evolves should correlate directly with careful IT planning that targets a phased approach based on use case priorities, such as *Change Management, Asset Management, Service Impact Management,* and even *Performance Management.*

The CMDB, whether a federated "citizen CMDB" or core, "integrated CMDB," is not a data warehouse optimized for high-volume data analytics. Rather, it is a resource aimed at capturing critical service interdependencies, relationships, and device and software configurations. Currently, few vendors offer the CMDB as a standalone solution, but typically embed it in other systems such as service desk with asset and change management, or service performance solutions vendors where CMDBs are optimized for more real-time usage.

Application Discovery and Dependency Mapping

The central value for all ADDM solutions is to discover, in as automated a fashion as possible, application-to-infrastructure and infrastructure-to-infrastructure interdependencies critical for the CMDB system and for effective service management overall. Cloud and virtualization have challenged, and continue to challenge, ADDM solutions to become more dynamic and adaptive to real-time, or near-real-time, changes.

ADDM solutions may be agentless, agent-based, or a combination of both. The varied approaches represent vendors' best efforts to get beyond thorny security issues, and even reach into **public cloud** environments (Fig. B.4).

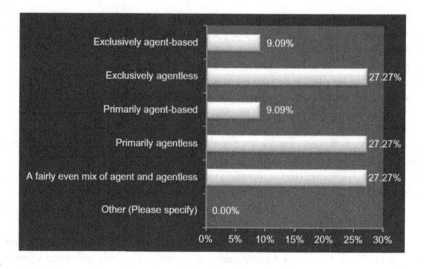

FIGURE B.4

ADDM solution approaches.

ADDM typically falls into either less real-time, configuration-centric capabilities more traditionally associated with CMDBs, or more transaction-aware, real-time capabilities with roots in performance management. Both are relevant for a CMS optimized to empower a true SKMS, and both are becoming more and more pervasive and effective in CMDB system deployments. Moreover, as the ADDM market evolves, we anticipate a gradual merging of ADDM values—in which real-time performance insights can directly become supportive of configuration and even asset interdependencies.

Other Discovery and Inventory Tools

Discovery and inventory tools can be correlated with CMDB deployments either dynamically or manually. In some cases, they are integrated with ADDM solutions to feed the CMDB system as a single package. They can range widely based on domain and use case, from network discovery to PC inventory, to security, to capacity planning, to monitoring tools that "discover" key pieces of infrastructure, and/or applications in support of event or performance-related analytics. We identified more than 50 discovery sources in some enterprises, while those with multiple geographical presences and localized buying preferences can escalate this number into the hundreds.

Automation

Little could be more critical to CMDB success than proactively phasing in automation, both in populating and maintaining the CMDB and in optimizing CMDB system insights in managing change, service performance, and even lifecycle asset values. Automation comes in multiple styles, ranging from what the market would call "configuration tools," to runbook and IT process automation, to triggering events based on shifting CI attributes for remediation and alerts. A partial list of options to consider for phased priorities over time might include:

- PC configuration, **patch management**, and audit capabilities
- System configuration, VM provisioning, and patch management
- Network configuration solutions
- Service desk workflow
- Development-centric simulation and design automation
- Automated application provisioning (DevOps) typically associated with cloud and virtualization
- Manifests for transitioning development models into production
- Security-related identity and access management solutions
- Runbook or IT process automation for stitching multiple automation capabilities together
- Load balancing and other performance-related capabilities
- Other cloud-specific or virtualized automation surrounding a whole new array of packaged solutions, including **software-defined data centers** and **software-defined networks**

Analytics

If the CMDB system is primarily about insight, then that insight needs to be fed and optimized through good analytic tools. These tools may have a range of capabilities, from advanced reporting to truly advanced heuristics, including self-learning algorithms, transaction analytics, and big data in various forms. "Big data for IT" and "operational analytics" have become buzzwords, but in some respects they do not do justice to the breadth and variety of analytic choices that can contribute meaningfully to CMDB-related initiatives. The following are just a few categories to consider:

- Self-learning predictive analytics, some of which already use service modeling to correlate performance anomalies with CMDB-related interdependencies
- Big data in the form of integrated data warehousing and data mining, ranging from visualization and search to more advanced trending over time for capacity, performance, and other insights
- Big data in terms of integrated data warehousing and data mining for IT financial planning and optimization for CapEx investments and OpEx efficiencies
- Transaction-centric analytics that may look not only at IT service performance, but also at user behaviors and business outcomes, including **user experience** insights

All of these analytic options are already being actively mapped to service modeling and integrated with CMDB systems in some deployments. Most analytic **integrations** favor ADDM over core CMDB for a variety of reasons, chief among them dynamic currency. Some analytic tools already have ADDM-like modeling built into them.

Dashboards and Visualization

Dashboards and other forms of visualization may be directly or indirectly affiliated with any of the above technology choices. Good visualization is where IT harvests and shares its insights within silos and, even more importantly, across domains.

Other Relevant Investments

Enabling and empowering the full CMDB system across multiple phases and use cases may well involve other technology investments beyond the general categories listed above. Two examples are project management and social IT, both of which ideally support better stakeholder planning and dialogue. Another relevant investment, the service catalog, deserves special attention as an outwardly-facing expression of CMDB modeling to empower automation and governance in provisioning (or enabling self-provisioning for) new IT services.

A LOOK AT THE BROADER CMDB SYSTEM AND THE SERVICE MANAGEMENT ECOSYSTEM IT SUPPORTS

As shown in Fig. B.5, the potential reach of the CMDB system in supporting what ITIL would call an SKMS is rich and diverse. Indeed, even Fig. B.5 is not meant to be complete or exhaustive; it is intended merely as a sketch of how different technology investments can come together to harvest the power of CMDB-driven insights over time.

EMA once labeled the two spheres in Fig. B.5 "the two CMDBs." The idea behind this naming was to show how real-time or near-real-time insights could provide strong value in concert with more process-centric systems, so changes can immediately be understood and validated in terms of infrastructure, application service, and business outcomes. Conversely, when problems arise, insights into how and where changes were made and managed could immediately be linked with performance-related issues.

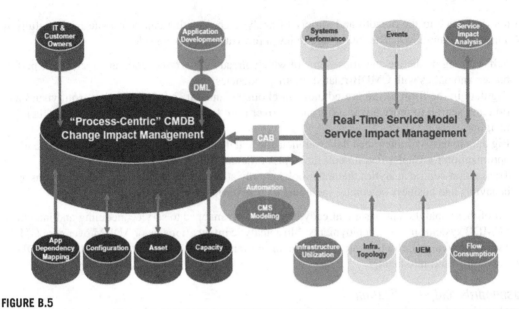

FIGURE B.5

ITIL support of SKMS.

However, the term "two CMDBs" no longer applies to the current market and industry taxonomy that buckets CMDB technology as a single, physical database. We are now using the term "real-time service model" to suggest how CMDBs, including federated CMDBs, may access critically relevant CI-related data without necessarily moving into a separate data store. This is a critical distinction because it centers the broader CMDB system less in database technology than in service modeling capabilities with reconciled data access.

A summary of what is included in Fig. B.6 is described in more detail with the following list:

- IT and customer owners—This phrase is shorthand for IT stakeholders, managers, and executives who have relevance to the broader CMDB initiative, as well as service and consumer owners outside of IT.
- Applications Development and the Definitive Media Library—These terms apply as the CMDB system evolves to support development and DevOps requirements for staging the introduction of new application services across the infrastructure. Analytic, automation, and service dependency insights are also key here.
- Application Dependency Mapping—This concept was discussed under "Application Discovery and Dependency Mapping" (ADDM). As CMDB systems evolve, the combination of real-time, transaction-centric ADDM tools with more traditional configuration-centric ADDM may serve as the spine for the broader system.
- Configuration—This term is shorthand for "configuration automation" solutions, such as those targeting network, systems, PCs, and other devices, as well as those that extend to provisioning new application systems. Note that here the arrow is drawn to show bidirectional interaction so

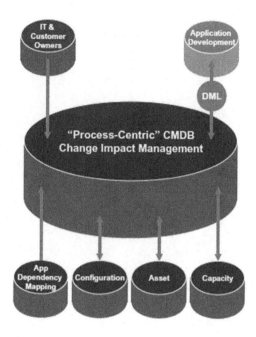

FIGURE B.6

A closer look at the process-centric CMDB, where most deployments begin.

that insights into larger service interdependencies can inform more point-optimized configuration tools while appropriate levels of detail and currency from these tools can update the CMDB based on policy.

- Asset—This term refers to asset-specific data, asset inventory tools, and/or an asset management database that houses financial information in greater detail than is appropriate for a core CMDB. Once again, the arrow is bidirectional so that appropriate asset-specific data can update the CMDB while service-relevant insights can help to deliver a baseline for more effective asset lifecycle optimization.
- Capacity—This term refers to one or multiple toolsets optimized for capacity planning analytics. Again, this is a critically bidirectional process ideally, in which capacity-related currency is maintained and service-related insights and interdependencies are shared.

Going clockwise from the top left in Figs. B.7 and B.8:

- Systems Performance—Refers to any number of systems management sources, from log files to time series data resident in monitoring and analytic sources.
- Events—Can come from any part of the application/infrastructure and once again, typically feed analytic engines.
- Service Impact Analytics—Link service interdependencies, change, and performance data together in a common analytic thread.
- Infrastructure Utilization—Refers to analytic tools that can harvest KPIs that impact shifting capacity requirements.

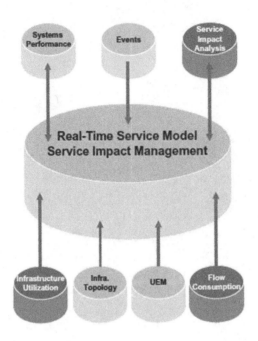

FIGURE B.7

Service impact management.

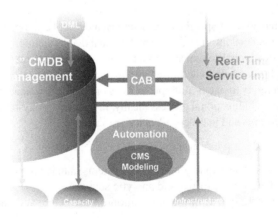

FIGURE B.8

Change advisory board (CAB) and automation.

- Infrastructure **Topology**—Keys on real-time awareness of the networked infrastructure (layers 2, 3, and above), as either integrated into an application dependency mapping tool or as a separate resource.
- UEM—Refers to **user experience management (UEM)** and what we call "the transactional stage," which can unify insights into application and business performance and business outcomes.
- Flow Consumption—Complements infrastructure utilization analytics with insights into how application traffic over the networked infrastructure may impact both performance and capacity-related issues. It may also provide insights into how and when applications are being used.

This is not meant to be a complete list, but it is a good departure point for planning.

Service Modeling: Where Logical and Physical Service Interdependencies Come Together

Fig. B.9 offers a logical depiction of the central requirement in the CMDB system: an adaptive service modeling system to bring together physical and logical interdependencies across the broader service

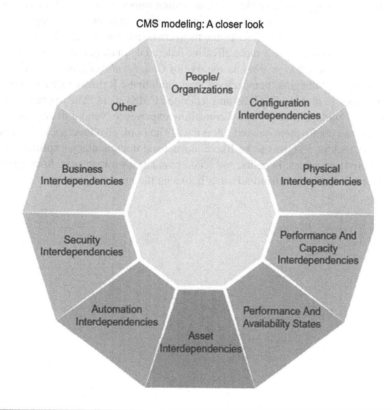

FIGURE B.9

Service modeling technology is at the very heart of CMDB system success.

landscape. This allows for data to reside in many different locations through a unified system of access. The beauty of associating logical (e.g., "customer" or "service provider") with physical infrastructure, middleware, and applications and their attributes is becoming increasingly more relevant as the extended IT organization becomes an ecosystem of partners, service providers, and, in some cases, suppliers.

SO WHERE DO I BUY ONE?

As inherently valuable as this modeling capability has become, no vendor actually markets just such a capability. To be clear, service modeling is often embedded in CMDB, ADDM, and service dashboard offerings, where it is presented as critical to functionality. However, most vendors approach service modeling with a tree-hugging reluctance once reserved for another innovative technology: **advanced operations analytics**. Service modeling also gained a bad name in many quarters due to the labors of customization, so it became necessary to make truly business-relevant service models appropriate for specific IT and business environments.

Nonetheless, some vendors actually worked to provide a cohesive and largely automated service modeling system that can support many elements, including imported insights on CIs and CI attributes from third-party sources. Moreover, there is a trend in some larger enterprises to adapt more fluid service modeling across multiple specific CMDB investments to create a broader unified system, a user-friendly "model of models" to help instantiate a more effective federated "manager of managers."

CMDB Systems: Making Change Work in the Age of Cloud and Agile is a unique combination of recommendations, industry insights, perspectives, and guidelines. It offers many diverse examples of how various approaches to making CMDBs and federated CMSs work. The overall goal is to provide both a landscape and a guide, drawing on past consulting experience, vendor dialogues and evaluations of vendor offerings, and deployment-related interviews. The book also leverages 10 years of research. In many places, the book is designed to be like a journalistic documentary, capturing many different first-person perspectives on issues, benefits, and recommendations for success. Such a rich and diverse set of sources place this book apart from all other books on the market today.

Appendix C

The NIST Definition of Cloud Computing

INTRODUCTION
AUTHORITY

The National Institute of Standards and Technology (NIST) developed this document in furtherance of its statutory responsibilities under the Federal Information Security Management Act (FISMA) of 2002, Public Law 107-347.

NIST is responsible for developing standards and guidelines, including minimum requirements, and for providing adequate information security for all agency operations and assets; but such standards and guidelines shall not apply to national security systems. This guideline is consistent with the requirements of the Office of Management and Budget (OMB) Circular A-130, Section 8b(3), "Securing Agency Information Systems," as analyzed in A-130, Appendix IV: Analysis of Key Sections. Supplemental information is provided in A-130, Appendix III.

This guideline has been prepared for use by federal agencies. It may be used by nongovernment organizations on a voluntary basis and is not subject to copyright, although attribution is desired.

Nothing in this document should be taken to contradict standards and guidelines made mandatory and binding on federal agencies by the secretary of commerce under statutory authority, nor should these guidelines be interpreted as altering or superseding the existing authorities of the secretary of commerce, director of the OMB, or any other federal official.

PURPOSE AND SCOPE

Cloud computing is an evolving paradigm. The NIST definition characterizes important aspects of cloud computing and is intended to serve as a means for broad comparisons of cloud services and deployment strategies and to provide a baseline for discussion from what is cloud computing to how to best use cloud computing. The service and deployment models defined form a simple taxonomy that is not intended to prescribe or constrain any particular method of deployment, service delivery, or business operation.

AUDIENCE

The intended audience of this document consists of system planners, program managers, technologists, and others adopting cloud computing as consumers or providers of cloud services.

THE NIST DEFINITION OF *CLOUD COMPUTING*

Cloud computing is a model for enabling ubiquitous, convenient, on-demand network access to a shared pool of configurable computing resources (e.g., networks, servers, storage, applications, and services) that can be rapidly provisioned and released with minimal management effort or service provider interaction. This cloud model is composed of five essential characteristics, three service models, and four deployment models.

Essential Characteristics

On-demand self-service. A consumer can unilaterally provision computing capabilities, such as server time and network storage, as needed automatically without requiring human interaction with each service provider.

Broad network access. Capabilities are available over the network and accessed through standard mechanisms that promote use by heterogeneous thin or thick client platforms (e.g., mobile phones, tablets, laptops, and workstations).

Resource pooling. The provider's computing resources are pooled to serve multiple consumers using a multitenant model, with different physical and virtual resources dynamically assigned and reassigned according to consumer demand. There is a sense of location independence in that the customer generally has no control or knowledge over the exact location of the provided resources but may be able to specify location at a higher level of abstraction (e.g., country, state, or datacenter). Examples of resources include storage, processing, memory, and network bandwidth.

Rapid elasticity. Capabilities can be elastically provisioned and released, in some cases automatically, to scale rapidly outward and inward commensurate with demand. To the consumer, the capabilities available for provisioning often appear to be unlimited and can be appropriated in any quantity at any time.

Measured service. Cloud systems automatically control and optimize resource use by leveraging a metering capability[1] at some level of abstraction appropriate to the type of service (e.g., storage, processing, bandwidth, and active user accounts). Resource use can be monitored, controlled, and reported, providing transparency for both the provider and consumer of the utilized service.

Service Models

Software as a Service (SaaS). The capability provided to the consumer is to use the provider's applications running on a cloud infrastructure.[2] The applications are accessible from various client devices through either a thin client interface, such as a web browser (e.g., web-based email), or a program interface. The consumer does not manage or control the underlying cloud infrastructure including network, servers, operating systems, storage, or even individual application capabilities, with the possible exception of limited user-specific application configuration settings.

Platform as a Service (PaaS). The capability provided to the consumer is to deploy onto the cloud infrastructure consumer-created or acquired applications created using programming languages, libraries, services, and tools supported by the provider.[3] The consumer does not manage or control

---

[1]Typically this is done on a pay-per-use or charge-per-use basis.

[2]A cloud infrastructure is the collection of hardware and software that enables the five essential characteristics of cloud computing. The cloud infrastructure can be viewed as containing both a physical layer and an abstraction layer. The physical layer consists of the hardware resources that are necessary to support the cloud services being provided, and typically includes server, storage and network components. The abstraction layer consists of the software deployed across the physical layer, which manifests the essential cloud characteristics. Conceptually the abstraction layer sits above the physical layer.

[3]This capability does not necessarily preclude the use of compatible programming languages, libraries, services, and tools from other sources.

the underlying cloud infrastructure including network, servers, operating systems, or storage but has control over the deployed applications and possibly configuration settings for the application-hosting environment.

Infrastructure as a Service (IaaS). The capability provided to the consumer is to provision processing, storage, networks, and other fundamental computing resources where the consumer is able to deploy and run arbitrary software, which can include operating systems and applications. The consumer does not manage or control the underlying cloud infrastructure but has control over operating systems, storage, and deployed applications; and possibly limited control of select networking components (e.g., host firewalls).

Deployment Models

Private cloud. The cloud infrastructure is provisioned for exclusive use by a single organization comprising multiple consumers (e.g., business units). It may be owned, managed, and operated by the organization, a third party, or some combination of them, and it may exist on or off premises.

Community cloud. The cloud infrastructure is provisioned for exclusive use by a specific community of consumers from organizations that have shared concerns (e.g., mission, security requirements, policy, and compliance considerations). It may be owned, managed, and operated by one or more of the organizations in the community, a third party, or some combination of them, and it may exist on or off premises.

Public cloud. The cloud infrastructure is provisioned for open use by the general public. It may be owned, managed, and operated by a business, academic, or government organization, or some combination of them. It exists on the premises of the cloud provider.

Hybrid cloud. The cloud infrastructure is a composition of two or more distinct cloud infrastructures (private, community, or public) that remain unique entities but are bound together by standardized or proprietary technology that enables data and application portability (e.g., cloud bursting for load balancing between clouds).

Index

Note: Page numbers followed by "f" indicate figures, "t" indicate tables and "b" indicate boxes.

Printed in the United States
By Bookmasters